Powershell Core 6.2 Cookbook

Leverage command-line shell scripting to effectively manage
your enterprise environment

Jan-Hendrik Peters

BIRMINGHAM - MUMBAI

Powershell Core 6.2 Cookbook

Commissioning Editor: Vijin Boricha
Acquisition Editor: Rohit Rajkumar
Content Development Editor: Ronn Kurien
Technical Editor: Prachi Sawant
Copy Editor: Safis Editing
Project Coordinator: Jagdish Prabhu
Proofreader: Safis Editing
Indexer: Priyanka Dhadke
Graphics: Tom Scaria
Production Coordinator: Saili Kale

First published: April 2019

Production reference: 1170419

Published by Packt Publishing Ltd.
Livery Place
35 Livery Street
Birmingham
B3 2PB, UK.

ISBN 978-1-78980-330-3

www.packtpub.com

`mapt.io`

Mapt is an online digital library that gives you full access to over 5,000 books and videos, as well as industry leading tools to help you plan your personal development and advance your career. For more information, please visit our website.

Why subscribe?

- Spend less time learning and more time coding with practical eBooks and Videos from over 4,000 industry professionals

- Improve your learning with Skill Plans built especially for you

- Get a free eBook or video every month

- Mapt is fully searchable

- Copy and paste, print, and bookmark content

Packt.com

Did you know that Packt offers eBook versions of every book published, with PDF and ePub files available? You can upgrade to the eBook version at `www.packt.com` and as a print book customer, you are entitled to a discount on the eBook copy. Get in touch with us at `customercare@packtpub.com` for more details.

At `www.packt.com`, you can also read a collection of free technical articles, sign up for a range of free newsletters, and receive exclusive discounts and offers on Packt books and eBooks.

Contributors

About the author

Jan-Hendrik Peters is an automation and DevOps professional by day, and a developer for the AutomatedLab framework by night. After working at an international retailer automating distributed POS support systems, he started working as a premier field engineer for Microsoft Germany, where he helps customers automate their infrastructure on-premises and in the cloud.

When he is not working, he likes to spend his time brewing his own beer, curing his own bacon, and generally doing manual labor.

About the reviewers

Jose Angel Muñoz is a systems engineer with more than 20 years' experience in Linux and Windows systems administration. He is currently working for RAET, where he has discovered the magic of automation and infrastructure as code. Jose Angel also collaborates with Ansible, creating new Python and PowerShell modules.

Previously, he collaborated with the Linux Magazine, where he published several technical articles on a variety of topics, including monitoring, security, virtualization, and development.

Friedrich Weinmann, a former Microsoft MVP for his engagement in the PowerShell community nowadays works as a Premier Field Engineer for Microsoft.

He speaks at international conferences on all things PowerShell, presents at usergroups and organizes a PowerShell usergroup himself. In his putatively spare time he contributes to open source projects and can be found hanging out in various PowerShell related communities.

Packt is searching for authors like you

If you're interested in becoming an author for Packt, please visit authors.packtpub.com and apply today. We have worked with thousands of developers and tech professionals, just like you, to help them share their insight with the global tech community. You can make a general application, apply for a specific hot topic that we are recruiting an author for, or submit your own idea.

Table of Contents

Preface

This PowerShell Core cookbook is a recipe-based approach in terms of learning about, and using, PowerShell Core in your organization. Whether you are using Windows, Linux, or macOS, PowerShell Core can be installed and used.

This book aims to show you typical infrastructure administration scenarios by means of short and concise recipes. You will explore everything from automating a release pipeline to managing Linux systems with PowerShell in the upcoming chapters.

With the release of PowerShell 7 that is slated for May 2019 this book will still be accurate and greatly help you with day to day tasks.

Who this book is for

This book is intended for system administrators who want to enhance their PowerShell scripting skills. Do you like to automate reoccurring tasks? Then this book is perfect for you. Do you manage Windows as well as Linux systems, but you are missing a common automation language? Then look no further. Do you want to work more with REST APIs but don't know where to start? Read this book.

To get the most out of this book, you should already be familiar with the basic terms of PowerShell. If necessary, read the book *Learn PowerShell Core*, by *David das Neves* and *Jan-Hendrik Peters*.

What this book covers

Chapter 1, *Introduction to PowerShell Core*, serves as an introduction and covers the very first steps with PowerShell Core.

Chapter 2, *Reading and Writing Output*, covers how to work with data and providers.

Chapter 3, *Working with Objects*, is an introduction to object-oriented programming and also shows you the benefits of using objects in your code.

Chapter 4, *Mastering the Pipeline*, is all about the pipeline and shows you how to work efficiently with large amounts of data in the pipeline.

Chapter 5, *Importing, Using, and Exporting Data*, is all about persisting and reading data from XML to JSON, and from REST to SQL.

Chapter 6, *Windows and Linux Administration*, compares different typical administrative tasks on Linux and Windows and demonstrates the benefits of PowerShell Core in these scenarios.

Chapter 7, *Windows Server Administration*, covers the pitfalls and the benefits of using PowerShell Core in a purely Windows environment. You will configure S2D, Docker, Active Directory Domain Services, and more.

Chapter 8, *Remoting and Just Enough Administration*, introduces remote debugging, *Just Enough Administration*, and the common information model.

Chapter 9, *Using PowerShell for Hyper-V and Azure Stack Management*, concentrates on the private cloud and shows you how to manage Hyper-V, deploy Azure Stack, and maintain your infrastructure workloads with PowerShell Core.

Chapter 10, *Using PowerShell with Azure and Google Cloud*, gives you two public cloud providers and compares the typical workloads, including storage and compute.

Chapter 11, *Accessing Web Services*, is all about REST. This chapter will not only show you how different actual REST APIs are accessed; it will also have you create your own!

Chapter 12, *High-Performance Scripting*, covers all the important concepts concerning the performance of your scripts. You will learn about true parallelization, efficient filtering, and more.

To get the most out of this book

To get the most out of this book, I recommend deploying this book's lab environment, which consists of the following:

- A Domain Controller/Router/Certificate Authority (recipes requiring Active Directory)
- Three file servers (SOFS and S2D recipes)
- Two Hyper-V hosts (Hyper-V and clustering recipes)
- A web server (IIS recipes) with SQL
- A CentOS 7.4 node (Linux recipes)

Should you decide to use your own infrastructure, please adapt the server names used in the recipes!

Lab requirements

To deploy the lab for the entire book, you need a Hyper-V host (recommended) or an Azure subscription (caution: deploying the lab will incur substantial costs if you do not deallocate the machines!). The requirements for your Hyper-V host are as follows:

- Windows 10/Server 2016
- A virtualization-enabled, modern processor (i5 or similar)
- At least 20 GiB RAM if all machines are up and running
- At least 50 GiB of free space on an SSD (no spinning disks)
- Deploy the lab using Windows PowerShell
- The Hyper-V feature needs to be enabled (requires a restart)
- One ISO file Windows Server 2016 Datacenter
- One ISO file SQL Server 2017 (Standard or Datacenter)
- One ISO file CentOS 7.4; a DVD image is recommended, since a network image requires an internet-connected host!

Deploying the lab will download the PowerShell module, AutomatedLab, which is used to aid rapid lab deployments. The entire lab will be built on the fly. If you are done with the lab and want to remove it, open an administrative PowerShell session and execute `Remove-Lab -Name PSCookBook`.

The lab deployment script can be found in the book's repository at `https://github.com/PacktPublishing/Powershell-Core-6.2-Cookbook/tree/master/Chapter00`.

Recipe recommendations

To follow all the recipes in this book, I recommend the following:

- Register for a free Azure DevOps account at `https://dev.azure.com` to follow the Azure DevOps recipes.
- Register for a free Microsoft Azure account at `https://azure.microsoft.com/en-us/free` to follow all Azure recipes.
- Register for a free Google Cloud account at `https://cloud.google.com` to follow all Google Cloud recipes.

Any code can be found at `https://github.com/PacktPublishing/Powershell-Core-6.2-Cookbook`.

Take care not to execute the scripts as a whole. I have added a throw statement to each recipe script so that you do not accidentally execute it entirely.

Download the example code files

You can download the example code files for this book from your account at `www.packt.com`. If you purchased this book elsewhere, you can visit `www.packt.com/support` and register to have the files emailed directly to you.

You can download the code files by following these steps:

1. Log in or register at `www.packt.com`.
2. Select the **SUPPORT** tab.
3. Click on **Code Downloads & Errata**.
4. Enter the name of the book in the **Search** box and follow the onscreen instructions.

Once the file is downloaded, please make sure that you unzip or extract the folder using the latest version of:

- WinRAR/7-Zip for Windows
- Zipeg/iZip/UnRarX for Mac
- 7-Zip/PeaZip for Linux

The code bundle for the book is also hosted on GitHub at `https://github.com/PacktPublishing/Powershell-Core-6.2-Cookbook`. In case there's an update to the code, it will be updated on the existing GitHub repository.

We also have other code bundles from our rich catalog of books and videos available at `https://github.com/PacktPublishing/`. Check them out!

Download the color images

We also provide a PDF file that has color images of the screenshots/diagrams used in this book. You can download it here: `https://www.packtpub.com/sites/default/files/downloads/9781789803303_ColorImages.pdf`.

Conventions used

There are a number of text conventions used throughout this book.

`CodeInText`: Indicates code words in text, database table names, folder names, filenames, file extensions, pathnames, dummy URLs, user input, and Twitter handles. Here is an example: "Mount the downloaded `WebStorm-10*.dmg` disk image file as another disk in your system."

A block of code is set as follows:

```
public Car(string make, string model, ConsoleColor color)
    {
        Color = color;
        Make = make;
        Model = model;
    }
```

When we wish to draw your attention to a particular part of a code block, the relevant lines or items are set in bold:

```
From
https://docs.microsoft.com/en-us/dotnet/api/system.boolean.tryparse
?view=netcore-2.2:
public static bool TryParse (string value, out bool result);
```

Any command-line input or output is written as follows:

```
$car = New-Object -TypeName Vehicle.Car
```

Bold: Indicates a new term, an important word, or words that you see on screen. For example, words in menus or dialog boxes appear in the text like this. Here is an example: "Select **System info** from the **Administration** panel."

Warnings or important notes appear like this.

Tips and tricks appear like this.

Sections

In this book, you will find several headings that appear frequently (*Getting ready*, *How to do it...*, *How it works...*, *There's more...*, and *See also*).

To give clear instructions on how to complete a recipe, use these sections as follows:

Getting ready

This section tells you what to expect in the recipe and describes how to set up any software or any preliminary settings required for the recipe.

How to do it...

This section contains the steps required to follow the recipe.

How it works...

This section usually consists of a detailed explanation of what happened in the previous section.

There's more...

This section consists of additional information about the recipe in order to make you more knowledgeable about the recipe.

See also

This section provides helpful links to other useful information for the recipe.

Get in touch

Feedback from our readers is always welcome.

General feedback: If you have questions about any aspect of this book, mention the book title in the subject of your message and email us at customercare@packtpub.com.

Errata: Although we have taken every care to ensure the accuracy of our content, mistakes do happen. If you have found a mistake in this book, we would be grateful if you would report this to us. Please visit www.packt.com/submit-errata, selecting your book, clicking on the Errata Submission Form link, and entering the details.

Piracy: If you come across any illegal copies of our works in any form on the internet, we would be grateful if you would provide us with the location address or website name. Please contact us at copyright@packt.com with a link to the material.

If you are interested in becoming an author: If there is a topic that you have expertise in, and you are interested in either writing or contributing to a book, please visit authors.packtpub.com.

Reviews

Please leave a review. Once you have read and used this book, why not leave a review on the site that you purchased it from? Potential readers can then see and use your unbiased opinion to make purchase decisions, we at Packt can understand what you think about our products, and our authors can see your feedback on their book. Thank you!

For more information about Packt, please visit packt.com.

Introduction to PowerShell Core 1

PowerShell Core, as the open source alternative to Windows PowerShell from which it evolved, is quickly becoming the automation engine of choice for many administrators and developers alike. As a true cross-platform shell, PowerShell Core is perfectly suited for many different operating system types and workloads.

While the next iteration of PowerShell Core at the time of writing was slated for May 2019 and will drop the Core this book and its recipes will remain accurate and useful. The release of PowerShell is merely a rebranding to unify PowerShell development. In the future we will continue to see rapid new iterations of PowerShell.

While installing PowerShell Core is a breeze, the first steps for people new to PowerShell can be quite challenging. In this chapter, I aim to bridge those little knowledge gaps and show you the ropes.

You'll learn all there is to know about installing and operating PowerShell Core and learn about the cmdlets necessary to find your way on any system running PowerShell Core. In addition to that, you'll discover how to get help without using the internet and do everything from within PowerShell.

This chapter is intended for beginners who are fairly new to PowerShell Core and will help you understand the very basics of PowerShell while the next chapters assume solid scripting knowledge.

In this chapter, we will cover the following recipes:

- Installing PowerShell Core on Windows
- Installing PowerShell Core on Linux
- Running PowerShell Core
- Getting help
- Getting around
- How do cmdlets work?
- Performing read-only operations

- Introducing change to systems
- Discovering the environment

Technical requirements

In order to follow the recipes in this chapter, you need a machine capable of running PowerShell Core that is connected to the internet.

Installing PowerShell Core on Windows

In this recipe, you'll learn how to provision PowerShell Core on a Windows system starting with Windows 6.1 (Server 2008 R2/Windows 7).

Getting ready

To follow this recipe, you'll need a Windows machine with at least Windows Server 2008 R2 or Windows 7. If this machine isn't connected to the internet, you'll need a way of transferring the installer to the machine.

How to do it...

Please perform the following steps:

1. In order to get the most recent release of PowerShell Core for Windows, browse to `https://github.com/powershell/powershell`:

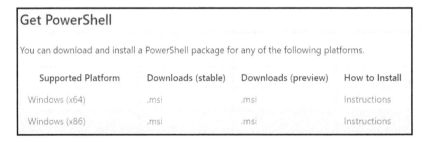

2. Download the release for your platform. I recommend using the stable 64 bit (x64) edition if possible.

3. Open the installer file, for example, `PowerShell-6.2.0-win-x64.msi`.

4. Follow the instructions on screen to install PowerShell Core

5. On the final page, you can directly enable PowerShell remoting if you want. Leave the option disabled for now; you'll configure it properly later on:

6. Start PowerShell Core by typing `pwsh` into the search bar!

How it works...

Using the standard MSI installer methods, PowerShell Core will be installed for your system in the 64 bit `Program Files` directory by default. It won't replace Windows PowerShell but will simply coexist peacefully and include the most recent updates to PowerShell.

If left on the default settings, an event manifest will be registered on the system, enabling an event log for PowerShell Core. The log file will be placed at `%SystemRoot%\System32\Winevt\Logs\PowerShellCore%4Operational.evtx` and can be found in the `Applications and Services Logs`.

By default, no remoting configuration will be made. We'll talk about remoting in `Chapter 8`, *Running Remote Commands and Understanding Just Enough Administration*, where you'll enable PowerShell remoting for a system.

There's more...

Besides the installer that you can download and install manually or through any software deployment solution, you can also use Chocolatey. Chocolatey is a NuGet package source for binary packages and can be used to bootstrap software on a system.

The following steps will install Chocolatey and PowerShell Core on a Windows system. These steps require using Windows PowerShell for the initial process:

1. Run the following command in Windows PowerShell (see `https://chocolatey.org/docs/installation` for details):

```
Set-ExecutionPolicy Bypass -Scope Process -Force
iex ((New-Object
System.Net.WebClient).DownloadString('https://chocolatey.org/instal
l.ps1'))
```

2. After the installation of Chocolatey, simply execute `choco install powershell /y`.
3. Start PowerShell Core by searching for `pwsh` in the search bar!

If you're so inclined, compiling the code from scratch is of course also an option. Simply follow the guidelines laid out in the GitHub repository to do so:

```
# Clone the repository
git clone https://github.com/powershell/powershell

Set-Location -Path .\powershell
Import-Module ./build.psm1

# Ensure you have the latest version of .NET Core and other necessary
components
Start-PSBootStrap

# Start the build process
Start-PSBuild

# Either run PowerShell directly...
& $(Get-PSOutput)

# ...or copy it to your favorite location (here: Program Files on Windows,
necessary access rights required)
$source = Split-Path -Path $(Get-PSOutput) -Parent
$target = "$env:ProgramFiles\PowerShell\$(Get-PSVersion)"
Copy-Item -Path $source -Recurse -Destination $target
```

See also

- PowerShell documentation: `https://docs.microsoft.com/powershell`
- Chocolatey documentation: `https://chocolatey.org/docs/installation`

Installing PowerShell Core on Linux

Since the arrival of PowerShell Core, its key feature has been the ability to run cross-platform and provide the exact same experience on any operating system. Installing PowerShell on Linux is nearly as easy as it is in Windows. If your distribution is among the list of supported distributions such as CentOS, openSUSE, or Ubuntu, the process is pretty straightforward.

Getting ready

In order to follow the recipe, you'll need any Linux distribution (even the Windows Subsystem for Linux) that's preferably connected to the internet and can download packages. In the recipe, I'm using CentOS and Ubuntu to show some very different approaches.

At the time of writing, the recipe was correct. However, check whether it still applies on the official installation page for your operating system, for example, `https://docs.microsoft.com/en-us/powershell/scripting/setup/installing-powershell-core-on-linux`.

How to do it...

On CentOS 7.x, perform the following steps:

1. Register the Microsoft RPM repository:

   ```
   curl https://packages.microsoft.com/config/rhel/7/prod.repo | sudo
   tee /etc/yum.repos.d/microsoft.repo.
   ```

2. Install the package: `sudo yum install -y powershell`.
3. Run PowerShell by executing `pwsh`, which is now installed.

On Ubuntu 18.10, perform the following steps:

1. Open the Ubuntu Software store.
2. Search for `powershell`:

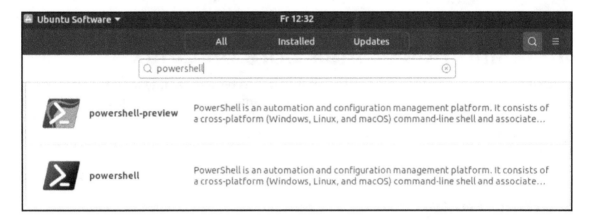

3. Install and run PowerShell Core:

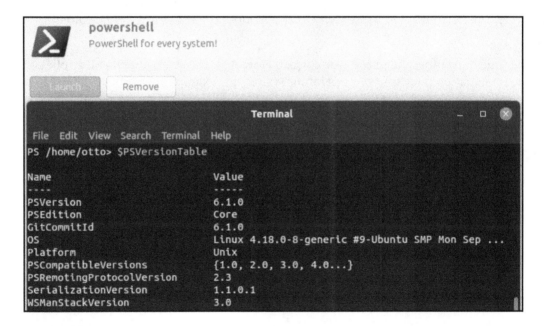

The steps to install PowerShell on other distributions are fairly similar as long as you can use your distribution's package management system, such as `rpm` or `dpkg`.

How it works...

Usually, the installation instructions for Linux require the registration of a package repository that's maintained by Microsoft and used to publish PowerShell Core. The repository settings include the URL, a reference to the GPG public key, and the status of the repository.

On Linux, binary packages are usually compiled using a makefile on the running OS and then, for example, linked or copied to one of the binary paths. The best example for this is probably Gentoo, where compiling your kernel and all components, libraries, and software is actually required. With RPM and DEB packages, developers can better resolve dependencies and include all necessary instructions to install a binary package or compile a source package.

With binary packages, the component is compiled for a specific architecture with general compilation flags set. While this won't allow the user to fine-tune every part of the installation, it'll provide the benefit of an easier deployment.

PowerShell comes pre-built in, for example, an RPM package for different OS architectures. By using the package management provider of the distribution, you ensure that all necessary dependencies are installed alongside the package itself.

With Ubuntu 18.10, PowerShell is available as a Snap package in the Ubuntu Software store. This allows a more user-friendly installation of PowerShell that doesn't require the command line at all—apart from using PowerShell, of course.

There's more...

There're many different flavors of Linux—there is macOS, Windows, and probably other platforms to come. Stay up-to-date by having a look at the official installation instructions at https://github.com/powershell/powershell.

In addition to traditional installation methods, you can also build your entire PowerShell from scratch.

See also

- Information on the Snap package format: https://snapcraft.io
- The official package source for PowerShell packages: https://github.com/powershell/powershell

Running PowerShell Core

Using PowerShell Core is very simple. This recipe will show you the very first steps and help you to run PowerShell Core after the installation.

Getting ready

In order to follow this recipe, you should have completed the installation of PowerShell Core for your operating system.

How to do it...

Let's perform the following steps:

1. On Windows, run `pwsh.exe`. On Linux or macOS, run `pwsh`.
2. Type your first cmdlet, `Get-Process`, to retrieve a list of running processes on the system and hit *Enter* to confirm.
3. Compare the output of the cmdlet with the output of `tasklist` (in Windows) and `ps` (in Linux):

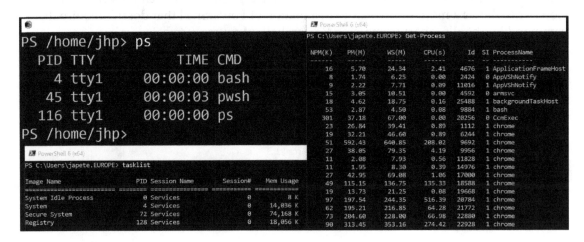

4. Type `Get-Date` and hit *Enter* to confirm.

5. Compare the output of this cmdlet with the output of `date /t` (in Windows) and `date` (in Linux):

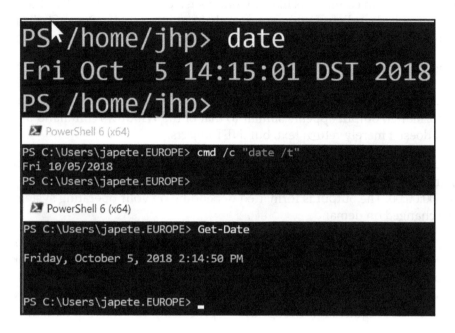

6. Execute the line: `Get-Process | Where-Object -Property WorkingSet -gt 100MB`.

7. Compare the output again with the output of `tasklist /FI "MEMUSAGE gt 102400"` (in Windows) and `ps -aux | awk -F" " '$5 > 102400'` (in Linux):

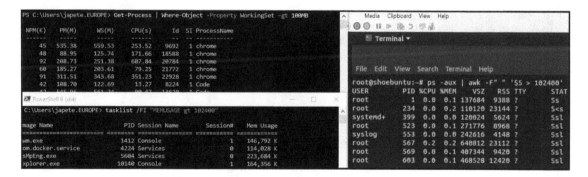

8. Lastly, execute this cmdlet: `Stop-Computer -WhatIf`. This time, there's no comparable command on either Windows or Linux.

How it works...

PowerShell works with commands like any other shell environment. Native PowerShell commands are called cmdlets. Unlike commands from other shells, PowerShell cmdlets should only serve one purpose and fulfill this purpose only. As always, there're exceptions to the rule. In some cases, command-line switches, called switch parameters, can be used to toggle additional functionality.

The first example, `Get-Process`, returns (`Get`) a list of running processes (`Process`). While the formatted output appears similar to that of the Windows command tasklist, PowerShell doesn't merely return text, but .NET objects.

Our second example, `Get-Date`, returns the current date and time as a .NET object again. In .NET, time is calculated with ticks, which are 100 nanosecond-intervals starting at 0001-01-01 00:00:00. The output is formatted depending on your operating system's culture and can be changed on demand.

The third example has you filter the output with PowerShell, which is extremely easy compared to Windows and Linux alike. Especially the endless possibilities of working with text in Linux make this a striking example. The `ps` command doesn't allow much filtering, so you need to rely on tools such as `awk` to process the text that is returned. This simple task without PowerShell requires knowledge of text processing and filtering with different tools.

The last cmdlet, `Stop-Computer`, demonstrates a very common parameter with many cmdlets called `WhatIf`. This parameter allows you to simply try a cmdlet before actually doing anything. This is an excellent way to test changes for general correctness, for example, before modifying your 10.000 Active Directory user accounts:

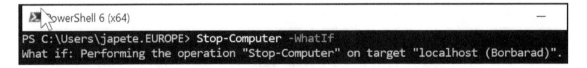

```
PowerShell 6 (x64)                                                          —
PS C:\Users\japete.EUROPE> Stop-Computer -WhatIf
What if: Performing the operation "Stop-Computer" on target "localhost (Borbarad)".
```

There's more...

There's plenty more to do and see in PowerShell—part of which will be covered in this book. Try to follow the upcoming recipes as well to find out about cmdlet discovery, the flow between cmdlets in the pipeline, and much more.

See also

- All official documentation regarding PowerShell: `https://docs.microsoft.com/powershell`
- *Learn PowerShell Core 6.0* by *David das Neves* and *Jan-Hendrik Peters*, as a supplementary book to really learn the language: `https://www.packtpub.com/networking-and-servers/learn-powershell-core-60`

Getting help

Help is never far away in PowerShell Core and, in this section, you'll learn how to utilize the help to your benefit.

Getting ready

In order to follow this recipe, you should have completed the installation of PowerShell Core for your operating system.

How to do it...

Please perform the following steps:

1. Open PowerShell Core.
2. Type the `Get-Help` cmdlet and hit *Enter*. The cmdlet displays help about the help system.

3. Use the `-?` parameter with any cmdlet, for example, `Start-Process -?`. Notice the output after this cmdlet. You can see the syntax of the cmdlet, as well as some additional remarks:

```
PowerShell 6 (x64)                                                                             □  ×
PS C:\Users\japete.EUROPE> start-process -?

NAME
    Start-Process

SYNTAX
    Start-Process [-FilePath] <string> [[-ArgumentList] <string[]>] [-Credential <pscredential>] [-WorkingDirectory
    <string>] [-LoadUserProfile] [-NoNewWindow] [-PassThru] [-RedirectStandardError <string>] [-RedirectStandardInput
    <string>] [-RedirectStandardOutput <string>] [-WindowStyle {Normal | Hidden | Minimized | Maximized}] [-Wait]
    [-UseNewEnvironment] [-WhatIf] [-Confirm] [<CommonParameters>]

    Start-Process [-FilePath] <string> [[-ArgumentList] <string[]>] [-WorkingDirectory <string>] [-PassThru] [-Verb
    <string>] [-WindowStyle {Normal | Hidden | Minimized | Maximized}] [-Wait] [-WhatIf] [-Confirm]
    [<CommonParameters>]


ALIASES
    saps
    start


REMARKS
    Get-Help cannot find the Help files for this cmdlet on this computer. It is displaying only partial help.
        -- To download and install Help files for the module that includes this cmdlet, use Update-Help.
        -- To view the Help topic for this cmdlet online, type: "Get-Help Start-Process -Online" or
           go to https://go.microsoft.com/fwlink/?LinkID=135261.


PS C:\Users\japete.EUROPE>
```

4. Type the `Get-Help Start-Process -Parameter FilePath` command. Note the output at that point. Only help for the `FilePath` parameter is returned. From the output, you can see that the parameter is mandatory, has two aliases, and doesn't like pipeline input:

```
PS C:\Users\japete.EUROPE> get-help start-process -parameter filepath

-FilePath <string>

        Required?                    true
        Position?                    0
        Accept pipeline input?       false
        Parameter set name           (All)
        Aliases                      PSPath, Path
        Dynamic?                     false
```

5. Type the `Get-Help Start-Process -Full` command. You can notice in the output that indeed no help files have been downloaded yet.

6. Type the `Update-Help -Scope CurrentUser` command to download all current help content.

7. Examine the folder contents of `$home\Documents\PowerShell\Help` in Windows and `~/.local/share/powershell` in Linux.

8. Type the `Update-Help -Module CimCmdlets -UICulture ja-jp,sv-se` command. Notice that not all modules provide localized help content—the content in `en-us` should be available for most modules, however.

9. Now that the help content has downloaded, try `Get-Help Start-Process -Full` again.

10. Notice that now the full content is available, allowing you to get additional information about a cmdlet.

How it works...

The help system of PowerShell Core can be used to update help files from the internet or from a `CIFS` share. Without updated help content, the help system always displays the name and syntax of a cmdlet as well as detailed parameter help for all parameters of a cmdlet.

In order to update help for modules on the local system, `Update-Help` will examine all modules in the `PSModulePath` environmental variable in order to find all modules that have the `HelpInfoUri` property set. It'll try to resolve the URI, which should point to a browsable website where it will then look for an XML file called `<ModuleName>_<ModuleGuid>_HelpInfo.xml`. Inside this XML file, the location of a cabinet file (`*.cab`) is stored, which will then be used to download the actual content.

With the new `Scope` parameter introduced in PowerShell Core, all help content will be placed in the personal user folder, for example, `C:\Users\<UserName>\Documents\PowerShell`, instead of a system-wide folder that would require administrative privileges, for example, `C:\Program Files\PowerShell`.

The `Update-Help` cmdlet will only download new content once per day if the cmdlet is called. In order to download the content more frequently, you can use the `Force` parameter.

There's more...

Help content can also be hosted on-premises by using the `Save-Help` cmdlet and distributing the content. On Windows systems, a group policy setting can be found that can control the default path for `Update-Help` as well. This setting is in **Administrative Templates** | **Windows Components** | **System** | **Windows PowerShell**. This setting is only valid for Windows PowerShell. Regardless of the edition, the `Update-Help` cmdlet supports the `SourcePath` parameter to specify from where the help content will be downloaded.

In order to provide your own help content properly, have a look at the PowerShell module, `PlatyPS`. This module makes it very easy to generate help content for your own modules, package it to the correct format, and much more.

`PlatyPS` supports markdown help, enabling you to write help content in a very easy way that feels more natural than creating large and complex `MAML` files.

See also

- Help overview: `https://docs.microsoft.com/en-us/powershell/module/microsoft.powershell.core/about/about_updatable_help?view=powershell-6`
- PowerShell module to generate help content: `https://github.com/powershell/platyps`

Getting around

In this section, you'll learn how to get around on any system running PowerShell Core through cmdlet discovery.

Getting ready

In order to follow this recipe, you should have completed the installation of PowerShell Core for your operating system.

How to do it...

Please perform the following steps:

1. Open PowerShell Core.
2. Type `Get-Command`. Notice that all available cmdlets on the system will be displayed. Depending on the modules installed on your system, this will be a lot.
3. Type `Get-Command New-Item -Syntax`. Notice that, this time, it's not the cmdlet that's returned, but the syntax that's displayed:

```
PS C:\Users\japete.EUROPE> Get-Command New-Item

New-Item [-Path] <string[]> [-ItemType <string>] [-Value <Object>] [-Force] [-Credential <pscredential>] [-WhatIf]
 [-Confirm] [<CommonParameters>]

New-Item [[-Path] <string[]>] -Name <string> [-ItemType <string>] [-Value <Object>] [-Force] [-Credential <pscrede
ntial>] [-WhatIf] [-Confirm] [<CommonParameters>]
```

4. Type `Get-Command -Verb Get -Module Microsoft.PowerShell.Utility`. Notice here that all read-only cmdlets of a specific module are returned, thereby greatly narrowing down the results:

```
PS C:\Users\japete.EUROPE> Get-Command        Get        Microsoft.PowerShell.Utility

CommandType     Name                                                Version    Source
-----------     ----                                                -------    ------
Cmdlet          Get-Alias                                           6.1.0.0    Microso
Cmdlet          Get-Culture                                         6.1.0.0    Microso
Cmdlet          Get-Date                                            6.1.0.0    Microso
Cmdlet          Get-Event                                           6.1.0.0    Microso
Cmdlet          Get-EventSubscriber                                 6.1.0.0    Microso
```

5. Type `Get-Command -CommandType Application`. This time, all external applications (in other words, binaries) are returned. Try to favor native PowerShell cmdlets over external applications where possible:

```
PS C:\Users\japete.EUROPE> Get-Command            Application

CommandType     Name                                          Version    Source
-----------     ----                                          -------    ------
Application     {A6D608F0-0BDE-491A-97AE-5C4B05D86E01}.bat     0.0.0.0    C:\WINDOWS\system32\{A6D608F0-0B...
Application     {EC94D02F-D200-4428-9531-05AF7F9799CB}.bat     0.0.0.0    C:\WINDOWS\system32\{EC94D02F-D2...
Application     {F33C3B9B-72AF-418A-B3FD-560646F7CDA2}.bat     0.0.0.0    C:\WINDOWS\system32\{F33C3B9B-72...
Application     adsiedit.msc                                  0.0.0.0    C:\WINDOWS\system32\adsiedit.msc
Application     AgentService.exe                              10.0.17... C:\WINDOWS\system32\AgentService...
```

6. Type `Get-Command -ParameterName ComputerName,CimSession,PSSession`. This is one of my favorites; with this parameter, only cmdlets that have certain parameters are returned. In this instance, all remote-capable cmdlets will be returned. This parameter, however, only searches through all cmdlets available in the current session:

```
PowerShell 6 (x64)
PS C:\Users\japete.EUROPE> Get-Command                ComputerName CimSession PSSession

CommandType     Name                                           Version    Source
-----------     ----                                           -------    ------
Alias           Disable-PhysicalDiskIndication                 2.0.0.0    storage
Alias           Disable-StorageDiagnosticLog                   2.0.0.0    storage
Alias           Enable-PhysicalDiskIndication                  2.0.0.0    storage
Alias           Enable-StorageDiagnosticLog                    2.0.0.0    storage
```

7. Type `Get-Command *Process,*Item`. Notice that, this time, a wildcard search is performed on all cmdlets that exist on the system.
8. Type `New-Alias -Name Start-Process -Value hostname` and then type `Get-Command Start-Process`. Only the alias will be returned now, effectively hiding the cmdlet, `Start-Process`.
9. Type `Get-Command Start-Process -All`. This time, the alias as well as the original cmdlet are returned.

How it works...

PowerShell and its incredibly flexible system are easily discovered with the help of `Get-Command`. Even for a seasoned PowerShell expert, `Get-Command` is invaluable as it works on any system, doesn't need additional content, and will save you precious time. Additionally, nobody is able to just know all existing cmdlets—sometimes, you just need to have a short look at the syntax.

Aliases are a part of PowerShell as well as cmdlets. Sometimes, an alias is introduced when the name of a cmdlet changes in order maintain backward compatibility to some degree. Other aliases are simply created to make working interactively faster or to ease the migration from another scripting language such as the aliases, `dir` and `ls`.

By inspecting module manifests and module definitions, Get-Command is able to discover the exported cmdlets of a module that make up the available cmdlets on a system. Additionally, the PATH environmental variable is used to discover external applications such as executables, libraries, and text files.

The output of Get-Command can simply be filtered with wildcards in order to discover cmdlets that have a certain purpose, for example, *Process will list all cmdlets that have something to do with processes.

One parameter that you should always use is the Syntax parameter. Reading the cmdlet syntax is one of the easiest ways to determine how the cmdlet can be used, what its mandatory parameters are, and what its parameter values should look like.

There's more...

Even if you're an advanced PowerShell user, Get-Command can help you. Just have a look at the amount of data you can access for each command by using Format-List. We'll later learn about Get-Member as well:

```
# Discover more about a cmdlet with Format-List
Get-Command New-Item | Format-List -Property *

# Examine additional properties that might be helpful
$cmd = Get-Command New-Item

# Where does the cmdlet's help content come from?
$cmd.HelpUri

# Quickly jump to the location of a cmdlet's module
Set-Location -Path $cmd.Module.ModuleBase

# How many parameters does a cmdlet have including the common parameters?
$cmd.Parameters.Count

# Discovering the data of a parameter, in this case realizing that
# New-Item allows empty strings or $null to be passed to the Name parameter
$cmd.Parameters.Name
```

Look at the following screenshot of how the output looks:

```
PowerShell 6 (x64)
PS C:\Users\japete.EUROPE> $cmd   Get-Command New-Item
PS C:\Users\japete.EUROPE> $cmd.Parameters.Name


Name             : Name
ParameterType    : System.String
ParameterSets    : {[nameSet, System.Management.Automation.ParameterSetMetadata]}
IsDynamic        : False
Aliases          : {}
Attributes       : {nameSet, System.Management.Automation.AllowNullAttribute,
                   System.Management.Automation.AllowEmptyStringAttribute}
SwitchParameter  : False
```

See also

- Information about command precedence and the way Get-Command displays its
  results: https://docs.microsoft.com/en-us/powershell/module/microsoft.
  powershell.core/about/about_command_precedence?view=powershell-6

How do cmdlets work?

In contrast to native OS commands such as ps on Linux or tasklist on Windows, PowerShell uses cmdlets. These cmdlets always follow the same, simple syntax. Moreover, specifying parameters and their values always works the same with every cmdlet as well.

This section will help you to understand how cmdlets work before diving into them in later chapters.

Getting ready

In order to follow this recipe, you should have completed the installation of PowerShell Core for your operating system.

How to do it...

Please perform the following steps:

1. Start PowerShell Core.
2. Type `New-Item -Path variable: -Name myVariable -Value "Isn't it great?`.
3. Type `$myVariable`. `$myVariable` is a variable—a temporary storage space for your data. Just executing the variable will place it on the output.
4. Type `Get-ChildItem $home *.*`. This cmdlet uses no parameter names, and only parameter values. `$home` is a built-in variable and `*.*` filters for all files with a dot in the name.
5. Type `Get-ChildItem *.txt $home`. Observe the error this time. You can't mix positional parameters.
6. Type `Get-ChildItem -Filter *.txt -Path $home`. By using the parameter names, the cmdlet works again.
7. Type `$processName = 'powershell'`. Assigning anything to a variable like this will store the result in the variable.
8. Type `Get-Process $processName`.
9. Type `Get-Process $pid`. As opposed to the process name, using an ID will fail the cmdlet.
10. Type `Get-Process -Id $pid`. By using the correct parameter, the cmdlet works again.
11. Type `Get-Command -Syntax -Name Get-Process`. Observe the syntax of the cmdlet; there's more than one way to execute a cmdlet. These are called parameter sets.

How it works...

Native PowerShell cmdlets should all follow the exact same syntax: verb-noun. The verb indicates the action and the noun indicates the recipient of that action. Whether it is a cmdlet such as `New-Item` or `Get-Process`, the syntax always follows the same principle.

With all of its different parameters used, a full cmdlet call might look like the following example:

```
Get-ChildItem $home -Filter *.txt -File
```

`Get-ChildItem` is the name of the cmdlet. `$home` is the value of a so-called positional parameter, `Path`. `-Filter` uses the parameter name, and `*.txt` is the value provided for that parameter. `-File` is something called a switch parameter, which resembles a command-line switch.

Performing read-only operations

Very often, PowerShell is used to gather data for reporting purposes, exporting and viewing configurations, and more. This is generally accomplished using the various `Get` cmdlets. In `Chapter 2`, *Reading and Writing Output*, we'll then see how to further process the gathered data.

Since the `Get` cmdlets won't change anything on your system, this is a great way to discover what PowerShell has to offer.

Getting ready

In order to follow this recipe, you should have completed the installation of PowerShell Core for your operating system. Some cmdlets are Windows-specific and require a Windows operating system.

How to do it...

Please perform the following steps:

1. On a Windows system, you can use many built-in cmdlets with PowerShell Core. Try `Import-Module Storage -SkipEditionCheck`.
2. On a Windows system, type `Get-Disk` to list all disks. The result should look similar to the following:

```
PS C:\Users\japete.EUROPE> Get-Disk

Number Friendly Name Serial Number    HealthStatus    OperationalStatus    Total Size Partition
                                                                                      Style
------ ------------- -------------    ------------    -----------------    ---------- ---------
0      SAMSUNG MZ... S1ZKNXAGB23001   Healthy         Online               476.94 GB  GPT
1      TOSHIBA-TR150 X6VB3077K8XU      Healthy         Online               447.13 GB  GPT
```

3. On a Windows system, use `Get-Disk -Number 0 | Get-Partition` to retrieve the partitions on the first disk:

```
PS C:\Users\japete.EUROPE> Get-Disk -Number 0 | Get-Partition


  DiskPath: \\?\scsi#disk&ven_samsung&prod_mz71n512hchp-000#4&1da3eea3&0&000000#{53f56307-b6bf-11d0-94f2-00a0c91efb8b}

PartitionNumber  DriveLetter  Offset                                Size Type
---------------  -----------  ------                                ---- ----
1                             1048576                             450 MB Recovery
2                             472907776                           100 MB System
3                             577765376                            16 MB Reserved
4                 C           594542592                        475.61 GB Basic
5                             511281463296                        789 MB Recovery
```

4. On any system, try the `Get-Uptime` cmdlet to calculate the system uptime.
5. Use `Get-Culture` and `Get-UICulture` to view the current language settings.
6. Review the result of `Get-PackageProvider`. On a Windows system, additional providers are visible.

How it works...

PowerShell provides access to several different data sources by means of the `Get` cmdlets. After retrieving the data, PowerShell wraps it into an object model to allow you to store, display, filter, and process the data.

The data sources can be anything from services, event logs, and files to functions and variables. Every item that's retrieved is called an object and will have different properties and methods, which we will see later on.

There's more...

Just explore `Get-Command -Verb Get` to find all read-only cmdlets and simply have a look at what the return values are. There's no harm in trying!

On your way to building a perpetuum mobile? Make PowerShell execute all `Get` cmdlets for some fun:

```
$ErrorActionPreference = 'SilentlyContinue'
Get-Command -Verb Get | ForEach-Object { & $_ }
```

The ampersand operator will invoke an expression. By iterating over each `Get` cmdlet that is returned by `Get-Command`, we try to read everything we can get our hands on. Please be aware that this will take some time.

Introducing change to systems

While reading data is usually fine, PowerShell is also a great automation engine that's able to change a system configuration. We'll explore a couple of cmdlets that will, in some form, change your system configuration.

Getting ready

In order to follow this recipe, you should have completed the installation of PowerShell Core for your operating system. You should prepare a virtual machine for testing purposes since the cmdlets used in this recipe will inadvertently change your system configuration.

How to do it...

Please perform the following steps:

1. Review the output of `Get-Command -Verb New,Set,Remove,Register,Unregister,Start,Stop` to review some of the more frequently used cmdlets.
2. Execute `$file = New-TemporaryFile` to create a temporary file.
3. Use `'SomeContent' | Set-Content -Path $file` to change the file contents.
4. Use `'More content!' | Add-Content -Path $file` to append data to the file.
5. Review the contents with `$file | Get-Item | Get-Content -Path`.
6. Lastly use `$file | Remove-Item -Verbose` to get rid of the file again.
7. Use `$ping = Start-Process -FilePath ping -ArgumentList 'packtpub.com' -PassThru`.
8. Use `$ping | Stop-Process -PassThru` to stop the background process.

9. Use `Start-Job -Name Sleepy { Start-Sleep -Seconds 100; Get-Date }`.

10. Have a look at the job with `Get-Job -Name Sleepy`—is it ready to deliver the data?

11. Use `Get-Job -Name Sleepy | Wait-Job` to wait for the results.

12. Lastly, use `Get-Job -Name Sleepy | Receive-Job -Keep` to gather the results.

13. As an alternative, try `$job = Get-ChildItem -Recurse -Force -Path $home &` and `$job | Wait-Job | Receive-Job`.

14. Clean up any remaining jobs by closing PowerShell or executing `$job | Remove-Job; Get-Job -Name Sleepy | Remove-Job`.

How it works...

There're many verbs in PowerShell that indicate changes such as `New`, `Set`, and `Remove`. Many of those cmdlets also return objects for the data that's altered or created. If one of those parameters doesn't provide output such as `Stop-Process`, you can try using the `PassThru` parameter if it is available. It usually means that objects will be returned.

In the recipe, you can see the usual flow between different cmdlets. The file can be created, modified, and removed using the pipeline and cmdlets related to each other. In `Chapter 2`, *Reading and Writing Output*, we'll see how pipeline input is usually processed.

With the new parameter, `&`, you can start a background job, much like the forking parameter on Linux. The job results can be collected later as well.

There's more...

There're countless cmdlets that change a running system, some of which we will see in this book. Be sure to have a look at the PowerShell repository on GitHub and the documentation on `https://docs.microsoft.com/en-us/` to get all available information before ruining your weekend or your colleague's on-call shift.

See also

- The official documentation: `https://docs.microsoft.com/powershell`
- The official code: `https://github.com/powershell/powershell`

Discovering the environment

PowerShell Core has plenty of built-in variables that give you immediate information about the environment you are working with. The following recipe will show you the most important ones.

Getting ready

In order to follow this recipe, you should have completed the installation of PowerShell Core for your operating system.

How to do it...

Please perform the following steps:

1. Review the output of `$PSVersionTable`. With this variable, you'll always know which version and edition you are running.
2. Try to execute `Set-Location $PSHome; Get-ChildItem`. This folder contains all PowerShell binaries necessary to run the shell.
3. Have a look at the value of `$pid`. This variable always points to your own PowerShell process.
4. Try running the `Get-Item DoesNotExist` cmdlet and afterward, view the contents of `$Error`. This variable collects errors that happen in your session. Not all errors collected here have been visible on the CLI.
5. Try the following: `$true = $false`. You'll be pleasantly surprised that these variables are so-called constants and can't be changed.
6. Have a look at the output of `Get-Process | Format-Table Name,Threads`. You'll notice that the threads always seem to stop at four elements.
7. Display the contents of the variable, `$FormatEnumerationLimit`. The value of four isn't a coincidence. This variable governs how list output is formatted.
8. Have a look at `$PSScriptRoot`. For some reason, this variable is empty. The reason is that this variable is only set when a script is executed. It then will point to the directory containing the script. `$PSCommandPath` will contain the entire script path.

9. Run the following command: `Set-Content -Path ~/test.ps1 -Value '$PSScriptRoot;$PSCommandPath'; ~/test.ps1`. Examine the output; the first line contains the script directory, whereas the second line will show the full script path you executed.

10. Lastly, try `Get-Variable *Preference`. These variables control the behavior of PowerShell regarding errors, warnings and more. In `Chapter 2`, *Reading and Writing Output*, we'll have a close look at those.

How it works...

Each time a new PowerShell session is started, a bunch of variables is registered and filled. You can always rely on those variables to exist and be present in your scripts. Many of those variables contain preferences for cmdlets, formatting, and output.

There's more...

In the following chapters, there'll be more. We'll continue using the built-in variables for different purposes.

Reading and Writing Output 2

Working with output and data is the most common thing you'll be doing in PowerShell. From generating data for reports, to quickly reviewing a system's status, to the bulk-insertion of values into a database table: everything has to do with data and output.

We'll cover a lot of ground in this chapter and, with simple recipes, you'll see how to access the certificate stores, the registry on a Windows machine and the filesystem on any OS. You'll also learn how to properly work with variables.

In this chapter, we'll cover the following recipes:

- Working with output
- Storing data
- Read-only and constant variables
- Variable scoping
- The six streams
- Stream redirection
- Working with the filesystem provider
- Working with the registry provider
- Working with the certificate provider
- Creating your own provider
- NTFS alternate data streams

Technical requirements

The code for this chapter can be found at `https://github.com/PacktPublishing/ Powershell-Core-6.2-Cookbook/tree/master/Chapter02.`

Working with output

This very basic recipe shows you the ropes when it comes to gathering simple output from a local system. In order to retrieve output, we usually use cmdlets with the verb `Get`. You'll notice, however, that other cmdlets that create, change, or remove items can also sometimes return data to work with.

Getting ready

To get ready, you need to have PowerShell Core installed. This recipe works on any operating system capable of running PowerShell Core.

How to do it...

Let's perform the following steps:

1. Open PowerShell.
2. Execute `Get-UICulture`, followed by `Get-Process`. Notice that the default formatting for these two cmdlets seems to be tabular, shown as follows:

```
PS C:\Users\japete.EUROPE> Get-UICulture

LCID            Name            DisplayName
----            ----            -----------
1033            en-US           English (United States)


PS C:\Users\japete.EUROPE> Get-Process       $pid

 NPM(K)    PM(M)      WS(M)     CPU(s)      Id  SI ProcessName
 ------    -----      -----     ------      --  -- -----------
     82    97.50     146.98       3.58   22332   1 pwsh
```

3. Execute `Get-TimeZone`, followed by `Get-Uptime`. This time, the default output formatting seems to be a list, shown as follows:

```
PS C:\Users\japete.EUROPE> Get-TimeZone


Id                          : W. Europe Standard Time
DisplayName                 : (UTC+01:00) Amsterdam, Berlin, Bern, Rome
StandardName                : W. Europe Standard Time
DaylightName                : W. Europe Daylight Time
BaseUtcOffset               : 01:00:00
SupportsDaylightSavingTime  : True




PS C:\Users\japete.EUROPE> Get-UpTime


Days           : 0
Hours          : 5
Minutes        : 56
Seconds        : 26
Milliseconds   : 0
```

4. Now, execute `Get-ChildItem -Path *DoesNotExist*`. With this cmdlet, you might get no output back at all.
5. Lastly, execute `New-Item -Name file -Value 'Test file'`. While this cmdlet doesn't use the verb `Get`, it still returns output to work with.

How it works...

When you execute a `Get` cmdlet, PowerShell will usually try to retrieve data from a data source. This can, for example, be processes running on a system, installed network adapters, and the current system uptime.

See also

- For more information on formatting, see the help topic: `Get-Help about_Format.ps1xml`
- For more information on the type system, see the help topic: `Get-Help about_Types.ps1xml`

Storing data

Having data on the output might be fine for some administrators but, with PowerShell, we want to interact with our data. This recipe will show you that the information you see on your screen has a lot more to offer by having a first look at objects in the context of PowerShell scripting.

Using variables, you can store a reference to one or more objects in order to access them later on. Not only is it convenient while interactively working on the command line, but it might also mean that your scripts execute faster since the data isn't retrieved unnecessarily.

In this recipe, we'll see that the output you can observe isn't at all what it seems.

How to do it...

Install and open PowerShell Core on any system you prefer and execute the following steps:

1. Type `Get-Help about_Variables`.
2. Execute the following lines to create three new variables:

   ```
   $timestamp = Get-Date
   $processes = Get-Process
   $nothing = $null
   ```

3. Executing your variable will simply place it on the output again:

   ```
   $timestamp
   ```

4. Enter `$timestamp.` and then press the *Tab* key in the CLI or *Ctrl* + Space in CLI and VS Code. Observe the different properties and methods that can be used here.
5. Try executing `$timestamp.DayOfWeek` and `$timestamp.IsDaylightSavingTime()`.
6. Accessing properties and methods on lists works just as well. Try executing the following:

   ```
   $processes.Name
   $processes.Refresh()
   ```

7. Be careful when using uninitialized variables, as the result may be potentially devastating:

```
# Properties will be $null as well
$nothing.SomeProperty

# Method calls will throw an error
$nothing.SomeMethod()

# Be extra careful with cmdlets like Get-ChildItem!
# The default path is the current working directory
Get-ChildItem -Path $nothing -File | Remove-Item -WhatIf
```

8. Lastly, you don't need to create a variable at all if you just need to access a property or method once:

```
# Accessing properties and methods while discarding the
# original object requires expressions, $( )
$(Get-TimeZone).BaseUtcOffset
$(Get-Process).ToString()
```

How it works...

PowerShell will store either the value or the reference of an object in your variables. We'll learn about value types and reference types in Chapter 3, *Working with Objects*. For now, you should remember the term **dot notation** and simply try it with every variable you can find.

Using dot notation, individual properties and methods of one or more objects can be accessed, using expressions you don't even need to create a new variable. The entire expression is evaluated and the result is then used to access a property or a method.

In this recipe you have seen that the output that is formatted on screen does not contain all possible properties and methods. It is always crucial to fully explore the returned data, for example using the dot notation, in order to know what you are dealing with.

Read-only and constant variables

On occasion, you might want to use read-only or constant variables in your code. This recipe will show you how to create variables with specific options, such as read-only or constant, and why you would use those. You will also see some important automatic variables that are, incidentally, also constants.

How to do it...

Install and start PowerShell Core and execute the following steps:

1. Try to execute the following code block:

```
$true = $false
$pid = 0
$Error = "I don't make mistakes!"
```

2. Execute the next cmdlet to see why *Step 1* didn't work as intended:

```
Get-Variable | Where-Object -Property Options -like *Constant*
```

3. You can create your own read-only and constant variables using `variable cmdlets`:

```
# Creating read-only and constants requires the variable cmdlets
$logPath = 'D:\Logs'
Set-Variable -Name logPath -Option ReadOnly
```

4. Modifying read-only variables is still possible with the `-Force` parameter:

```
Set-Variable -Name logPath -Value '/var/log' -Force
```

5. The `Option` parameter is useful for other purposes as well, such as creating private and global variables:

```
Get-Help -Name New-Variable -Parameter Option
```

How it works...

`variable cmdlets` allow a bit more control over how variables are created than the simple assignment, `$variable = "Value"`, you saw in the previous recipe. By specifying options, you can control where the variable will be visible and whether it's read-only or constant.

Constant variables can only be declared when creating them with `New-Variable`, and can only be changed or removed by creating a new PowerShell session.

There's more...

If you're interested in more advanced topics regarding variables, take a look at the help topic `about_Variables`, which includes a link to further variable-related help topics as well.

Variable scoping

Scopes are important in your day-to-day scripting and they control the visibility of your variables, functions, and aliases. While PowerShell does a great job of handling scopes automatically in a way that feels very natural to the user, you can also use scopes implicitly in your scripts.

How to do it...

Install and start PowerShell Core and execute the following steps:

1. Execute the following code block:

```
$outerScope = 'Variable outside function'

function Foo
{
    Write-Host $outerScope
    $outerScope = 'Variable inside function'
    Write-Host $outerScope
}

Foo
Write-Host $outerScope
```

You should see the following output:

```
Variable outside function
Variable inside function
Variable outside function
PS /home/jhp> 
```

2. Modify the code a little bit to use scope modifiers like **private**, **script**, and **local** and try it again:

```
<#
  By explicitly using scopes, you can alter the state of virtually
any variable
  The following scopes are available. Inner scopes can access
variables from outer scopes
    global: The outermost scope, i.e. your current session
    script: The scope of a script or module
    local: The scope inside a script block
    private: In any scope, hidden from child scopes
    using: This one is special.
#>
$outerScope = 'Variable outside function'
$private:invisible = 'Not visible in child scopes'

function Foo
{
    Write-Host $outerScope
    $script:outerScope = 'Variable inside function'
    $local:outerScope = 'Both can exist'
    Write-Host "Private variable content can't be retrieved:
$invisible"
    Write-Host $outerScope
}

Foo
Write-Host $outerScope
```

This time, you'll notice that you can create multiple variables with the same name in different scopes.

3. Try the following code next, to see how the using scope works:

```
$processName = 'pwsh'
$credential = New-Object -TypeName pscredential -ArgumentList
'user',$('password' | ConvertTo-SecureString -AsPlainText -Force)
Start-Job -ScriptBlock { Get-Process -Name $processName} | Wait-Job
| Receive-Job # Error
Start-Job -ScriptBlock { Get-Process -Name $using:processName} |
Wait-Job | Receive-Job # Works
Start-Job -ScriptBlock {
$($using:credential).GetNetworkCredential().Password } | Wait-Job |
Receive-Job # Works as well
```

As you have seen in the output of the previous cmdlet, the using scope allows access to variables from within a script block.

How it works...

PowerShell usually handles variable scoping automatically. When you're working interactively on the CLI, you'll automatically be using the global scope. Calling a script will execute the script in its own scope, the script scope. Executing a function or a script block in general will launch it into another scope, the local scope.

By explicitly using scope modifiers, you can change variables, aliases, and functions that are usually outside of your current reach. While this allows you to work outside your normal boundaries, you have to be careful not to overwrite the code of your users by using the global scope to a large extent.

There's more...

Scoping can lead to some issues when not taken care of, for example, with dot-sourcing. Dot-sourcing a script with `. 'Full Script Path.ps1'` will mean that the entire script with all of its contents will be imported into your current scope. However, this also means that the script might overwrite your variables, aliases, functions, cmdlets, and so on.

The six streams

PowerShell has radically changed the way we automate, by not providing us with exit codes like many have grown used to. Instead, PowerShell exclusively uses different streams to convey output, errors, warnings, and more. Mastering those streams enables you to write more powerful and versatile scripts.

Working with the six streams happens to be so common that cmdlets support the so-called common parameters that all cmdlets share. In this recipe, you will be working with streams like *Output, Error, Warning, Verbose, Debug* and *Information*.

How to do it...

Install and start PowerShell Core and execute the following steps:

1. Try the following cmdlets and observe the result:

```
# This command will return both an error and one output object
Get-Item -Path $home,'doesnotexist'

# This command usually returns nothing. The Verbose parameter
however enables another stream.
Remove-Item -Path $(New-TemporaryFile) -Verbose
```

2. The `Verbose` parameter was actually part of the common parameters. Run the next lines of code and observe what happens now:

```
Get-Item -Path $home,'doesnotexist' -ErrorAction SilentlyContinue -
OutVariable file -ErrorVariable itemError
$file.FullName # Yes, it's your file
$itemError.Exception.GetType().FullName # This sure looks like your
error
```

3. Like the `Verbose` and `Debug` streams, the information stream isn't visible by default. Try executing the following code to see the versatility of the information stream:

```
function Get-AllTheInfo
{
    [CmdletBinding()]param()

    Write-Information -MessageData $(Get-Date) -Tags
Dev,CIPipelineBuild
    if ($(Get-Date).DayOfWeek -notin 'Saturday','Sunday')
    {
        Write-Information -MessageData "Get to work, you slacker!"
-Tags Encouragement,Automation
    }
}

# Like the Verbose and Debug streams, Information isn't visible by
default
# Working with the information is much improved by cmdlets that
actually process the tags
Get-AllTheInfo -InformationVariable infos
Get-AllTheInfo -InformationAction Continue

# Information can be filtered and processed, allowing more
```

sophisticated messages in your scripts

```
$infos | Where-Object -Property Tags -contains 'CIPipelineBuild'
```

4. Streams can also be controlled globally through the `Preference` variables as the next sample shows:

```
$ErrorActionPreference = 'SilentlyContinue'
$VerbosePreference = 'Continue'
Import-Module -Name Microsoft.PowerShell.Management -Force
Get-Item -Path '/somewhere/over/the/rainbow'
```

5. Additional parameters exist for the purpose of risk mitigation. You might already know them as `WhatIf` and `Confirm`. Take a look at the following example:

```
Remove-Item -Path (New-TemporaryFile) -Confirm
Remove-Item -Path (New-TemporaryFile) -WhatIf

# WhatIf and Confirm are governed by automatic variables as well
$WhatIfPreference = $true
New-TemporaryFile

$WhatIfPreference = $false # Reset to default
$ConfirmPreference = 'Low' # None, Low, Medium, High
New-TemporaryFile
```

6. As a cmdlet developer, try to use the `Write` cmdlets (apart from `Write-Host`) to write to different streams:

```
Write-Warning -Message 'A warning looks like this'
Write-Error -Message 'While an error looks like this'
Write-Verbose -Message 'Verbose, Debug and Information are hidden
by default'
```

How it works...

When a cmdlet is executed, PowerShell automatically uses the different streams to convey information. It's mostly up to the developer to make use of those streams. With a scripted cmdlet, this means using the `Write` cmdlets. By using the common parameters, the availability of a stream can be controlled.

Apart from controlling the availability of a stream, the entire stream can also be stored in a variable before allowing it to continue through the pipeline.

The reason why we try not to use `Write-Host` when developing a script is that the `Write-Host` cmdlet won't write to any of the streams. Instead, the console host is used to display text. The problem with this behavior is that the user has no control over the visibility of the host messages.

There's more...

If you want to add your own `WhatIf` and `Confirm` parameters, you don't need to implement them like normal parameters, shown as follows:

```
# Do not do this
function Test-WrongRiskMitigation
{
    param
    (
        [switch]
        $WhatIf
    )

    if ($WhatIf)
    {
        Write-Host "Simulating shredding of evidence"
    }
}
```

Instead, you can make use of the `CmdletBinding` attribute, which automatically enables all common parameters and is able to add `WhatIf` and `Confirm` properly:

```
function Test-RiskMitigation
{
 [CmdletBinding(SupportsShouldProcess)]
 param ( )

 if ($PSCmdlet.ShouldProcess('Target object, here: The evidence','Action,
here: Shred'))
 {
 Write-Host -ForegroundColor Red -Object 'Shredding evidence...'
 }
}

Test-RiskMitigation -WhatIf
Test-RiskMitigation
```

This way, you can simply react to the cmdlet emitting a confirmation message as a user. There's no additional implementation necessary apart from using the cmdlet binding and the automatic `PSCmdlet` variable.

Stream redirection

While it isn't used very often with PowerShell, stream redirection is used now and then for different purposes. External applications, especially, tend to confuse the error and the output stream. This obstacle can be overcome quite easily with stream redirection.

In the last recipe, you learned about stream numbers. All numbered streams can be redirected with the redirection operators, > and >>. This recipe will show you how and when to use the redirection operators instead of the common parameters like `ErrorAction` or `Verbose`.

How to do it...

Install and start PowerShell Core and execute the following steps:

1. All streams can be redirected, thereby creating a new file, as in the following example:

   ```
   Get-Item -Path $home,'nonexistant' 2> error.txt 1> success.txt
   Get-Content -Path error.txt, success.txt
   ```

2. You can also append different streams to files by using the >> operator:

   ```
   Get-Item -Path $home,'nonexistant' 2>> error.txt 1>> success.txt
   Get-Content -Path error.txt, success.txt
   ```

3. Streams can also be combined into the output by using the >&1 operator:

   ```
   # This helps e.g. with misbehaving external applications
   Get-Module -Verbose -List -Name 'PackageManagement','nonexistant'
   2>&1 4>&1
   ```

4. Combining streams into the output will pollute the output, however:

   ```
   $modules = Get-Module -Verbose -List -Name
   'PackageManagement','nonexistant' 2>&1 4>&1
   $modules.Count # This should contain only one...
   $modules[0] # This definitely doesn't look like a module
   ```

How it works...

Stream redirection works very differently compared to the `Variable` parameters you saw in the previous recipe. Redirection, as it's implemented in many operating systems, will redirect an entire stream such as `Error` to either a file or to the output stream. There's hardly a productive use for this apart from applications feeding the wrong streams.

As you have seen in *Step 4*, the usage of stream redirection to other streams should be used with care. The output of the `Get-Module` cmdlet has been polluted with an error record. This is a completely different data type and will certainly get in your way.

Working with the filesystem provider

PowerShell is extended by different providers that allow access to different data stores. The most ubiquitous one, however, is the filesystem provider. We use it automatically in many scripts and while working interactively on the command line.

This recipe introduces PowerShell providers and shows you what the filesystem provider can and can't do.

Getting ready

Install and start PowerShell Core. If you want to map a CIFS share, ensure that you can connect to one.

How to do it...

Let's perform the following steps:

1. As soon as you start PowerShell Core, the filesystem provider starts working and imports your mounted drives. You'll usually be placed in your own home directory or—as an administrator—in your system root.

2. Have a look at the output of `Get-PSProvider` to see all available providers, as shown as follows:

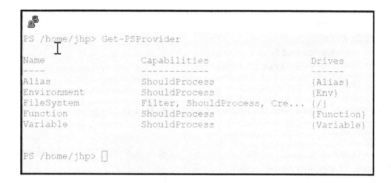

```
PS /home/jhp> Get-PSProvider

Name                 Capabilities                   Drives
----                 ------------                   ------
Alias                ShouldProcess                  {Alias}
Environment          ShouldProcess                  {Env}
FileSystem           Filter, ShouldProcess, Cre...  {/}
Function             ShouldProcess                  {Function}
Variable             ShouldProcess                  {Variable}


PS /home/jhp>
```

3. To see which cmdlets support providers, execute the following code:

```
# cmdlets that work with providers
Get-Command -Noun Location, Item, ItemProperty, ChildItem, Content,
Path
```

4. Different providers map different drives by default. Have a look at some of them by executing the following code:

```
# Providers usually automatically mount their drives
Get-PSDrive
```

5. Providers allow you to use the same basic operations, such as `Set-Location`, on any path. Try it out with the filesystem:

```
# Navigate the filesystem
Set-Location -Path $home
```

6. With the filesystem provider, the `Get-ChildItem` cmdlet can use additional parameters. Have a look at some of them with the next code sample:

```
# The File and FollowSymlink parameters are only available when the
filesystem provider is used
Get-ChildItem -Recurse -File -FollowSymlink
Get-ChildItem -Path env: # Only default parameters here

# Globbing is supported regardless of the operating system and
provider
Get-ChildItem -Path /etc/*ssh*/*config
Get-ChildItem -Path C:\Windows\*.dll
Get-ChildItem -Path env:\*module*
```

7. It pays to have a look at the syntax of a cmdlet with `Get-Command` syntax first. Take a look at the following code block:

```
# Take a look at the syntax for easier operations
# e.g. Creating multiple items from an array
$folders = @(
    "$home/test1"
    "$home/test2/sub1/sub2"
    "$home/test3"
)
New-Item -Path $folders -ItemType Directory -Force

# or creating a file in multiple locations
New-Item -Path $folders -Name 'someconfig.ini' -ItemType File -
Value 'key = value'
```

8. The filesystem provider behaves like the usual filesystem management tools of your operating system, but your results may vary when, for example, comparing the output of the Windows Explorer properties window with the number of files returned by `Get-ChildItem`:

```
New-Item $home\hidden\testfile,$home\hidden\.hiddentestfile -
ItemType File -Force
$(Get-Item $home\hidden\.hiddentestfile -Force).Attributes =
[System.IO.FileAttributes]::Hidden
Get-ChildItem -Path $home\hidden # .hiddentestfile won't appear
Get-ChildItem -Path $home\hidden -Hidden # Only shows the hidden
file
Get-ChildItem -Path $home\hidden -Force # Retrieves all files
```

9. The `Include` and `Exclude` parameters can be powerful filter parameters with `Get-ChildItem`:

```
# The Include and Exclude parameters can be useful filters
# / on Windows defaults to system drive
# Enables more complex filters than the Filter parameter
Get-ChildItem -Path $pshome -Recurse -Include *.dll,*.json -Exclude
deps.ps1
```

10. `content cmdlets` allow you to modify anything. With the filesystem, you would usually use them to read and modify file contents:

```
# This works for other Provider cmdlets as well
Get-Content -Path $pshome/Modules/PackageManagement/* -Include
*.psm1
Set-Content -Path $home\testfile -Value "File content`nMultiple
lines"
Add-Content -Path $home\testfile -Value 'Another new line'
Get-Content -Path $home\testfile
```

11. Lastly, execute the following code to map a new CIFS share with PowerShell:

```
# The filesystem provider is one that allows mounting more provider
drives
New-PSDrive -Name onlyInShell -Root \\someserver\someshare -
PSProvider FileSystem
Get-ChildItem -Path onlyInShell:
Remove-PSDrive -Name onlyInShell
```

How it works...

Depending on your operating system, there'll be the following providers:

- **Alias**: Allowing access to aliases
- **Environment**: Allowing access to environmental variables
- **Function**: Allowing access to function script blocks
- **Variable**: Allowing access to variables
- **FileSystem**: Allowing access to the filesystem and the mounting of CIFS shares
- **Certificate**: Currently Windows-only, allowing access to certificate stores
- **Registry**: Windows-only, allowing access to the Windows registry
- **WSMan**: Currently Windows-only, allowing access to WinRM configuration via WSMan

This is a non-exhaustive list, as new providers are added through modules or can be created with the module SHiPS, which we'll see in the recipe, *Create your own provider*.

The provider code implements different cmdlets such as `Get-ChildItem` and uses its own logic in the code to do what the cmdlet name implies. Not all providers implement all operations. While it's perfectly fine to use `New-Item` in the filesystem, it'll work differently with the certificate provider, which only allows creating new certificate stores.

Working with the registry provider

The registry provider is a Windows-only provider that allows access to the local registry of a host. All local hives can be navigated like a filesystem, with the usual provider cmdlets.

How to do it...

Install and start PowerShell Core on Windows and execute the following steps:

1. Execute the following code to list items in the local machine registry hive:

```
# Like the filesystem, the local registry hives can be browsed.
# ACLs apply, so AccessDenied errors aren't uncommon
Get-ChildItem HKLM:\SOFTWARE
```

2. Since there're no additional filters, you don't have much control over Get-ChildItem, which only returns registry keys and displays their values. Trying to enumerate values this way fails:

```
# Get-ChildItem returns Keys and their values by default
Get-ChildItem -Recurse -Path
'HKLM:\SOFTWARE\Microsoft\Windows\CurrentVersion\Run'
```

3. To enumerate registry values, the Get-ItemProperty cmdlet is used. Try the following code sample:

```
# To retrieve only properties, Get-ItemProperty is used instead
# Without a name, Get-ItemProperty returns all values in a given
path
Get-ItemProperty -Path 'HKLM:\SOFTWARE\Microsoft\Windows
NT\CurrentVersion'

# If only the property value is used
Get-ItemPropertyValue -Path 'HKLM:\SOFTWARE\Microsoft\Windows
NT\CurrentVersion' -Name ProductName

# While this is used predominantly for Registry access, it can be
used for the file
# system as well. However, this approach is very cumbersome
Get-ItemProperty -Path $(Get-Command -Name pwsh).Source -Name
LastWriteTime
```

4. Creating new items works similarly to the filesystem. Notice that registry keys are created, not values:

```
# In order to create new keys, you can use New-Item
New-Item -Path HKCU:\Software -Name MyProduct
```

5. In order to work with values, the ItemProperty cmdlets are used. Try the next code sample to see how new values are created and existing values are changed:

```
<#
To create new values, use New-ItemProperty. Values for PropertyType
include:
String (REG_SZ): Standard string
ExpandString (REG_EXPAND_SZ): String with automatic environment
variable expansion
Binary (REG_BINARY): Binary data
DWord (REG_DWORD): 32bit binary number
MultiString (REG_MULTI_SZ): String array
QWord (REG_QWORD): 64bit binary number
#>
New-ItemProperty -Path HKCU:\Software\MyProduct -Name Version -
Value '0.9.9-rc1' -PropertyType String
New-ItemProperty -Path HKCU:\Software\MyProduct -Name SourceCode -
Value $([Text.Encoding]::Unicode.GetBytes('Write-Host "Cool, isnt
it?"')) -PropertyType Binary

# Test it ;)
[scriptblock]::Create($([Text.Encoding]::Unicode.GetString($(Get-
ItemPropertyValue -Path HKCU:\Software\MyProduct -Name
SourceCode)))).Invoke()

# Change an item
Set-ItemProperty -Path HKCU:\Software\MyProduct -Name SourceCode -
Value $([Text.Encoding]::Unicode.GetBytes('Stop-Computer -WhatIf'))
[Text.Encoding]::Unicode.GetString($(Get-ItemPropertyValue -Path
HKCU:\Software\MyProduct -Name SourceCode))
```

6. Removing items is straightforward. Try the next code sample to remove your key again:

```
# The default removal cmdlet works just as well
Remove-Item -Path HKCU:\Software\MyProduct -Verbose
```

7. Note that the registry provider is unable to map remote registries—you need to use .NET to be able to do that.

```
# Not capable of using credentials
Get-PSProvider -PSProvider Registry

# Mapping local hives is fine
New-PSDrive -Name HKCR -PSProvider Registry -Root HKEY_CLASSES_ROOT
Get-ChildItem -Path HKCR:
Remove-PSDrive -Name HKCR
```

How it works...

Like the filesystem provider, the registry provider implements the provider cmdlets. This allows you to interact with the registry in your scripts. To overcome the issue of not being able to map a remote registry hive, the `Invoke-Command` cmdlet can be used.

While the filesystem works with files and folders, the registry works with keys and values. This structure may look like the filesystem, but the implementation is slightly different. In order to access files, any `Item` cmdlet will do. To access registry values, the `Item` cmdlets certainly work, but to retrieve only the content of a value, you need to use the `ItemProperty` cmdlets.

There's more...

While `Invoke-Command` via web service management and Windows remote management should be your preferred way of accessing remote registry keys, serialization and other issues can occur. Using .NET, you can also simply access a remote registry hive via **Distributed Component Object Model** (**DCOM**) and **Remote Procedure Calls** (**RPC**) from your local session. To get started, have a look at the following code sample:

```
$remoteKey =
[Microsoft.Win32.RegistryKey]::OpenRemoteBaseKey('LocalMachine', 'MyHost',
'Registry64')
$remoteUserKey =
[Microsoft.Win32.RegistryKey]::OpenRemoteBaseKey('CurrentUser', 'MyHost',
'Registry64')
```

The previous lines opened two remote hives, HKLM and HKCU. With the next lines, you can get value names in a key and get a specific value from said key:

```
$remoteKey.OpenSubKey('SOFTWARE\Microsoft\Windows
NT\CurrentVersion').GetValueNames()
$remoteKey.OpenSubKey('SOFTWARE\Microsoft\Windows
NT\CurrentVersion').GetValue('ProductName')
```

To create remote sub keys and remote values, you can use the following lines. Notice the Boolean parameter value for the OpenSubKey method. The key needs to opened with write access, the default is read-only:

```
$remoteUserKey.OpenSubKey('SOFTWARE',$true).CreateSubKey('MyProduct').SetVa
lue('Version','1.2.3.4', 'String')
$remoteUserKey.OpenSubKey('SOFTWARE\MyProduct').GetValue('Version')
$remoteUserKey.DeleteSubKeyTree('Software\MyProduct')
```

While not strictly necessary, you should always free up any references to .NET objects so that the garbage collection can clean up and free up resources:

```
$remoteKey.Dispose()
$remoteUserKey.Dispose()
```

Working with the certificate provider

Like the registry provider, the certificate provider is Windows-only. It allows you to access your certificate stores for the computer and user accounts, with some additional filtering methods available to you.

As with the registry provider, there are some things to consider.

How to do it...

Install and start PowerShell Core on a Windows host and execute the following steps:

1. Use the provider cmdlet to list certificate stores and certificates inside a store:

```
# Another Windows-only provider, allowing access to local cert
stores
Get-PSProvider -PSProvider Certificate

# Again, the default cmdlets apply
# List all certificate stores
Get-ChildItem -Path Cert:\CurrentUser
```

```
# List all certificates of the user's personal store
Get-ChildItem -Path Cert:\CurrentUser\my
```

2. The extended parameters of the `Get-ChildItem` cmdlet help to apply additional filters:

```
# The parameters offered by the Certificate provider are very
interesting
# on Windows PowerShell, additional parameters like -EKU and -
SslServerAuthentication will be available
Get-ChildItem -Path Cert:\CurrentUser\my -CodeSigningCert
```

3. With PowerShell Core, not all additional parameters of `Get-ChildItem` that you might know from Windows PowerShell can be used. `Where-Object` is still your friend:

```
$certificate = Get-ChildItem -Path Cert:\CurrentUser\my | Select-
Object -First 1

# Filter on the OIDs. If OID can't be resolved, use the numeric
object ID instead of the friendly name!
# The OID is more reliable and not subject to localization
$certificate.EnhancedKeyUsageList

# for example searching for all client authentication certificates
Get-ChildItem -Path cert:\currentuser\my | Where-Object -
FilterScript {$_.EnhancedKeyUsageList.ObjectId -eq
'1.3.6.1.5.5.7.3.2'}

# Not unimportant; Filter on certificates where the private key is
accessible, i.e. to digitally sign documents
Get-ChildItem -path Cert:\CurrentUser\my |
    Where-Object -Property HasPrivateKey |
    Format-table -Property Subject,Thumbprint,@{Label='EKU';
Expression = {$_.EnhancedKeyUsageList.FriendlyName -join ','}}

$certificate.HasPrivateKey
```

4. Not all `Item` cmdlets are implemented for the certificate provider:

```
# While New and Set cmdlets aren't implemented for certificates,
Remove can be used for some spring cleaning
Get-ChildItem -Path Cert:\CurrentUser\my |
    Where-Object -Property NotAfter -lt $([datetime]::Today) |
    Remove-Item -WhatIf
```

5. But you can still create new certificate stores:

```
# New-item can be used for new stores - but this is rarely done
New-Item -Path Cert:\LocalMachine\NewStore
Remove-Item -Path Cert:\LocalMachine\NewStore
```

How it works...

Like the other providers, the cmdlets implement their own functionality and allow access to certificates in your personal store. Although the functionality is quite limited, the `Get-ChildItem` and `Get-Item` cmdlets are useful to filter certificates and remove expired certificates if they aren't pruned automatically.

Creating your own provider

Creating your own provider can be a very useful (and fun) skill to learn as well. The PowerShell module SHiPS enables you to map any existing data structure in order to access it as a drive. At the moment, SHiPS only supports the `Get-Item` and `Get-ChildItem` cmdlets to retrieve data.

SHiPS is used, for example, with PowerShell in Azure Cloud Shell (https://shell.azure.com), as well as with the popular lab automation module, AutomatedLab (https://github.com/automatedlab/automatedlab).

How to do it...

Install and start PowerShell Core and execute the following steps:

1. In order to be able to develop your own provider, you need to install SHiPS from the gallery first. Alternatively, you can follow the steps outlined at https://github.com/powershell/ships to compile it yourself with .NET Core:

```
# Install SHiPS
Install-Module -Name SHiPS -Force -Scope CurrentUser
```

2. SHiPS is based on PowerShell classes. First of all, you might want to add your root container:

```
# SHiPS providers are based around PowerShell classes.
# To create a new directory, or container, your class needs to
# inherit from the class ShipsDirectory
class MyContainerType : Microsoft.PowerShell.SHiPS.SHiPSDirectory
{
    # Your new container should now implement the function
GetChildItem() at the very least.
    # In order to actually return child items, your container needs
content!
    MyContainerType([string]$name): base($name)
    {
    }

    [object[]] GetChildItem()
    {
        $obj = @()
        $obj += [MyFirstLeafType]::new();
        return $obj;
    }
}
```

3. Add another container that is nested in your root, as well as one or two leafs:

```
# Leafs are the child items of your containers that can't contain
any more items themselves.
# Containers are still allowed to contain more containers though.
class MyFirstContainerType :
Microsoft.PowerShell.SHiPS.SHiPSDirectory
{
    MyFirstContainerType([string]$name): base($name)
    {
    }
}

class MyFirstLeafType : Microsoft.PowerShell.SHiPS.SHiPSLeaf
{
    MyFirstLeafType() : base ("MyFirstLeafType")
    {
    }

    [string]$LeafProperty = 'Value'
    [int]$LeafLength = 42
    [datetime]$LeafDate = $(Get-Date)
}
```

4. Lastly, store your provider definition as a module and import it:

```
# Take a look at the sample code
psedit .\ShipsProvider.psm1

# In order to mount your provider drive, you can simply use New-PSDrive
Import-Module -Name .\ShipsProvider -Force
```

 `psedit` is a handy function available in Visual Studio Code to open files in the editor! If you are working in another IDE, you might need a different command to view the code. Try `Get-Content` instead.

5. With SHiPS and your module imported, you can mount your drive. Notice that the root of your drive relates to the root class that contains your hierarchy:

```
New-PSDrive -Name MyOwnDrive -PSProvider SHiPS -Root
"ShipsProvider#MyContainerType"
```

6. Examine it with the `item` cmdlets:

```
# Now you can use the item cmdlets at your leisure
Get-ChildItem -Path MyOwnDrive:\MyFirstContainerType
Get-ChildItem -Path MyOwnDrive: -Recurse
```

7. Notice how your leafs and containers are displayed, as follows:

```
PS C:\> Get-ChildItem       MyOwnDrive:


    Directory: MyOwnDrive:


Mode   Name
----   ----
.        MyFirstLeafType  ◄─────────────────── Leaf object
+        MyFirstContainerType  ◄─────────────── Container object


    Directory: MyOwnDrive:\MyFirstContainerType


Mode   Name
----   ----
.        MyFirstLeafType
```

How it works...

SHiPS allows you to map out a read-only data structure of your choice, limited only by your programming skills. While you can't use cmdlets such as Remove-Item, you can define your own object methods or expose functions that call cmdlets or .NET methods internally. Your own provider might also return .NET objects from existing classes, such as the System.IO.FileInfo object returned from the filesystem provider.

Your data can still be processed with the Object cmdlets, piped and otherwise, worked with in PowerShell. Just be aware that, to retrieve the data, only Get-Item and Get-ChildItem can be used, and that all of the other provider-aware cmdlets simply aren't implemented.

There's more...

If you feel up to it, you can add dynamic parameters to your provider. Remember the File parameter for the FileSystem provider or CodeSigningCertificate for the Certificate provider? You can add your own parameters easily with SHiPS:

```
class MyDynamicParameter
{
    [Parameter()]
    [switch]
    $DispenseCandy
}

class MyContainerType : Microsoft.PowerShell.Ships.SHiPSDirectory
{
    ...
    [object] GetChildItemDynamicParameters()
    {
        return [MyDynamicParameter]::new()
    }
    ...
}

New-PSDrive -Name MyOwnDrive -PSProvider SHiPS -Root
ShipsProviderAdvanced#MyContainerType
Get-ChildItem MyOwnDrive: -Recurse -DispenseCandy
```

This isn't only limited to switch parameters, but to any parameter type you can think of. This includes parameter validation as well, allowing you, for example, to define a ValidateSet parameter for Get-ChildItem and your own provider.

See also

- For more documentation on SHiPS, see `https://github.com/powershell/ships`.
- To learn more about classes, either peruse the book *Learn PowerShell Core 6.0* by *David das Neves* and *Jan-Hendrik Peters* or have a look at the official documentation at `https://docs.microsoft.com/en-us/powershell/module/microsoft.powershell.core/about/about_classes?view=powershell-6`.

NTFS iternate data streams

While not exactly related to the streams such as output and error, which we've seen so far, there's a special type of stream that's quite interesting to play around with: the NTFS alternate data stream. This recipe is specific to NTFS-formatted volumes and will show you why the `Unblock-File` cmdlet exists in the first place.

How to do it...

Install and start PowerShell Core and execute the following steps:

1. Download a file to play around with:

```
# To get started, download any file to an NTFS-formatted volume.
# This lab assumes that you're storing downloads in $home\Downloads
$downloadRoot = "~\Downloads"

# Download any file, for example a release of the popular lab
automation framework AutomatedLab
start
https://github.com/AutomatedLab/AutomatedLab/releases/download/v5.1
.0.153/AutomatedLab.msi
```

2. Examine the file with `Get-Item`. Do you notice any irregularities? Let's see:

```
# At first glance, this file appears normal
Get-Item $downloadRoot\AutomatedLab.msi
```

3. Now try `Get-Item` again, with the `-Stream` parameter. What is different now? Let's see:

```
Get-Item $downloadRoot\AutomatedLab.msi -Stream *
```

The previous line of code displays what you can see in the filesystem properties dialog. The stream called `Zone.Identifier` is responsible for creating this message in the UI!

 All NTFS files contain a data stream and additional streams such as the zone identifier for file downloads.

4. Streams can be processed with the `Item` and `Content` cmdlets:

```
# Streams can be processed with the Content-cmdlets
# The data stream is of course returned by default
Get-Content -Path C:\windows\logs\cbs\cbs.log -Stream ':$DATA'

# The zone identifier specifies if the file was downloaded from the
Internet or another zone
# You can find out all kinds of information from this, like the
content URL in this example.
```

```
# At the time of writing, the HostUrl resided on the S3 storage by
Amazon and used an
# access signature to set the link expiration date
Get-Content -Path $downloadRoot\AutomatedLab.msi -Stream
Zone.Identifier
```

5. You can't only read them, you can also create your own:

```
# Let's try the other content cmdlets now...
Set-Content -Path .\TestFile -Value 'A simple file'
$bytes = [Text.Encoding]::Unicode.GetBytes('Write-Host "Virus
deployed..." -Fore Red')
$base64script = [Convert]::ToBase64String($bytes)

# We have now hidden a script inside an inconspicuous file
Set-Content -Path .\TestFile -Stream Payload -Value $base64script

# And of course we can execute it in this beautiful one-liner
[scriptblock]::Create($([Text.Encoding]::Unicode.GetString($([Conve
rt]::FromBase64String($(Get-Content .\TestFile -Stream
Payload)))))).Invoke()
```

6. You can also clear stream contents as well as remove streams:

```
# You can clear the stream manually as well
Clear-Content -Path .\TestFile -Stream Payload

# And you can remove the entire stream
Remove-Item -Stream Payload -Path .\TestFile
```

7. For the zone identifier stream, the Unblock-File cmdlet makes removal easier:

```
# The Unblock-File cmdlet does exactly the same with the stream
Zone.Identifier
Unblock-File -Path $downloadRoot\AutomatedLab.msi
Get-Item -Path $downloadRoot\AutomatedLab.msi -Stream *
```

How it works...

NTFS alternate data streams are, as the name implies, alternative streams where data can be stored. Since this lends itself to malware deployment similar to what you tried in the recipe, these streams are used more often than you might think.

The zone identifier is the easiest and most readily available example since it's usually written when you download a file by traditional means in your browser. The individual streams for your reference are as follows:

Zone ID	Zone display name
0	My computer
1	Local intranet
2	Trusted sites
3	Internet
4	Restricted sites

There's more...

Windows components such as the File Server Resource Manager or products such as DropBox are using an alternate data stream to store information as well. In the case of DropBox, this stream is called `com.dropbox.attributes`, which seems to be used to store data about the machine the file was synced from, as shown as follows:

```
PS C:\> get-content 'C:\Users\japete.EUROPE\dropbox\Daleks Exterminate.mp3'     com.dropbox.attributes
x▯▯VJ)▯/H▯▯O▯▯I▯L▯▯▯ON▯Q▯R▯V▯ML▯▯▯▯%▯▯▯▯R▯K▯▯▯%▯J▯▯▯t▯B77▯▯▯@▯?▯▯ ▯r[[▯▯▯Z ▯D▯\
```

I hope your curiosity is now piqued, so go ahead and have a look at your files to see what lies hidden in the depths of your drives:

```
Get-ChildItem -Path ~ -Recurse -File | Where-Object -FilterScript {
    $($_ | Get-Item -Stream *).Stream -notmatch ':\$DATA|Zone\.Identifier'
}
```

3
Working with Objects

Whenever we use PowerShell, we are bound to be using objects. Knowing the basics of .NET and Object-Oriented Programming plays a vital role in your ability to master PowerShell.

In this chapter, you will learn the very basics of .NET. The last few recipes are geared more toward experienced users who want to unlock the full potential of PowerShell.

In this chapter, we will cover the following recipes:

- Introduction to Object-Oriented Programming
- Exploring object properties
- Exploring object methods
- Using static class members
- Creating classes
- Using custom objects
- Manipulating and extending objects
- [ref], [out], and delegates

Technical requirements

The code for this chapter can be found in this book's GitHub repository at `https://github.com/PacktPublishing/Powershell-Core-6.2-Cookbook/tree/master/Chapter03`.

Introduction to Object-Oriented Programming

In this recipe, you will be given an introduction to Object-Oriented Programming. Since this is half theory, half practice, not all of the steps will give you instructions/code that you need to execute.

Getting ready

Download and start an editor you are comfortable with. For the best experience, try Visual Studio Code, which is free and open source: https://code.visualstudio.com/.

How to do it...

Perform the following steps:

1. Open your favorite editor and examine the following C# code:

```csharp
namespace Vehicle
{
    public class Car
    {
        public string Make {get; set;}
        public string Model {get; set;}
        public ConsoleColor Color {get; set;}
        public UInt16 TireCount {get;set;}
        public UInt16 Speed {get; private set;}

        public Car()
        {
            TireCount = 4;
        }

        public Car(string make, string model, ConsoleColor color)
        {
            Color = color;
            Make = make;
            Model = model;
        }
    }
}
```

2. Notice the `namespace` keyword right at the beginning. Namespaces are collections of classes, enumerations, and other types. If you want to compare this to Java, think of a package:

```
namespace Vehicle
```

3. There are usually one or more classes inside a `namespace`. Classes are templates for new objects that are created. Think of the `Get-Process` cmdlet – every time you execute this cmdlet, data is pulled from the operating system and figuratively molded by the template into an output you can then use:

```
public class Car
```

4. Classes usually possess properties (or fields), methods, events, and more. Each new object that's created from this class, often called an instance of a class, automatically possesses every property, method, and so on that the class template has defined. Add the following properties to the body of your class inside curly braces:

```
public string Make {get; set;}
public string Model {get; set;}
public Nullable<ConsoleColor> Color {get; set;}
public UInt16 TireCount {get;set;}
public UInt16 Speed {get; private set;}
```

5. Execute the following command:

```
$car = New-Object -TypeName Vehicle.Car
```

6. Examine your new object by outputting it. At the moment, it looks pretty bare, apart from some default values:

```
$car
<# Will output:
Make :
Model :
Color :
TireCount : 4
Speed : 0
#>
```

7. Classes usually contain a so-called constructor. The constructor in C# is automatically generated, but can be redefined to allow passing parameters, as you can see in the following example:

```
$car = New-Object -TypeName Vehicle.Car -ArgumentList
'Opel','GT','Red'
$car
<#
Make : Opel
Model : GT
Color : Red
TireCount : 4
Speed : 0
#>
```

8. A shortcut to creating new objects is to execute the constructor directly with the static new method. To learn more about static methods, read through this chapter! Use the new method of the Vehicle.Car class to create a new car:

```
[Vehicle.Car]::new('Opel','GT','Red')
```

How it works...

.NET is an Object-Oriented Programming language, and like Java and others is a high language. Unlike other programming languages such as C, Assembler, and others, developers do not need to concern themselves with memory management and machine-specific things.

Through a wealth of different classes for all kinds of things such as IO, networking, text processing, and much, much more, C# and .NET are a popular choice for many developers. But it should become a popular choice for administrators as well: PowerShell Core is based on .NET Core and can access the full range of .NET Standard functionalities, giving you access to many powerful and useful classes.

In *Steps 1* through *4*, you examined a C# code snippet that was imported using the Add-Member cmdlet. In PowerShell, the New-Object cmdlet is used to create an instance of a class. In some instances, you have to call this cmdlet yourself to create your objects, as you saw in *Step 5*. More often, though, a cmdlet will create instances of classes for you when executed.

As we saw in this recipe, .NET classes are organized into namespaces.When we work with .NET, we usually use classes that are defined somewhere in the System namespace and its child namespaces, for example, System.IO or System.Management.Automation.

Every class will have a combination of properties and methods, among other types, like events. Those class members can be publicly accessible or only accessible to the class itself.

In the following recipes, we will gradually discover more and more aspects of the .NET Framework and its use in PowerShell.

See also

- For more information on the .NET Framework, see `https://docs.microsoft.com/en-us/dotnet/` and for C# specifically
- Introduction to C#: `https://docs.microsoft.com/en-us/dotnet/csharp/tutorials/intro-to-csharp`

Exploring object properties

You know by now that everything we do in PowerShell will eventually generate objects. But how can you make use of this behavior? In the following recipe, we will thoroughly examine objects with the `Get-Member` cmdlet. Along with `Get-Command` and `Get-Help`, `Get-Member` is going to be the most important cmdlet in your toolkit.

Getting ready

Install and start PowerShell Core.

How to do it...

Perform the following steps:

1. Instantiate a new object and store it in a variable:

   ```
   $folder = Get-Item -Path .
   ```

2. To find out what the object can offer, we can use the `Get-Member` cmdlet:

   ```
   # Either pipe a collection of objects to get member
   $folder | Get-Member

   # or pass a single object to the parameter InputObject
   Get-Member -InputObject $folder
   ```

3. To filter the output to properties only, we can use the `MemberType` parameter:

```
# Filter the output a bit with the MemberType parameter
$folder | Get-Member -MemberType Properties
```

4. Let's examine some members of this class: `FullName`, `Exists`, `Parent`, and `*Time`:

```
# Select only a subset of member with the Name parameter
$folder | Get-Member -Name FullName,Parent,*Time, Exists
```

Notice the definition of each number in the output of *Step 4*. `FullName`, `Exists`; the different `Time` properties are simple data types such as string, Boolean values, and timestamps. The `Parent` property, however, is of the `System.IO.DirectoryInfo` data type:

Name	Type
FullName	System.String
Parent	System.IO.DirectoryInfo
CreationTime	System.DateTime
LastAccessTime	System.DateTime
LastWriteTime	System.DateTime
Exists	System.Boolean

Try passing the `Parent` property to `Get-Member` next – what do you notice when comparing the output with *Step 2*?

```
# As long as an object exists on the output, you can deploy Get-Member
$folder.Parent | Get-Member
```

If you are not sure which data type an object has, there is always the `GetType` method. This method exists on any .NET object and is inherited from the base class `System.Object`:

```
# Our $folder is apparently of the same data type as its parent.
# This should not come as a surprise, since the parent is also a directory.
# You can see the type of any object with GetType()
$folder.GetType().FullName # System.IO.DirectoryInfo
$folder.Parent.GetType().FullName # System.IO.DirectoryInfo
```

Try the following code and examine the following object properties and methods as well:

```
# Everything is an object, really.
42 | Get-Member

# External applications will always return string arrays
# Whether it is Linux
mount | Get-Member
$(mount).GetType().FullName # System.Object[] - a list of strings, one for
each line

# or Windows
ipconfig | Get-Member
$(ipconfig).GetType().FullName # System.Object[] - a list of strings, one
for each line

# Are you missing the exit code of your external application? It is
recorded automatically
$LASTEXITCODE
```

The most basic data types that we use on a day-to-day basis are as follows:

```
# The most basic classes that we use have so-called type accelerators
[bool] # System.Boolean, the boolean values 0,1,$false,$true
[int16] # Also referred to as short: 16bit integers
[int] # 32bit integers
[int64] # Also referred to as long: 64bit integers
[string] # A series of UTF16 code units or characters
[char] # A single UTF16 code unit or character
[datetime] # A timestamp
[timespan] # A timespan
[array] # A list of objects
[hashtable] # A collection of key-value-pairs
```

The aforementioned list is, of course, non-exhaustive. You will find yourself using other data types frequently as well.

How it works...

The Get-Member cmdlet is used to find all publicly visible class members through reflection. Most of the time, these members will be properties and methods. Don't be surprised to find events here as well. Events can be used for some more advanced scripting where you would like to react to object events. This could, for example, be a FileSystemWatcher that fires an event as soon as a file is changed.

When examining the output of Get-Member, you often see in the member definition that certain members are read-only. Take the following example of a file or directory. While the full name can only be read (get;), the creation time can be modified (get; set;). Changing the FullName property is only possible by executing the MoveTo method:

```
FullName Property string FullName {get;}
CreationTime Property datetime CreationTime {get;set;}
```

There's more...

When you learned about the basic data types that we frequently use, you will have noticed that most of them were so-called value types. In .NET, we differentiate between value types and reference types. Value types are created in the stack, whereas reference types are a reference to the heap.

Value types such as integers or Boolean values do not possess any properties other than their own value. Their structures usually provide a variety of conversion methods, such as the ubiquitous ToString method on every object, or the ToDateTime method on an integer.

Reference types like System.Diagnostics.Process are stored on the heap and undergo garbage collection by the language runtime. Be careful when working with reference types. Since only a reference to an object on the heap is stored in a variable, copying the variable will only copy the reference, and not the value itself.

Try the following bit of code to visualize the difference between value and reference types:

```
# Value types and reference types
# Vale types like integers are stored in the stack
$intA = 4
$intB = $intA
$intB = 42
$intA -eq 4 # still true

# Reference types like arrays are pointing to the heap
$arrayA = 1,2,3,4
$arrayB = $arrayA
$arrayB[0] = 'Value'
$arrayA[0] -eq 1 # This is now false! arrayA has been changed as well as
arrayB
```

See also

- Value and reference types: `https://docs.microsoft.com/en-us/dotnet/visual-basic/programming-guide/language-features/data-types/value-types-and-reference-types`
- .NET API documentation: `https://docs.microsoft.com/en-us/dotnet/api/?view=netcore-2.2`

Exploring object methods

Alongside object properties, we also often need object methods to manipulate objects or access information. Like properties, methods are members of a class that each object will offer. Through reflection, `Get-Member` can also provide detailed information about methods of a class or an object.

We commonly use object methods to accomplish tasks for which there are no built-in cmdlets available, such as writing NTFS access control entries. Object methods are also commonly used to alter object properties that would otherwise be read-only, like the full name of a file, which can be changed with the `MoveTo` method.

Getting ready

Install and start PowerShell Core.

How to do it...

Perform the following steps:

1. The `Get-Member` cmdlet is again an indispensable tool when working with .NET classes. Try the following bit of code to list all object methods of the `File` and `Directory` objects:

   ```
   Get-ChildItem | Get-Member -MemberType Methods
   ```

2. Execute the following commands:

   ```
   # Accessing methods
   $file = New-TemporaryFile
   $parentPath = Split-Path -Path $file.FullName -Parent
   $newPath = Join-Path -Path $parentPath -ChildPath newFileName
   ```

```
# With arguments
$file.MoveTo($newPath)
$file.FullName # The MoveTo method is a way of changing the
FullName property, which is read-only.

# and without arguments
$file.Delete()
```

3. Be careful when accessing methods that do not exist, or methods of objects that do not exist. Try to do so now by calling a method that does not exist:

```
# Careful with empty objects or non-existing methods
# Method does not exist. Throws a terminating MethodNotFound error
$file.DoStuff()

# Object does not exist. Throws an InvokeMethodOnNull exception.
($null).Delete()
```

4. Execute the following code:

```
# Finding possible arguments
# CopyTo has two overloads
($file | Get-Member -Name CopyTo).Definition

# A handy shortcut is simply leaving the parentheses off
$file.CopyTo
```

5. Now execute the following code:

```
# Performance of .NET calls versus cmdlets
Measure-Command -Expression {
    Get-ChildItem -Recurse -File -Path /
}

Measure-Command -Expression {
    $root = Get-Item -Path /
    $options = [System.IO.EnumerationOptions]::new()
    $options.RecurseSubdirectories = $true
    $root.GetFiles('*', $options)
}
```

6. Methods may or may not return objects. If they do, Get-Member will display the data type that is returned for each overload:

```
# Method calls may or may not return values
$process = Get-Process -Id $PID
$process | Get-Member -Name WaitForExit
```

```
# The WaitForExit method has two overloads
# When passing a timeout to WaitForExit, it returns a boolean value
indicating if the process
# has exited in the allotted timeout.
$pingProcess = if ($IsWindows)
{
    Start-Process -FilePath ping -ArgumentList 'microsoft.com','-n
10' -PassThru
}
else
{
    Start-Process -FilePath ping -ArgumentList 'microsoft.com','-n
10' -PassThru
}

# Waiting 500ms should return false, since our 10 ICMP request will
most likely not be done
if( -not $pingProcess.WaitForExit(500))
{
    Write-Host -ForegroundColor Yellow "Pinging not yet
complete..."
}

# The other overload has no return type (void) and will wait
indefinitely
$pingProcess.WaitForExit()
```

How it works...

Accessing members of a class, whether they are properties or methods, is usually achieved through dot notation. In the case of methods, a pair of parentheses is also necessary. Please note that there should not be any whitespace characters between the method name and the parentheses.

You started off in *Step 1* by using Get-Member to discover properties and methods. Executing a method is different from accessing a property. Method calls always require parentheses and can optionally accept parameters. You did this in *Step 2* by using the MoveTo method with arguments and the Delete method without arguments.

As you saw in *Step 1*, there are plenty of methods to choose from. Some methods you will encounter will have more than one way of calling it. These are called overloads. The CopyTo method of a file, for example, allows you to specify either the file path or the file path and a Boolean flag, indicating whether the destination will be overwritten. In *Step 4*, you used Get-Member as well as dot notation to see method definitions.

Method calls can improve your script performance, sometimes significantly. Unfortunately, this doesn't mean that your code will be more readable. In *Step 5*, you tried two different methods of listing files to see the difference between native PowerShell and .NET.

If a method accepts arguments, they are inserted into parentheses, separated by a comma. Even when calling .NET methods, PowerShell will attempt to convert your arguments into the correct data types if possible. Use parentheses to form expressions if you are using the return value of a cmdlet as input, as follows:

```
$process.WaitForExit($(New-TimeSpan -Seconds 30).TotalMilliseconds)
```

There's more...

Did you know that `ForEach-Object` can also initiate method calls? If you take a look at the syntax of `ForEach-Object`, you will notice a second parameter set that has a `MemberName` parameter. It does not matter if the member you are accessing is a method or a property. Try it now by spawning 10 processes! Take care to use another process, for example gedit if you are on Linux and use Gnome Desktop:

```
# Foreach-Object and members
# We create 10 notepads and use the WaitForExit method on all of them
$notepads = 1..10 | ForEach-Object {Start-Process -FilePath notepad -
PassThru}

# We execute the WaitForExit method with one argument, the timeout
$notepads | ForEach-Object -MemberName WaitForExit -ArgumentList 500
$notepads | ForEach-Object -MemberName Kill
```

Using static class members

.NET classes do not only expose object properties and methods, but also static properties and methods. While object members require an object to be accessed, static members do not. These members are defined in the class alongside object members, and often contain helpful methods and properties.

Getting ready

Install and start PowerShell Core.

How to do it...

Perform the following steps:

1. Static members do not require an object. To use them, however, we still need to reference the class we are using a member from. To access a method, the type name needs to inserted into square brackets and a double colon needs to be used:

```
# Using a static method
[Console]::Beep(440, 1000)

# Accessing a static property
[System.IO.Path]::PathSeparator
```

2. Get-Member can help discover static members, as well with the Static parameter:

```
# Using Get-Member to find static properties of .NET types
# of objects
Get-Process | Get-Member -Static
[System.Diagnostics.Process]::GetCurrentProcess()

# and of types
[datetime] | Get-Member -Static
[datetime]::Parse('31.12.2018',[cultureinfo]::new('de-de'))
[datetime]::IsLeapYear(2020) # Finally, February 29th is back!
```

3. There are many helpful .NET classes that you can use to your advantage, for example, the path class in the System.IO namespace:

```
# The path class is very helpful
$somePath = '/some/where/over/the.rainbow'
[IO.Path]::GetExtension($somePath)
[IO.Path]::GetFileNameWithoutExtension($somePath)
[IO.Path]::GetTempFileName() # Which is where your New-
TemporaryFile is coming from
[IO.Path]::IsPathRooted($somePath)
```

4. File and Directory classes can be used to accomplish most file- and directory-related tasks:

```
# Ever wanted to test your monitoring?
$file = [IO.File]::Create('.\superlarge')
$file.SetLength(1gb)
$file.Close() # Close the open handle
Get-Item $file.Name # The length on disk is now 1gb
Remove-Item $file.Name
```

```
# In order to lock a file for your script, the file class offers
methods as well
$tempfile = New-TemporaryFile
$fileHandle = [IO.File]::OpenWrite($tempfile.FullName)
# Try to add content now - the file is locked
'test' | Add-Content $tempfile.FullName
# The method Write can be used now as long as you keep the handle
# Using another static method to get the bytes in a given string
$bytes = [Text.Encoding]::utf8.GetBytes('Hello :)')
$fileHandle.Write($bytes)
$fileHandle.Close() # Release the lock again
Get-Content -Path $tempfile.FullName
```

5. The `DriveInfo` class can be used with the `GetDrives` method to retrieve all enabled drives:

```
# Ever needed to validate drives?
[IO.DriveInfo]::GetDrives()

if (-not $IsWindows)
{
    [IO.DriveInfo]'/'
    [IO.DriveInfo]'/sausage' # A valid, but non existent drive will
show IsReady = $false
}
else
{
    [IO.DriveInfo]'C'
    [IO.DriveInfo]'Y' # A valid, but non existent drive will show
IsReady = $false
}
```

6. Other static properties can even affect the behavior of cmdlets, such as `Invoke-WebRequest` and `Invoke-RestMethod`:

```
$originalProtocol = [Net.ServicePointManager]::SecurityProtocol
[Net.ServicePointManager]::SecurityProtocol =
[Net.SecurityProtocolType]::Tls12
[Net.ServicePointManager]::SecurityProtocol = $originalProtocol
```

How it works...

Static members of classes often contain helper methods and useful properties. There is one static method that most people with even a very short background in programming will know of, and that is `public static void main (string[] args)`, which is used as the main entry point in a program in Java and C#.

In this recipe, you have used various static methods and properties to your advantage. You started in *Step 1* by accessing the static method `Beep` in the console class to emit a sound. While not necessarily very useful, it is an easy example of a static method, or a method that does not require an object to work.

In *Step 2*, you saw that `Get-Member` is also available for discovering static members of a class. *Steps 3* to *5* showed you different useful static members for day-to-day tasks. In the last step, you saw that some static properties can even change the behavior of cmdlets. By modifying the `SecurityProtocol` property of the `ServicePointManager` class, you can change the behavior of `Invoke-WebRequest` and `Invoke-RestMethod` for an entire session.

It would take more than a single recipe to show you all the helpful .NET types you can encounter. So, just stop from time to time, use `Get-Member -Static`, and examine the output!

There's more...

You will also find a special static member when a developer has applied the Singleton pattern, where only one instance of a class can exist. This static property will contain the instance of the class itself and is only created once.

Creating classes

To create your own classes in PowerShell, you have two options. You can use either .NET with C# to create your class, or you can use the PowerShell class language element.

Both have their pros and cons, which we will see in the following recipe.

Getting ready

Install PowerShell Core and start an editor of your choice, for example, Visual Studio Code, with PowerShell and C# extensions.

How to do it...

Perform the following steps:

1. We will start by creating a fully-fledged .NET class to store information in. To do this, start with a new file with the ending .cs. This will be the starting point for your own class library.

2. Next, add the three classes you will find in 05 - ClassesDotNet.cs to your new, empty C# file, or simply use this file:

   ```
   using System.Collections.Generic;

   namespace com.contoso
   {
       public enum DeviceType
       { }
       public class Device
       { }

       public class Desktop : Device
       { }

       public class Server : Device
       { }
   }
   ```

3. By using Add-Type, you can load the library into your current session:

   ```
   # Compile and import C# code on the fly
   Add-Type -Path '.\05 - ClassesDotNet.cs'
   ```

4. As an alternative, you can use Add-Type to compile simple libraries:

   ```
   # Or save the compiled result for posterity
   Add-Type -Path '.\05 - ClassesDotNet.cs' -OutputAssembly Device.dll
   Add-Type -Path .\Device.dll
   ```

5. By using PowerShell classes, we can be more flexible. Refer to 05 – Classes.ps1 and load the classes into memory by highlighting them and pressing *F8* in an editor (or the hotkey that is bound to Run Selection):

```
enum DeviceType
{ }

class Device
{ }

class Desktop : Device
{ }

class Server : Device
{ }
```

6. By using parameter validation, we can apply some additional checks to our parameter values:

```
[ValidatePattern(' (EMEA|APAC)_\w{2}_\w{3,5}')]
[string] $Location
[ValidateSet('dev.contoso.com','qa.contoso.com','contoso.com')]
[string] $DomainName
```

7. You can instantiate both classes by calling their constructors. Remember to use Get-Member to view the parameters that the constructor accepts:

```
# Instantiate classes with New-Object or the new() method
$desktop = New-Object -TypeName com.contoso.Desktop -ArgumentList
'AssetTag1234','Desktop'
$serverDotNet = New-Object -TypeName com.contoso.Server -
ArgumentList 'AssetTag5678','EMEA_DE_DUE', 'contoso.com','Server'
$serverPsClass = [Server]::new('AssetTag5678','EMEA_DE_DUE',
'contoso.com','Server')
```

8. Using the Get-Member cmdlet on both objects shows slight differences:

```
# Notice that our members look a bit different
# IsDomainJoined cannot be marked private for our PowerShell Class
$serverDotNet, $serverPsClass | Get-Member -Name IsDomainJoined

# While our .NET class does not show its private methods
# our PowerShell class cannot hide its hidden method any longer
$serverDotNet, $serverPsClass | Get-Member -Force -MemberType
Methods
```

How it works...

Using C# to create your class libraries will allow you to reap the benefits of compiled assembly, such as greater execution speed, with the trade-off of having to acquire more software development skills. If you don't require all C# language features, such as LINQ, full control over member visibility and others, then PowerShell classes might be more suitable for you.

PowerShell classes lend themselves to serving as property bags and classes with simple properties and methods. PowerShell classes can contain static methods and inherit from other classes and interfaces, and combine the best of both worlds for many use cases.

In this recipe, you wrote your own class step by step by first adding class definitions to your code. Then, you applied parameter validation. Lastly, you saw that PowerShell classes are instantiated exactly like normal .NET classes are.

There's more...

PowerShell classes are also used with **Desired State Configuration** (**DSC**) resources. At the time of writing, the adoption is still fairly low since using class-based resources restricts the host's PowerShell version to anything greater than or equal to (Windows) PowerShell 5.

See also

- To read more about classes, check out the help content: `https://docs.microsoft.com/en-us/powershell/module/microsoft.powershell.core/about/about_classes?view=powershell-6`

Using custom objects

Easier than developing a full class, simple property bags that do not provide class methods are often already enough. As a quite literal bag of properties, these objects are very useful for preparing data for CSV export or simply collecting data from multiple sources in one object.

Other than that, custom objects are also useful as return values for functions and cmdlets.

Getting ready

Install and start PowerShell Core.

How to do it...

Perform the following steps:

1. Custom objects often make use of the PSCustomObject data type. To create a new custom object, you can use the type-casting operator to cast a hashtable into a PSCustomObject:

```
# Use the typecasting operator to create one
[PSCustomObject]@{
    DeviceType = 'Server'
    DomainName = 'dev.contoso.com'
    IsDomainJoined = $true
}

# Alternatively, New-Object might be used
New-Object -TypeName pscustomobject -Property @{
    DeviceType = 'Server'
    DomainName = 'dev.contoso.com'
    IsDomainJoined = $true
}
```

2. Custom objects only have the properties you have defined. Have a look at the output that Get-Member will now show:

```
# Using Get-Member with the output again shows more
# Notice the methods that exist, even though they have not been
implemented by you?
# PSCustomObject, like many classes, inherits from the class Object
[PSCustomObject]@{
    DeviceType = 'Server'
    DomainName = 'dev.contoso.com'
    IsDomainJoined = $true
} | Get-Member
```

3. When `Get-Member` is used in the pipeline, custom objects have no immediate disadvantage:

```
# Provided you supply the correct property names, you can use these custom
# objects in the pipeline as well.
Get-Help Get-Item -Parameter Path
[pscustomobject]@{ Path = '/'} | Get-Item
```

4. Using custom objects for CSV export can be a good way to share data with people who are unfamiliar with PowerShell:

```
# Especially when being exported, the custom object really shines
$someLogMessages = 1..10 | ForEach-Object {
    [pscustomobject]@{
        ComputerName = 'HostA', 'HostB', 'HostC' | Get-Random
        EntryType = 'Error', 'Warning', 'Info' | Get-Random
        Message = "$_ things happened today"
    }
}
$someLogMessages | Export-Csv -Path .\NiceExport.csv
psedit .\NiceExport.csv
```

5. Have a look at the data type of the objects that have been imported from any CSV file:

```
# When importing any csv, examine the data type
Get-Date | Export-Csv .\date.csv
Import-Csv .\date.csv | Get-Member
Remove-Item .\date.csv
```

6. To apply your own data type to a custom object, you can use the `PSTypeName` property:

```
# You can even apply your own type name to your custom object
$jhp = [PSCustomObject]@{
    PSTypeName = 'de.janhendrikpeters.awesomeclass'
    TwitterHandle = 'NyanHP'
    Born = [datetime]'1987-01-24'
}
$jhp | Get-Member
$jhp.GetType().FullName
# This method still knows the gory details
```

7. PowerShell also allows you to add your own type name nearly everywhere:

```
# You can even add your own type to anything
$item = Get-Item -Path /
$item.PSTypeNames.Insert(0,'JHP')
$item | Get-Member
```

How it works...

In this recipe, you used custom objects with the `PSCustomObject` data type by using both the type-casting operator `[PSCustomObject]` as well as the `New-Object` cmdlet to create a new instance.

In the steps that followed, you saw how easy these objects are to work with. Custom objects can be very useful, especially in a pipeline. In the last two steps, you even injected a .NET type name into your own object as well as a .NET object.

See also

- For more information on C# and .NET, have a look at another great cookbook: `https://www.packtpub.com/application-development/c-7-and-net-core-cookbook`

Manipulating and extending objects

In this recipe, we will get our hands dirty and use reflection to examine objects and change read-only properties. You will learn the difference between properties and fields and what they are normally used for.

You will also learn how to extend objects on-the-fly using `Add-Member`. We will explore the different member types and how they can be used.

Getting ready

Install and start PowerShell Core.

How to do it...

Perform the following steps:

1. For this recipe, let's start with the humble `FileInfo` object and its members:

```
# To get started, we need something to manipulate
$tempFile = Get-Item -Path $(New-TemporaryFile).FullName

# The ubiquitous Get-Member shows all relevant details - for now
$tempFile | Get-Member
```

2. Even with the `Force` parameter, there are no additional details that might help:

```
# Using the force does not provide more useful output
$tempFile | Get-Member -Force
```

3. The `GetType` method, however, returns some useful methods that we can leverage:

```
# With reflection, we can dive deep into our objects
$tempFile.GetType() | Get-Member -Name Get*
```

4. Try retrieving all the fields from your directory. Fields are usually private properties that can neither be read nor written to directly:

```
$tempFile.GetType().GetFields([Reflection.BindingFlags]::NonPublic
-bor [Reflection.BindingFlags]::Instance) |
    Format-Table -Property FieldType, Name

# To see the value of a field, try using the GetField method
$field = $tempFile.GetType().GetField('_name',
[Reflection.BindingFlags]::NonPublic -bor
[Reflection.BindingFlags]::Instance)
$field.GetValue($tempFile)
```

5. Let's have some fun and modify the full name of a file:

```
$fullName = $tempFile.GetType().GetField('FullPath',
[Reflection.BindingFlags]::NonPublic -bor
[Reflection.BindingFlags]::Instance)
$fullName.GetValue($tempFile)
$fullName.SetValue($tempFile,
'C:\Users\japete.EUROPE\AppData\Local\Temp\WHATISHAPPENING')
```

6. Observing the output, it doesn't look that bad:

```
$tempFile.FullName # Oh boy...
$tempFile # File still looks like before
$tempFile | Get-Member # Get-Member also looks normal
```

7. However, `object` methods now fall apart:

```
$tempFile.CopyTo('D:\test')
Exception calling "CopyTo" with "1" argument(s): "Could not find
file 'C:\Users\japete.EUROPE\AppData\Local\Temp\WHATISHAPPENING'."
At line:1 char:1
+ $tempFile.CopyTo('D:\test')
+ ~~~~~~~~~~~~~~~~~~~~~~~~~~~~
+ CategoryInfo : NotSpecified: (:) [], MethodInvocationException
+ FullyQualifiedErrorId : FileNotFoundException
```

8. Using `Add-Member` is a bit less disruptive and still very useful. Try adding a note property and observe the output:

```
# Note properties are like yellow sticky notes - they are loosely
attached to the object
$tempFile | Add-Member -NotePropertyName MyStickyNote -
NotePropertyValue 'SomeValue'
$tempFile.MyStickyNote
# Note properties have a changeable data type
$tempFile.MyStickyNote = Get-Date
```

9. A `script` property is a self-calculating property that might be useful as well:

```
# ScriptProperties are dynamic properties that calculate
themselves.
# By using this, we are referencing the current instance of the
class
$tempFile | Add-Member -MemberType ScriptProperty -Name Hash -Value
{Get-FileHash -Path $this.PSPath}
$tempfile.Hash
```

10. Lastly, a `script` method allows you to define something similar to an `object` method, with a script block as its payload:

```
# ScriptMethods are similar to object methods and can accept
parameters as well
$tempFile | Add-Member -MemberType ScriptMethod -Name GetFileHash -
Value {Get-FileHash -Path $this.PSPath}
$tempFile.GetFileHash()
```

How it works...

Reflection provides .NET objects that contain information about assemblies and data types. While this in itself is already useful, reflection can also be used to dynamically generate new data types at runtime or to change otherwise read-only properties of objects, also known as fields. Fields are usually referred to when we talk about private class members that can neither be read nor set from outside the object. To read or also change field values, they are often wrapped in properties that allow access to get and set methods. A set method is also a great place to apply some additional validation before a field is modified.

Using reflection opens up a whole new world, with even more things that would normally not be possible. Even if you do not regularly modify private fields, knowing how to use `Add-Member` to simply add members is a great skill. The `Add-Member` cmdlet allows you to easily extend existing objects so that they contain more information temporarily.

There's more...

There is much more you can do with `Add-Member`. Take a look at the following example, which adds data values from an event log entry to the event so that the latter can be exported easier:

```
# as one practical example, take the Windows event log
$oneEvent = Get-WinEvent -FilterHashtable @{
 LogName = 'Security'
 ID = 4624
} -MaxEvents 1

$oneEvent | Add-Member -NotePropertyName SubjectUserName -NotePropertyValue
($oneEvent.Properties[1].Value)
$oneEvent.SubjectUserName
```

When retrieving objects remotely or from jobs, `Add-Member` is an invaluable tool as well, as the following example shows:

```
$deserializedEvent = Start-Job { Get-WinEvent -FilterHashtable @{
    LogName = 'Security'
    ID = 4624
} -MaxEvents 1 | Add-Member -MemberType ScriptProperty -Name EventXml -
Value {[xml]$this.ToXml()} -PassThru } | Wait-Job | Receive-Job
$deserializedEvent.EventXml # Useful
$deserializedEvent.EventXml.Event.EventData.Data # Everything is there to
use
$deserializedEvent.ToXml() # Error - this method does not exist any longer
```

See also

- For more information on reflection, please visit the following link: https://docs.microsoft.com/en-us/dotnet/csharp/programming-guide/concepts/reflection

- For more information on the different member types, please visit the following link: https://docs.microsoft.com/en-us/dotnet/standard/design-guidelines/member

[ref], [out], and delegates

You can introduce more .NET into scripts by using more advanced techniques, such as delegate methods. This recipe will also show you what [ref] and [out] types are and what to do when an object method expects such data types.

Getting ready

Install and start PowerShell Core.

How to do it...

Perform the following steps:

1. Let's start with a seemingly simple static method, TryParse, in the Boolean class:

   ```
   [bool] | Get-Member -Static -Name TryParse
   ```

2. To be able to use this method, the parameter modifier [out] is needed. [Out] indicates that a parameter value is passed as a reference that will be used as output, for example, to a variable:

   ```
   $parsedValue = $null
   $parseSuccess = [bool]::TryParse('False', [ref]$parsedValue)
   Write-Host "Parsing 'False' to boolean was successful:
   $parsesuccess. The parsed boolean is $parsedValue"
   ```

3. The output of Get-Member is a bit misleading. While a reference is indeed passed, [out] and [ref] are not the same:

```
From
https://docs.microsoft.com/en-us/dotnet/api/system.boolean.tryparse
?view=netcore-2.2:
public static bool TryParse (string value, out bool result);
```

The keyword ref indicates that a reference to the heap is passed as a function parameter instead of the actual value itself.

4. Ref can be used in PowerShell as the data type of a cmdlet parameter, enabling you to use [ref] in PowerShell as well:

```
# [ref] in PowerShell
function ByReference
{
    param(
        [ref]
        $ReferenceObject
    )

    $ReferenceObject.Value = 42
}

$valueType = 7
ByReference -ReferenceObject ([ref]$valueType)
$valueType.GetType() # Still a value type, but the value has been
changed
```

5. In C#, developers also regularly use delegate methods. Most prominently, they are used with LINQ, which are language-integrated queries:

```
# Delegate methods like Actions and Funcs are often used in C#, but
you can also use them in PowerShell
# The LINQ Where method in C# looks like this:
# processes.Where(proc => proc.WorkingSet64 > 150*1024);

# The proper type cast is important. The output of Get-Process is
normally an Object array!
[System.Diagnostics.Process[]]$procs = Get-Process

# The delegate type that LINQ expects is a Func. This type expects
two
# parameters, a Type parameter indicating the source data type,
e.g. Process as well as a predicate, the filter
[Func[System.Diagnostics.Process,bool]] $delegate = { param($proc);
```

```
return $proc.WorkingSet64 -gt 150mb }
[Linq.Enumerable]::Where($procs, $delegate)

# The same delegate can be used with e.g. First, which filters like
where and returns the first object
# matching the filter
[Linq.Enumerable]::First($procs, $delegate)
```

How it works...

Passing parameters by reference with the [out] and [ref] keywords is sometimes necessary. Knowing what those keywords mean is therefore very important. Since only a reference to an object is passed, the value that has been referred to is changed – the original object.

In the case of the many TryParse methods, this behavior is actually desirable. A variable to store the result is provided, allowing each TryParse method to return two results: the result of the conversion method, as well as the actual resulting value after the conversion.

Delegates such as the LINQ lambda expression or an Action delegate are used for UI events when a task is processing data in the background and an action is used to work with the dispatcher to modify UI components.

Ref, out, and delegates are only infrequently used in PowerShell, but you will stumble upon them often; the TryParse methods are the most prominent example of where you will see them.

See also

- For more information on delegates, check out https://www.red-gate.com/ simple-talk/dotnet/net-framework/high-performance-powershell-linq/

4
Mastering the Pipeline

The pipeline plays a vital role in almost every PowerShell script. By learning the most important pipeline cmdlets, you will start to master the pipeline.

After the usual pipeline processing cmdlets, we will have a look at more advanced topics, such as enabling pipeline input for your own cmdlets, as well as designing scripts with performance in mind.

In this chapter, we will cover the following recipes:

- What is a pipeline?
- Sorting data efficiently
- Selecting subsets of data
- Grouping large data sets
- Filtering data
- Processing data
- Enabling pipeline input
- High-performance pipelines

Technical requirements

The code for this chapter can be found at `https://github.com/PacktPublishing/Powershell-Core-6.2-Cookbook/tree/master/Chapter04`.

What is a pipeline?

The pipeline in PowerShell is characterized by the | pipeline character, and, generally speaking, it connects the output of one cmdlet with the input of another. When processing pipeline input, cmdlets have two ways of accepting data from the pipeline – we will see both in action.

By observing the flow between Get and Set cmdlets, we can learn much about the pipeline, which is what this first recipe is all about.

Getting ready

Install and start PowerShell Core.

How to do it...

Perform the following steps:

1. In my opinion, the most used cmdlet in a pipeline might be Get-Member. Try it yourself by simply piping cmdlet output to Get-Member:

   ```
   Get-Process | Get-Member
   Get-Date | Get-Member -Static -MemberType Methods
   ```

2. Often, the Get and Set cmdlets are connected with a pipeline. Observe the flow on Windows by combining Get-Service and Set-Service in a pipeline:

   ```
   # Pipelines connect input and output
   # Often Get and Set cmdlets are connected
   Get-Service -Name spooler | Set-Service -Status Stopped
   ```

3. Usually, piping empty collections simply means that the next cmdlets in the pipeline will not get executed at all. Try piping an empty list of objects to another cmdlet:

   ```
   # The pipeline also works with empty collections. In this case,
   Set-PSSessionConfiguration does not need to be called
   # This cmdlet only works in an administrative context.
   Get-Process -Name *Idonotexist* | Stop-Process -WhatIf
   ```

4. Piping more than one object to another cmdlet will result in each individual object being processed by the receiving cmdlet. Execute the same combination of the Get and Set cmdlets with different values to see the difference:

```
# Regardless of how many objects Get-Process returns,
# Stop-Process processes each individual one
Get-Process -Id $pid | Stop-Process -WhatIf
Get-Process | Stop-Process -WhatIf
```

5. Pipeline input can be accepted by value. Take a look at the InputObject parameter of Get-Process:

```
# How do cmdlets take pipeline input?
# Either by value - entire objects progress down the pipeline
Get-Help Get-Process -Parameter InputObject
```

6. Pipeline input can also be accepted by property name. See the difference by using Get-Help on the Id and Name parameters of Get-Process:

```
# Or by property name - only the individual object properties are
being used
Get-Help Get-Process -Parameter Id
Get-Help Get-Process -Parameter Name
```

7. Parameters can also accept input both ways, like the Path parameter of the Get-Item cmdlet. Try the Get-Item cmdlet both with the correct object type, as well as with an object that just has the correct property:

```
# One example of ByValue and ByPropertyName is Get-Item
# The parameter Path accepts input by value as well as by property
name
Get-Help Get-Item -Parameter Path
'/' | Get-Item

# ByPropertyName enables scenarios like this
Get-Process -Id $Pid | Get-Item

# Any object with the correct property will do
[pscustomobject]@{
    Id = 0
} | Get-Process
```

8. If a cmdlet parameter has one or more aliases, those can be used in the pipeline as well. Try it now by using `Get-ADComputer` and objects with the `CN` property:

```
# Sometimes, a cmdlet might even have parameter aliases that allow
you to pipe more object types
Get-Help Stop-Computer -Parameter ComputerName
(Get-Command Stop-Computer).Parameters.ComputerName.Aliases

# With this in mind and with access to the AD cmdlets, you can use
Get-ADComputer
# to retrieve objects that have the property CN which binds to
ComputerName
Get-ADComputer -SearchBase 'OU=RebootOU,DC=contoso,DC=com' -
Properties CN -Filter * | Stop-Computer -WhatIf
```

9. You can execute the last bit of code to review cmdlet parameter aliases. This is optional, and will just give you a list of cmdlets and their parameter aliases:

```
# Have a look at all cmdlets and their parameter aliases
$ignoredParameters =
'WhatIf','Confirm','ErrorAction','ErrorVariable','WarningAction','I
nformationAction','OutBuffer','WarningVariable','OutVariable','Pipe
lineVariable','InformationVariable','Verbose','Debug'

$FormatEnumerationLimit = -1 # To enable formatted lists of more
than 4 elements for the current session
Get-Command |
Where-Object { try{$_.Parameters.GetEnumerator() | ForEach-Object
{$_.Value.Aliases.Count -gt 0 -and $_.Key -notin
$ignoredParameters}}catch{}} |
Format-Table Name,@{
    Label = 'Aliases'
    Expression = {
        $_.Parameters.GetEnumerator() | ForEach-Object {
            if ($_.Value.Aliases.Count -gt 0 -and $_.Key -notin
$ignoredParameters)
            {
                '{0}: {1}' -f $_.Key,($_.Value.Aliases -join ',')
            }
        }
    }
} -Wrap
```

How it works...

Cmdlets in general should be designed to enable pipeline input. With that in mind, it is still a good idea to examine cmdlet parameters with `Get-Help` for a more verbose output, or with `Get-Command` to find any parameter that accepts pipeline input.

The steps to bind parameter values to parameters are always the same, regardless of the way the pipeline is used:

1. Bind all named parameters.
2. Bind all positional parameters.
3. Bind from the pipeline by value with exact type match.
4. Bind from the pipeline by value with conversion.
5. Bind from the pipeline by name with exact type match.
6. Bind from the pipeline by name with type conversion.

Understanding these steps is important: if you pass values down the pipeline, you cannot use the parameters as named or positional that should be bound from the pipeline. This behavior also explains which parameter set of a cmdlet will be used if an object is of the correct type (`ByValue`) pretty well, and additionally has the correct properties (`ByPropertyName`).

Fortunately, only entire objects or individual object properties will be used in the pipeline – nothing else. How the receiving cmdlet will internally process all objects is another thing entirely. A cmdlet developer might decide not to process each individual entry sequentially at all, but implement parallel processing, for example.

There's more...

There's more regarding this topic in the *Enabling pipeline input* recipe in this chapter, where you will enable pipeline input for your own cmdlet.

See also

You can execute the `Get-Help` cmdlet with the `about_Pipelines` parameter value, as it contains everything you need to know about pipelines – or just keep on reading this chapter.

Sorting data efficiently

Sorting data in PowerShell is something that is done very frequently, and is one of PowerShell's strengths. As with many cmdlets, sorting objects can start very simple but will get increasingly difficult.

In this recipe, you will sort input for other cmdlets and observe the difficulties that you will inevitably face when sorting output. There are often times where sorting data is important, for example, to identify the five most memory-consuming processes in case of an issue. Other than that, sorting is often only done for display purposes.

How to do it...

Perform the following steps:

1. When sorting objects, we mostly start with something that can be sorted. Sort a simple list of strings now:

   ```
   'POSHDC1', 'POSHWEB1', 'POSHFS1', 'POSHDC2' | Sort-Object
   ```

2. With the addition of the Descending parameter, the sort order is reversed. Reverse the sorting by applying the Descending parameter:

   ```
   'POSHDC1', 'POSHWEB1', 'POSHFS1', 'POSHDC2' | Sort-Object -
   Descending
   ```

3. When sorting more complex objects, such as a process or a service, you can select one or more properties to sort on. Try sorting by name and memory consumption next:

   ```
   # Since property accepts an object[], you can pass comma-separated
   values
   Get-Process | Sort-Object -Property Name, WorkingSet64
   ```

4. `Sort-Object` also includes the handy `Top` and `Bottom` parameters. Try listing only the last five objects:

```
# One improved over Windows PowerShell was the inclusion of Top and
Bottom
# That way you can get to your information even faster
Get-Process | Sort-Object -Property WorkingSet64 -Bottom 5
```

5. Sometimes, the sort order seems to be wrong. Try sorting the services by their status and then by their name. Scroll through the output and you will notice the issue:

```
# The status Running should not be output after the status Stopped
- so what gives?
Get-Service | Sort-Object -Property Status, Name
```

6. This is because certain data types are not sorted as we intend them to be, or cannot be sorted at all. To find the root of this, use `Get-Member` on the `Status` property and have a look at the data type:

```
# The property type is not a simple string, but an enumeration
Get-Service | Get-Member -Name Status
(Get-Service -Name spooler).Status.GetType().BaseType.FullName #
System.Enum

# If we examine all values, we can see their string content
[enum]::GetNames([System.ServiceProcess.ServiceControllerStatus])

# Converting Running and Stopped to integers shows the root of the
problem
# demonstrating that Sort-Object actually worked well, just not as
we intended
[int][System.ServiceProcess.ServiceControllerStatus]::Stopped # 1
[int][System.ServiceProcess.ServiceControllerStatus]::Running # 4
```

7. One way to solve this problem is to use script blocks as calculated properties – the result of the script block is used for sorting. Try sorting your services with a script block instead of a property name:

```
# The variable $_ or $PSItem point to each individual element in
the pipeline
Get-Service | Sort-Object -Property {$_.Status.ToString()}, Name
```

8. Using a hashtable is also possible, allowing you to modify the sort order for individual properties. Use a hashtable to reverse the sort order for the Status property:

```
# With a hashtable, you can specify a sort order for individual
properties, which
# would also solve our conundrum.
# Valid keys of this hashtable are Expression, Descending and
Ascending
Get-Service | Sort-Object -Property @{
    Expression = 'Status'
    Descending = $true
}
```

9. Sort-Object is not the most efficient choice when dealing with larger collections. You can see its impact by executing the Sort method of a .NET list in comparison to Sort-Object:

```
# Certain data types like lists support sorting as well, often
being more efficient than Sort-Object
[int[]]$randomNumbers = 1..10000 | Foreach-Object {Get-Random}
Measure-Command -Expression {
    $intList = New-Object -TypeName
System.Collections.Generic.List[int]
    $intList.AddRange($randomNumbers)
    $intList.Sort()
} # 8ms, including assembly import

Measure-Command -Expression {
    $randomNumbers | Sort-Object
} # 172ms, over 20 times slower, but less cumbersome to use
```

How it works...

Sort-Object examines each individual object and determines the sort order. Sort-Object will try to use the object's Compare method if it is implemented, and will otherwise use an alphanumeric sorting. When using object properties to sort a collection of objects, always try to find something that can easily be sorted, such as strings, integers, and dates.

If the object cannot be sorted as easily, a script block or a hashtable may be used. With a script block as well as with a hashtable, we can make use of the built-in $_ parameter and its alias, $PSItem. $_, always points to the current element in the pipeline. In case a collection of objects is being piped, $_ will point to each individual object. This means that all object properties and methods can be used inside a script block as well, such as $_.Status.ToString(), which is a method that's called on the object's Status property.

See also

Executing the Get-Help Sort-Object -Full cmdlet has you covered, with more information and examples on sorting objects.

Selecting subsets of data

After sorting a collection, we often want to select only a subset of the collection, such as the first couple of elements. This is often done when only a small amount of objects are needed, or to simply select the first one.

This recipe will show you how you can select elements from the top or bottom of a list, or from somewhere in-between, using an index. Especially when examining output, you often only need the first couple of elements to see what they look like, and not the entire collection.

How to do it...

Perform the following steps:

1. Usually, we use Select-Object to select subsets of objects that have been filtered, sorted, and processed before. Select that last five items of a collection:

   ```
   # After having sorted and filtered, objects are often selected
   Get-Process |
       Sort-Object -Property WorkingSet64 |
       Select-Object -Last 5
   ```

2. A handy shortcut is often `Select-Object -First 1`. Try the following example as one way of viewing object property values:

```
# This only displays the properties of one object instead of
hundreds
Get-Process | Select-Object -First 1 | Format-List *
```

3. Try using the `Index` parameter to extract elements from collections by referring to their zero-based index:

```
# Using the Index parameter, you can also extract indices from
collections
1..100 | Select-Object -Index 1,5,10
'1.10.122.27' -split '\.' | Select-Object -Index 3
```

4. The `Skip` parameter allows you to skip elements; try it now:

```
1..10 | Select-Object -Skip 5
```

5. By combining it with `First` and `Last`, you can specify which elements will be skipped. Try selecting items from a short list with different combinations of `First, Last, Skip,` and `SkipLast`:

```
# Skip 5 from the bottom, select last remaining
1..10 | Select-Object -Skip 5 -Last 1
# Skip 5 from top, select first remaining
1..10 | Select-Object -Skip 5 -First 1

# The parameter SkipLast simply cuts off the last couple of
elements off a list
# This behavior can also be achieved with -Skip n -Last n
1..10 | Select-Object -SkipLast 7
1..10 | Select-Object -Skip 7 -Last 100
```

6. Like `Sort-Object`, `Select-Object` has a `Unique` parameter. However, with `Select-Object`, this parameter is case-sensitive. Try it now and select the unique items from a list:

```
# Select (like Sort) has a Unique parameter. Unlike other cmdlets,
this is case-sensitive
'apple','Apple' | Select-Object -Unique
```

How it works...

In all parameter sets, the Select-Object cmdlet allows you to select a subset of elements. If you are using the First and Index parameters, it does that by stopping the cmdlet that is delivering data. This can sometimes lead to errors if a cmdlet does not take kindly to being canceled in the middle of an operation. If that is the case, you can work with the Wait parameter to force Select-Object to wait for all elements to be delivered first.

Other than selecting and skipping elements, Select-Object is also used to select and exclude properties, and expand values of single properties. Since this effectively recreates the objects with a different type, and with no properties apart from the selected ones, you have to be careful. Objects that had properties selected are often not usable in the pipeline any longer – their data type is always lost, and in case of input by property name, the correct property might not have been selected.

Grouping large data sets

The Group-Object cmdlet is a powerful tool as well, allowing you to group collections of objects by the objects' property values. Like the other object cmdlets, Group-Object can, of course, also work with constructed properties to be even more flexible.

I use Group-Object often to get a grip on large collections, or to group output from different remote hosts. This recipe will show you how you can effectively group larger collections into manageable groups, step by step.

Getting ready

Install and start PowerShell Core.

If you want to follow along with Windows-specific cmdlets (of which there should not be too many), feel free to create the PowerShell Workshop – HyperV lab, which is part of AutomatedLab. You can get started with the following code in Windows PowerShell to create the lab environment:

```
Install-Module AutomatedLab -AllowClobber -Force
Import-Module AutomatedLab # A question regarding telemetry will pop up,
please read it carefully
Enable-LabHostRemoting -Force
New-LabSourcesFolder -Drive C
```

For more information on AutomatedLab, please see `https://github.com/AutomatedLab/AutomatedLab/wiki`.

How to do it...

Perform the following steps:

1. `Group-Object` is able to group collections of objects based on one or more properties:

   ```
   Get-Service | Group-Object -Property Status
   Get-WinEvent -LogName System -MaxEvents 100 | Group-Object -
   Property LevelDisplayName
   ```

2. Of course, grouping on multiple properties is possible as well:

   ```
   # Especially when working remotely on multiple systems, grouping
   can help
   # each background job and each remote execution will add a property
   called PSComputerName
   # which contains the machine the data originated on.
   $computers = Get-Content -Path .\MassiveComputerList.txt
   Invoke-Command -ComputerName $computers -ScriptBlock {
       Get-WinEvent -LogName System -MaxEvents 100
   } |
       # Grouping on PSComputerName, or as seen here a combination of
   Hostname and Level
   Group-Object -Property PSComputerName, LevelDisplayName
   ```

   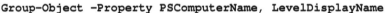

    `PSComputerName` is very useful with remote commands and jobs – try this to easily work with large object collections that have been retrieved remotely.

3. Using the `AsHashtable` parameter will return a hashtable from your grouped data, with the keys being the grouped property values and the values being the actual grouped objects.

   ```
   # The parameter AsHashtable will create a hashtable, with the keys
   being the grouped property values
   Get-Process | Group-Object Name -AsHashTable
   $groupedProcs = Get-Process | Group-Object Name -AsHashTable
   $groupedProcs.svchost # on Windows
   $groupedProcs.systemd # on Linux with Systemd
   ```

4. Don't forget the `AsString` parameter, though – many object properties are not simple strings or integers, and you might benefit from converting them:

```
# Depending on the data type of your property, adding the parameter
AsString is helpful.
# This parameter indicates that the property values will be
converted to strings
$withoutAsString = Get-Service | Group-Object -Property Status -
AsHashTable
# This is not possible
$withoutAsString.Running
# This would work - but do you really want this?
$withoutAsString[([System.ServiceProcess.ServiceControllerStatus]::
Running)]


# AsString helps
$withAsString = Get-Service | Group-Object -Property Status -
AsHashTable -AsString
$withAsString.Running
```

5. Constructed properties will again allow you to use anything as a property – for example, the file hash:

```
# With constructed properties, you can again group on anything
$files = 1..100 | % {$f = New-TemporaryFile; Set-Content -Value
(Get-Random -min 1 -max 100) -Path $f.FullName; $f}

# Grouping files by hash is a quick and easy way to identify
duplicates in the file system
$files | Group-Object -Property {(Get-FileHash $_.FullName).Hash}

# Combined with cmdlets like where object, the results can be
narrowed down further
$files |
    Group-Object -Property {(Get-FileHash $_.FullName).Hash} |
    Where-Object -Property Count -gt 1
```

6. Rather Windows-specific, you can, for example, group Active Directory users by their parent organizational unit:

```
# Constructed properties are also very useful for things like this
# an object DN in the Active Directory can be used to quickly group
user
# by parent OU, with the format being
CN=someuser,OU=someOu,DC=contoso,DC=com
# The RegEx pattern replaces "CN=...," , leaving only the OU string
intact.
Get-ADUser -Filter * |
```

```
            Group-Object -Property @{
            Expression = {
                $_.distinguishedName -replace 'CN=\w+,'
            }
        }
```

How it works...

The `Group-Object` cmdlet simply expands property values that you select and tries to group all objects based on those property values. In the rare case that a property value cannot be used to group the objects, you can opt to use constructed properties again.

Do keep performance in mind though, since, of course, the script block, or expression that's used for your constructed properties, will have to be evaluated for each object that's passed through the pipeline.

The `AsHashtable` and `AsString` parameters are extremely useful, as boxing the results into a hashtable makes accessing the grouped data easier. With hashtables, you can simply use dot-notation, which is very convenient. And, of course, results can still be counted:

```
$events = Get-WinEvent -LogName System -MaxEvents 100 | Group-Object -
Property LevelDisplayName
$events.Error.Count
```

Filtering data

Another very powerful cmdlet that is being used regularly is `Where-Object` – the filtering cmdlet. With `Where-Object` in particular, performance is always an issue that we will examine more in the last recipe.

This recipe will show you how to use `Where-Object` to your advantage, and how the `Where` method might be used instead.

Getting ready

Install and start PowerShell Core.

How to do it...

Perform the following steps:

1. Starting off with the `Where-Object` syntax, we can see that there are an unusual amount of parameter sets. Try to find out how many different ways there are of using `Where-Object` by using `Get-Command`:

```
# Every comparison is implemented not case-sensitive and case-
sensitive
Get-Command Where-Object -Syntax
```

2. The usual mode of operation is to compare single property values to a reference. Try to filter all running processes for the ones that consume more than 100 MiB of memory:

```
# The syntax is very easy to comprehend if you just read it out
loud
# from left to right:
# Get all processes where the property value of WorkingSet64 is
greater than 100 megabyte
Get-Process | Where-Object -Property WorkingSet64 -gt 100mb
```

3. Be careful when typing, and use tab completion if possible, since misspelled property names will result in empty collections. Observe the result by purposefully mistyping `Length` as `Lenght`:

```
# Be careful with spelling mistakes: You will not notice them
# Length is misspelled, returning an empty result set
Get-ChildItem | Where-Object -Property Lenght -gt 1
```

4. Filtering multiple object properties or properties of properties requires another parameter, the `FilterScript` parameter. Try using it now to compare only the weekday of a given date with a list of entries:

```
# If you recall the syntax, only one property can compared at any
given time
# To compare more properties or complex properties, you will need
the FilterScript
Get-ChildItem -Path $home |
    Where-Object -FilterScript {
    # The filter script should return a boolean value
        $_.CreationTime.DayOfWeek -in 'Saturday','Sunday'
    }
```

5. The `Where` method that has been introduced in PowerShell 4 adds much flexibility, and is faster than `Where-Object`. Try using the `Where` method instead of `Where-Object` to see how they are different:

```
# The syntax is Where({ expression } [, mode [, numberToReturn]])
# where the mode can be First, Last, SkipUntil, Until, Split
(Get-Process).Where(
  {$_.WorkingSet64 -gt 150mb}
)
```

6. With its included operation modes, you can emulate the use of `Where-Object` and `Select-Object` in one single method call. Now, you don't need to call two cmdlets, and can simply use a fast method. Select the first five filtered objects now:

```
(Get-Process).Where(
    {$_.WorkingSet64 -gt 150mb}, 'First', 5
)
```

7. Using a mode like `Split`, the return values can be stored in two variables; one containing the objects that passed the filter, the other one containing the rest. Split the result by using the `Split` operator:

```
$matchingProcesses, $rest = (Get-Process).Where(
  {$_.WorkingSet64 -gt 150mb}, 'Split'
)
```

How it works...

The `Where-Object` cmdlet is PowerShell's mighty filtering cmdlet. While it is not the fastest way to filter collections of things, it is very flexible and comparatively easy to use. To accomplish this task, `Where-Object` examines every object that passes down the pipeline individually, applies any filters that have been selected, and sends the filtered data on the output stream.

This also means that `Where-Object` will apply its filters after all objects have been retrieved, making it slow by design. Be aware of that fact when filtering large collections of objects, as it might take some time.

Processing data

When working with object collections in PowerShell, they are often used as input for the `ForEach-Object` cmdlet, the `foreach` method, or the `foreach` statement.

This recipe will show you when to use the cmdlet, the method, or the statement, and the key differences between all of them.

Getting ready

Install and start PowerShell Core. If you want to try the Active Directory example, please have a look at the book Preface and the section *How to get the most out of this book* in order to deploy the lab environment.

How to do it...

Perform the following steps:

1. The `ForEach-Object` cmdlet is usually used with a single script block that is executed for each object in the pipeline. Try using the output of `Get-ChildItem` with `ForEach-Object` now:

```
Get-ChildItem -File | ForEach-Object -Process {Get-FileHash -Path
$_.FullName}
```

2. Using the `..` range operator, you can have a very simple collection to use with `ForEach-Object`. Try executing the `New-TemporaryFile` cmdlet ten times in a row:

```
# The output of Foreach-Object will be whatever is returned in the
script blocks
$files = 1..10 | ForEach-Object -Process {New-TemporaryFile}
```

3. You can also use the `MemberName` parameter to execute methods and expand property values. Try to access the `BaseName` property and the `ToString` method with an argument list:

```
# Foreach-Object can also be used, albeit a bit too complicated, to
expand property values
# or execute methods by specifying the name of the member
Get-ChildItem | ForEach-Object -MemberName BaseName
Get-Process | ForEach-Object -MemberName ToString
(Get-ChildItem).LastWriteTime | ForEach-Object -MemberName ToString
-ArgumentList 'F',([cultureinfo]'de-de')
```

4. `ForEach-Object` has additional script blocks that can be used as well. Try using the `begin` and `end` blocks:

```
# Foreach-Object can accept multiple script block arguments
# Begin and End are only executed once
$files | ForEach-Object -Begin {
    Write-Host -ForegroundColor Yellow "Starting pipeline
processing"
} -Process {
    Get-FileHash -Path $_.FullName
} -End {
    Write-Host -ForegroundColor Yellow "Finished pipeline
processing"
}
```

5. The `Foreach` method can be used very similarly to `ForEach-Object`, with some minor differences. It will execute faster than the cmdlet. Try it now with a script block, a member name, and a type conversion operator:

```
# Like the Where method, the Foreach method can be used instead of
Foreach-Object
# Arguments are script blocks, member names or data types to
convert to
$files.ForEach({Get-FileHash -Path $_.FullName})
# Method calls
$files.ForEach('ToString')
# Type conversions for collections
$files.LastWriteTime.ForEach([string])
```

6. Often seen with loops of any kind are progress bars. Keep in mind that drawing UI always takes some time. Try `Write-Progress` in a nested loop:

```
$counter = 0
$collection = Get-Process
$collection | ForEach-Object -Begin {
    Write-Progress -Id 1 -Activity 'Starting things' -Status
'Really doing it' -PercentComplete 0
    Start-Sleep -Milliseconds 100
} -Process {
    $counter++
    Write-Progress -Id 1 -Activity 'Working on things' -Status
"Processing $($_.Name)" -PercentComplete
($counter/$collection.Count * 100)
    Start-Sleep -Milliseconds 100
}
```

7. The `foreach` statement is another way to iterate over collections of objects. Try the `foreach` statement now with the Active Directory module, if you have access to it:

```
# In addition to Foreach-Object and Foreach(), there is also the
foreach statement
# It often looks a lot cleaner, and it will not add the overhead
that a cmdlet does
$events = foreach ( $domain in (Get-ADForest).Domains)
{
    # Caution: Do not use a filter * when accessing the AD unless
you have to.
    # Think of a select * from a large table - you wouldn't do
that...
    $computers = Get-ADComputer -Server $domain -Filter * |
ForEach-Object -MemberName DnsHostName
    Invoke-Command -ComputerName $computers -ScriptBlock {
        # Collecting data on all machines
        Get-WinEvent -LogName Security -MaxEvents 10
    }
}
```

8. Dictionary data types such as hashtables cannot be used like arrays when using loops or other pipeline cmdlets. Try using a hashtable with ForEach-Object:

```
$hashtable = @{
    Key1 = 'Value'
    Key2 = 'Another key, another value'
    Key3 = 'Yet another key'
}

# While there is output, it looks wrong - the entire hashtable is
used as a single object
# This is because hashtables do not use a traditional zero-based
index
$hashtable | ForEach-Object {Write-Host "Key: $($_.Key), Value
$($_.Value)"}

# With an Enumerator, we can start the iteration for real
$hashtable.GetEnumerator() | ForEach-Object {Write-Host "Key:
$($_.Key), Value $($_.Value)"}
```

How it works...

The ForEach-Object cmdlet, the Foreach method, and the foreach statement are all used to iterate over collections of objects. It doesn't matter if the collection that is used is empty or just contains one single element. With an empty collection, no iteration will happen. A single element will only trigger a single iteration.

The Begin, Process, and End blocks that you have used in this recipe are incidentally also used in pipeline cmdlets for the very same purpose.

Using the cmdlet will always include a slight decrease in performance. In case a large collection will be processed, the foreach method or the foreach statement will be a better fit. Take a look at this code sample and the time it took to process a simple collection of 1,000 integers:

```
Measure-Command {1..1000 | ForEach-Object {$_}} | Select TotalMilliSeconds
# 43ms
Measure-Command {(1..1000).Foreach( {$_})} | Select TotalMilliSeconds #
33ms
Measure-Command { # 12ms
    foreach ($i in 1..1000)
    {
        $i
}} | Select TotalMilliSeconds
```

Enabling pipeline input

As a general rule of thumb, cmdlets should provide the ability to bind parameters from the pipeline, as this will enable more people to use a function in any way they want to. As a script developer, enabling pipeline input is not a very complicated task, but it does require some thought going into the design of the cmdlet.

In this recipe, we will explore how to enable pipeline input by property name, as well as by value.

Getting ready

Install and start PowerShell Core. Open up an editor of your choice, for example, Visual Studio Code.

How to do it...

Perform the following steps:

1. The simplest form of pipeline input can be enabled with a choice of three variables: $Input, $_, and $PSItem. Create a small test function that simply uses $Input:

```
function Test-PipelineInput
{
 Get-Item $Input
}

'/', $home, $PSHOME | Test-PipelineInput
```

2. Since the function seems to have the wrong functionality, we need an additional element. To process values from the pipeline, one named script block is mandatory. Add a process block to your cmdlet to see how it works:

```
function Test-PipelineInput
{
    process
    {
        # The process block is mandatory for pipeline input.
        # The variable input enumerates all objects in the pipeline
        Write-Host "
        `$_ is $_
        `$PSItem is $PSItem
```

```
      `$Input is $Input
       "
    }
}

'/' | Test-PipelineInput
```

3. The optional `Begin` and `End` blocks can be used to execute code before the pipeline processing has started. These blocks are ideal for preparation and clean-up tasks. Add them now and generate some messages with `Write-Host`:

```
function Test-PipelineInput
{
    begin
    {
        # The optional begin block at this point only sees an empty
$Input variable
        Write-Host "Starting with processing"
    }

    ...

    end
    {
        # The optional end block also cannot use $Input
        Write-Host "Processing finished"
    }
}

'/', $Home, $PSHOME | Test-PipelineInput
```

4. Pipeline input is usually processed either by property name or by value, giving you more control over the parameters than the rather anonymous `$Input` variable. Let's start with input by value – add a `Parameter` attribute and a parameter:

```
function Test-PipelineByValue
{
    # While the cmdlet binding attribute is not necessary, it is
one component
    # that lets functions behave like cmdlets
    [CmdletBinding()]
    param
    (
        # Each parameter taking values from the pipeline needs to
be decorated
        # with a parameter attribute
```

```
        [Parameter(ValueFromPipeline)]
        [string[]]
        $Path
    )
}
```

5. With the `ValueFromPipeline` attribute property set, the cmdlet now needs a process block. Inside the process block, the piped content can be used. Add a process block that just executes `Get-Item`:

```
function Test-PipelineByValue
{
    # While the cmdlet binding attribute is not necessary, it is
one component
    # that lets functions behave like cmdlets
    [CmdletBinding()]
    param
    (
        # Each parameter taking values from the pipeline needs to
be decorated
        # with a parameter attribute
        [Parameter(ValueFromPipeline)]
        [string[]]
        $Path
    )

    process
    {
        Get-Item @PSBoundParameters
    }
}
```

6. With the optional `Begin` and `End` blocks used to prepare the result, the finished cmdlet might look like this:

```
function Test-PipelineByValue
{
    [CmdletBinding()]
    param
    ( ... )

    begin
    { ... }

    process
    { ... }

    end
```

```
    { ... }
}
```

7. Now, test your new cmdlet both ways:

```
'/', $Home, $PSHOME | Test-PipelineByValue
Test-PipelineByValue -Path '/', $Home, $PSHOME
```

8. The parameter attribute with a `ValueFromPipelineByPropertyName` property will enable your cmdlet to also accept property values from the pipeline. Add this setting now:

```
function Test-PipelineByPropertyName
{
    [CmdletBinding()]
    param
    (
        [Parameter(ValueFromPipeline,
ValueFromPipelineByPropertyName)]
        [string[]]
        $Path
    )

    ...
}
```

9. Now, test the cmdlet again, this time using arbitrary objects that just have the right properties:

```
Get-Process -Id $pid | Test-PipelineByPropertyName
Test-PipelineByPropertyName -Path '/', $Home, $PSHOME
```

How it works...

In this recipe, you built your own pipeline-capable function. While, at first, you used `$Input`, you quickly progressed to a proper pipeline cmdlet that makes use of the `Begin`, `Process`, and `End` blocks and can accept parameter values from the pipeline.

When PowerShell processes pipeline input, the parameters are bound in a specific order. If you recall our first recipe in this chapter, *What is a pipeline?*, the important steps are:

1. Bind from the pipeline by value with exact type match.
2. Bind from the pipeline by value with conversion.
3. Bind from the pipeline by name with exact type match.
4. Bind from the pipeline by name with type conversion.

When processing pipeline input, PowerShell first tries to bind entire objects to parameters. First of all, this is done with an exact type match. For example, the output of `Get-Process` will be bound to the `InputObject` parameter of the `Stop-Process` cmdlet. If an exact match is not possible, a type conversion will be attempted.

If no parameters can be bound by value, the binding of properties is attempted instead. Again, PowerShell first tries to do an exact match, and afterwards will attempt a type conversion. You need to be aware of the binding order when designing your own pipeline-aware cmdlets.

High-performance pipelines

Performance is very important in automation scenarios. Often, scripts and cmdlets work with more than a few objects and connect to more than a few remote systems to collect data.

The performance of the pipeline, especially when working with the `Where-Object` cmdlet, can be impacted heavily. In many cases, this is not necessary and can be corrected with very few, simple modifications to your code.

This recipe demonstrates the importance of filters when accessing the filesystem, as well as the Windows event log.

Getting ready

Install and start PowerShell Core. If you want to follow along with the Windows event log example, please use a virtual machine with a Windows version that is compatible with PowerShell Core.

How to do it...

Perform the following steps:

1. First of all, remember `Get-Command` and the `ParameterName` parameter. While this is, incidentally, also a useful `Filter` parameter, it will help you locate cmdlets that are able to filter without using `Where-Object`. Use `Get-Command` now:

   ```
   Get-Command -ParameterName *Filter*
   ```

2. While using `Where-Object` to filter objects based on certain criteria is a popular choice, it is often the slowest choice, even for a small set of objects, as the following step shows. Try filtering for DLLs with `Where-Object`:

   ```
   $files = Get-ChildItem -File -Recurse -Path $PSHOME | Where-Object
   -Property Extension -eq '.dll'
   (Get-History)[-1].Duration
   ```

3. By simply replacing `Where-Object` with the `Filter` parameter, we can cut down the time needed to execute the same functionality by one-third or more. Try it now by using the `Filter` parameter:

   ```
   $files = Get-ChildItem -File -Recurse -Path $PSHOME -Filter *.dll
   (Get-History)[-1].Duration
   ```

4. Many cmdlets have a filter parameter that should make it an obvious candidate to effectively filter data. But even with a filter parameter, there are still differences in execution time and efficiency. Try using `Get-WinEvent` next:

   ```
   Get-WinEvent -LogName System | Where-Object -Property Id -in
   6005,6006
   ```

5. `Get-WinEvent` has multiple filter parameters. Observe the output of `Get-Command`:

   ```
   Get-Command -Syntax Get-WinEvent
   ```

   ```
   Get-WinEvent [[-LogName] <string[]>] [-MaxEvents <long>] [-
   ComputerName <string>] [-Credential <pscredential>] [-FilterXPath
   <string>]
   ```

   ```
   Get-WinEvent [-FilterHashtable] <hashtable[]> [-MaxEvents <long>]
   [-ComputerName <string>] [-Credential <pscredential>] [-Force] [-
   Oldest] [<CommonParameters>]
   ```

```
Get-WinEvent [-FilterXml] <xml> [-MaxEvents <long>] [-ComputerName
<string>] [-Credential <pscredential>] [-Oldest]
[<CommonParameters>]
```

6. We are using these filter parameters to filter events based on their XML structure.
   Have a look at the following sample event and try to spot the fields that we need
   for our simple query:

7. Let's start with the `FilterHashtable` parameter. This parameter can be used to
   define which logs, IDs, categories, and so on should be retrieved from the event
   log. You can immediately feel that the output is delivered faster. Try `Get-
   WinEvent` now:

```
Get-WinEvent -FilterHashtable @{
    LogName = 'System'
    ID = 6005, 6006
}
```

8. You often need to apply additional filters, especially with the Windows event log, such as filtering for specific event data entries with the case-sensitive `FilterXPath` parameter. Use the `FilterXPath` parameter to navigate the XML tree for each event to find events matching the filter:

```
Get-WinEvent -LogName System -FilterXPath '*[System[EventID=6005
or EventID=6006]]'
```

9. As you can see in the following screenshot, your filter directly relates to the Event XML:

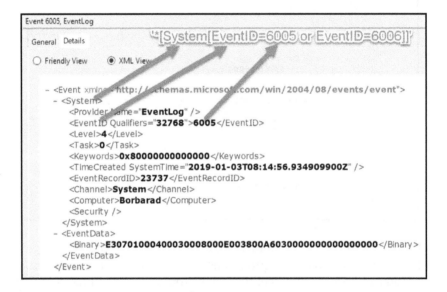

10. When comparing execution speed and efficiency, the `FilterHashtable` and `FilterXpath` parameters clearly win. Please execute each `Get-WinEvent` call individually to be able to use the cmdlet history. The `Duration` property is not available in Windows PowerShell. Compare the three different filters for `Get-WinEvent`:

```
$eventsWhere = Get-WinEvent -LogName System | Where-Object -
Property Id -in 6005,6006
$eventsXpath = Get-WinEvent -LogName System -FilterXPath
'*[System[EventID=6005 or EventID=6006]]'
$eventsHash = Get-WinEvent -FilterHashtable @{
    LogName = 'System'
    ID = 6005, 6006
}
```

```
$historyEntries = (Get-History)[-3..-1]

Write-Host ("
Where-Object: {0}
FilterXpath: {1}
FilterHashtable: {2}
" -f
$historyEntries[-3].Duration,$historyEntries[-2].Duration,$historyE
ntries[-1].Duration)

# Output:
# Where-Object: 00:00:11.4915062
# FilterXpath: 00:00:00.1191566
# FilterHashtable: 00:00:00.1043507
```

How it works...

This recipe showed you step-by-step why filtering early is important. You started by using the Filter parameter of Get-ChildItem and moved on to the different, more complex filter parameters of Get-WinEvent.

Many cmdlets have parameters that have filter in their name. As a rule of thumb, if a cmdlet allows you to filter as one of its parameters, this should be the most efficient way to narrow down the result set. Filtering with the Where-Object cmdlet is, generally speaking, always the slowest choice.

When it comes to performance in the pipeline, you are also well advised to look at parameters, such as AsJob, or at modules, such as SplitPipeline. While you cannot always use background jobs for different reasons, splitting the load into separate runspaces, as SplitPipeline does, should always be possible. The performance bonus will be most noticeable with CPU intensive processing that can be spread over different threads.

There's more...

Even when not working with `Where-Object`, there is often a performance impact with pipeline processing. Take a look at the following example, where file hashes are calculated for 1,000 objects:

```
$manyFiles = 1..1000 | foreach {$tmp = New-TemporaryFile | Get-Item; $tmp |
Set-Content -Value (1..50 | foreach {Get-Random}); $tmp}

# Method 1 uses the beginners approach: Pipe to foreach and process each
item individually
$manyHashes = $manyFiles | ForEach-Object -Process {$_ | Get-FileHash}
(Get-History)[-1].Duration # 320ms

# Method 2 uses Get-FileHash in the pipeline for all objects - very
efficient when compared to Foreach-Object
$manyHashes = $manyFiles | Get-FileHash
(Get-History)[-1].Duration # 140ms

# Method 3 uses the Split-Pipeline module to split processing of long-
running operations
Install-Module -Name SplitPipeline -Scope CurrentUser -Force
$manyHashes = $manyFiles | Split-Pipeline {process{ Get-FileHash
$_.FullName }}
(Get-History)[-1].Duration
```

Importing, Using, and Exporting Data

5

Importing, exporting, and using data in PowerShell is another essential skill. Whether you are using simple **Comma-Separated Values** (**CSV**) or you interact with RESTful APIs, PowerShell has got you covered. Many tools are able to export CSV and XML data, and management software very often exposes RESTful APIs. The following recipes will show you how to work with different types of data that you will usually encounter.

In this chapter, we will cover the following topics:

- Working with CSV
- Making objects transportable with XML
- Modern data structures – JSON and YAML
- Interacting with RESTful APIs
- Interacting with MS SQL
- Interacting with PostgreSQL and other database engines
- Encrypting data

Technical requirements

The code for this chapter can be found at `https://github.com/PacktPublishing/ Powershell-Core-6.2-Cookbook/tree/master/Chapter05`.

Working with CSV

The humble comma-separated file might be frowned upon by many, but there are some benefits to using these simple data structures. Whether you are using them to import configuration data for a bunch of hosts or you are using them to present data to end users, CSV is easy to use.

Often enough, CSV files are a very easy medium to convey information that has been gathered through automation.

Getting ready

Install and start PowerShell Core.

How to do it...

Let's perform the following steps:

1. There are not many cmdlets that work with CSV. Find them with `Get-Command`:

   ```
   # Let's review Get-Command
   Get-Command -Noun Csv
   ```

2. In general, CSVs are only ever useful for two-dimensional data structures with simple property types and values. Try `ConvertTo-Csv` to see what these structures can look like:

   ```
   # The thread collection is formatted using the ToString() method.
   Get-Process -Id $PID |
    Select-Object -Property Name, Id, Threads |
    ConvertTo-Csv
   ```

3. The standard delimiter is a comma. Use your system locale's delimiter by using the `UseCulture` parameter:

   ```
   # Using the default delimiter, a comma
   Get-Item / | Export-Csv -Path .\Default.csv
   Get-Content -Path .\Default.csv

   # Using the system delimiter is just one parameter
   Get-Item / | Export-Csv -UseCulture -Path .\WithSytemDelim.csv
   Get-Content -path .\WithSytemDelim.csv
   ```

4. Of course, you can define arbitrary, single-character delimiters as well. Try it now with a tabulator instead of a comma:

```
Get-Item / | Export-Csv -Delimiter "`t" -Path .\WithCustomDelim.csv
```

5. During the export, you will invariably experience information loss: all property values are converted into strings. Depending on the property type, the result will simply be the type name, as you can see in the following screenshot:

```
"Name","Id","Threads"
"pwsh","18128","System.Diagnostics.ProcessThreadCollection"
PS C:\Users\japete.EUROPE\source\repos\PacktPowerShellCookbook>
```

6. A very useful parameter when dealing with CSV is the `Append` parameter. If the object properties match the CSV headers, the object will be appended to the table. With the `Force` parameter, missing properties will be ignored. Try it now and append a CSV file:

```
$objectA = [PSCustomObject]@{
    Column1 = 42
    Column2 = 'Value'
}
$objectB = [PSCustomObject]@{
    Column1 = 1337
 Column2 = 'Another value'
}
$objectC = [PSCustomObject]@{
 Column1 = 666
}
$objectA | Export-Csv -Path sequentialexport.csv
$objectB | Export-Csv -Append -Path .\sequentialexport.csv
$objectC | Export-Csv -Append -Path .\sequentialexport.csv
$objectC | Export-Csv -Append -Path .\sequentialexport.csv -Force

Import-Csv -Path .\sequentialexport.csv
```

7. When importing from a CSV file, the data type will be a simple custom object. All properties will become `NoteProperty` types and are strings. Confirm this now by executing the `Get-Member` cmdlet:

```
Import-Csv -Path .\sequentialexport.csv | Get-Member
```

8. If you just need to convert between CSV and objects, the `ConvertTo-Csv` and `ConvertFrom-Csv` cmdlets have you covered. Try both of them now:

```
# To prepare data on the fly, for example to pass it to other tools
# the conversion cmdlets can be used
$objectA | ConvertTo-Csv

# If you receive comma-separated values from applications, try
using the Header parameter
'Value1, Value2, Value3' | ConvertFrom-Csv -Header Col1, Col2, Col3
```

9. To narrow down the object properties to export, you do not have to use `Select-Object`. Try `Select-PSFObject` from the `PSFramework` module with its awesome conversion syntax:

```
# Through non-standard modules, you can easily extend or modify the
objects that you want to export
Install-Module -Name PSFramework -Force -Scope CurrentUser
Get-ChildItem -File -Path / -Recurse -Depth 2 |
 Select-PSFObject Name, 'CreationTime.DayOfWeek as CreatedOn to
string' |
 Export-Csv -Path ./exportedfiles.csv
```

How it works...

This recipe demonstrated the use of the `ConvertTo-Csv`, `ConvertFrom-Csv`, `Export-Csv`, and `Import-Csv` cmdlets to create two-dimensional tables from PowerShell objects.

The CSV export and import cmdlets are very straightforward. All first-level object properties will be exported by converting the object properties into strings. This usually means a loss of information if you consider data types such as collections and `System.Diagnostics.ProcessStartInfo`.

CSV files are especially useful if you want to hand over your exported data to people unfamiliar with PowerShell. CSV files can be opened in many popular spreadsheet applications to sort, group, or otherwise process data.

Making objects transportable with XML

Apart from CSV, **Extensible Markup Language (XML)** is also a popular format. While XML is not well-suited for human-readable exports, it can be used to transport objects between systems.

Through .NET, you can invoke the conversion of objects to XML directly as well, forgoing storing the data in a file. This recipe will show you how to work with the CLIXML (command-line interface XML) format as well as standard XML formats that might be used.

Getting ready

Install and start PowerShell Core.

How to do it...

Let's perform the following steps:

1. As with CSV, there are some cmdlets that help you to deal with XML structures. Discover them now with `Get-Command`:

```
Get-Command -Noun Clixml,Xml
```

2. Converting objects into XML with the `Export-CliXML` cmdlet will start a process called serialization. Try it now and export the current date:

```
# XML can contain a lot of information
Get-Date | Export-Clixml -Path .\date.xml
(Get-Content .\date.xml).Count
```

3. Importing the objects from CLIXML will immediately look different from CSV: the default format is still being used. Compare both now:

```
Get-Date | Export-Csv -Path .\date.csv
Import-Csv .\date.csv
Import-Clixml -Path .\date.xml
```

4. Exporting objects to CLIXML means subjecting them to the process of serialization. When being imported or deserialized, the objects invariably change. Use `Get-Member` to find out more:

```
Import-Clixml -Path .\date.xml | Get-Member
Get-Process -Id $Pid | Export-Clixml -Path .\process.xml
Import-Clixml -Path .\process.xml | Get-Member -MemberType Methods
Import-Clixml -Path .\process.xml | Get-Member -Name
ProcessName,Threads
```

5. With the `ConvertTo-Xml` cmdlet, you can convert objects on the fly into CLIXML. The output type is an XML document that you can navigate. Try it now and access the result with dot-notation:

```
$xmlDate = Get-Date | ConvertTo-Xml
$xmlDate.Objects.Object.'#text'
```

6. The process of serialization can also be triggered using the static `Deserialize` method of the `PSSerializer` class. Try to use it now, for example, as an alternative to `ConvertTo-Xml`:

```
$serializedDate =
[System.Management.Automation.PSSerializer]::Serialize((Get-Date))
[System.Management.Automation.PSSerializer]::Deserialize($serialize
dDate)
[System.Management.Automation.PSSerializer]::DeserializeAsList($ser
ializedDate)
```

7. It is the same process when you retrieve objects in jobs or from remote systems. Try using `Get-Member` on the output of a PowerShell job:

```
$proc = Start-Job -ScriptBlock {Get-Process -Id $pid} | Wait-Job |
Receive-Job -Keep
$proc | Get-Member -MemberType Methods
```

8. Conveniently, this process adds new members as well. Try to find out which members have been added automatically with `Get-Member`:

```
$proc | Get-Member -Name
PSShowComputerName, PSComputerName, RunspaceId
```

How it works...

This recipe taught you the difference between XML and CSV by examining the output visually and with `Get-Member`. You experienced first-hand what deserialization looks like in practice.

Serialization and deserialization are commonly used by developers as a means to transport data, for example, between services, or to save the state of an object. Very often, XML serialization is used to accomplish this. Depending on the type of service, other data structures, such as JSON, are more suitable due to less overhead.

When executing scripts remotely, it is important to remember that all objects that are created have to be transported over the wire. To make those objects transportable, they are serialized to an XML string that is reconstructed (deseralized) on the receiving system.

This recipe had you export and import CSV and XML files. You should have seen that both have their pros and cons. Every time that objects have to be transport, for example, in a remote session, XML will be used automatically and is not meant for human consumption. Using cmdlets such as `Get-Member` will help you to identify whether an object has been imported from a different source, and what the source was.

Modern data structures – JSON and YAML

Apart from CSV and XML, new data structures, such as **YAML Ain't Markup Language** (**YAML**), are gaining more traction. On the other hand, formats such as **JavaScript Object Notation** (**JSON**) that have been around for a long time are especially popular with web services.

Both are data structures that can be used to serialize and deserialize data, albeit with a loss of information. Neither JSON nor YAML can fully serialize objects like an XML serializer does.

Getting ready

Install and start PowerShell Core.

How to do it...

Let's perform the following steps:

1. PowerShell is natively capable of working with JSON. Try converting a simple object into JSON with the `ConvertTo-Json` cmdlet. Use it now as follows:

```
$customObj = [PSCustomObject]@{
    StringProperty = 'StringValue'
    IntProperty = 42
    ArrayProperty = 1,2,3
}

$jsonString = $customObj | ConvertTo-Json
$jsonString
```

2. When being converted back, basic data types will be fully reconstructed. Confirm this by looking at the output:

```
$jsonString | ConvertFrom-Json
```

3. The `Invoke-RestMethod` cmdlet will automatically return JSON—try calling a REST service:

```
Invoke-WebRequest -uri https://jsonplaceholder.typicode.com/todos/1

# Invoke-RestMethod does the parsing for you as a custom object
$response = Invoke-RestMethod -Method Get -Uri
https://jsonplaceholder.typicode.com/todos/1
$response | Get-Member
```

4. Methods such as PUT and POST also work with JSON to transfer data to a REST endpoint. Try using the POST method with the REST endpoint:

```
$jsonBody = @{
    SomeData = 'Some Content :)'
} | ConvertTo-Json

Invoke-RestMethod -Method Post -Uri
https://jsonplaceholder.typicode.com/posts -Body $jsonBody -
ContentType application/json
```

5. You can make more of JSON with modules such as Newtonsoft.Json, a popular library used in many .NET projects as well as PowerShell Core:

```
Install-Module -Name newtonsoft.json -Scope CurrentUser
Get-Date | ConvertTo-Json | ConvertFrom-Json
Get-Date | ConvertTo-JsonNewtonsoft | ConvertFrom-JsonNewtonsoft
```

6. YAML essentially goes in the same direction. While there is no integrated YAML support, you can use the PowerShell YAML module. Try it now by installing it and using `Get-Command` on the installed module:

```
# YAML suppport is not included with PowerShell
Install-Module PowerShell-yaml -Scope CurrentUser
Get-Command -Module powershell-yaml
```

7. Converting back and forth with YAML will leave you with lean text and a dictionary that contains your original object's properties. Try it now with a simple custom object as the input:

```
$customObj = [PSCustomObject]@{
    StringProperty = 'StringValue'
    IntProperty = 42
    ArrayProperty = 1,2,3
}

$yamlString = $customObj | ConvertTo-Yaml
$yamlString

# Converting the object back from YAML generates a dictionary
instead of a custom object
$yamlString | ConvertFrom-Yaml
```

How it works...

In this recipe, you used JSON and YAML as different data types that are often preferred over XML. You started by learning the syntax of JSON through some cmdlets and then looked at YAML as an alternative. Since YAML is not supported by default, it is your choice which format to use. This recipe should have given you enough information to decide whether or not an additional module is worth it.

PowerShell cmdlets, such as `ConvertTo-Json`/`ConvertFrom-Json` and `Invoke-RestMethod`, have been able to work with JSON since Windows PowerShell 3, which was released in 2012. In PowerShell Core, the JSON conversion cmdlets have been improved, allowing greater control over the values that are returned.

The process of serialization and deserialization works similar to the XML serialization. Both YAML and JSON have a lot less overhead while still being able to convey enough information for modern RESTful web services.

There's more...

Explore how YAML and JSON are used in practice with the project DscWorkshop at `https://github.com/automatedlab/dscworkshop`. Utilizing the powerful module, Datum, developed by Gael Colas, YAML is used to generate configuration data for desired state configuration.

See also

- Learn more about Datum at `https://github.com/gaelcolas/datum`.

Interacting with RESTful APIs

Working with RESTful APIs has been essential for Dev and Ops people alike for many years now. From custom application to standard software, monitoring stack to asset management, many products offer web-based consoles, and, of course, a RESTful API to interact with.

Like Windows PowerShell, PowerShell Core is well-suited to work with web services in a very uniform way through REST. This recipe will use the GitHub API as an example.

Getting ready

Install and start PowerShell Core.

How to do it...

Let's perform the following steps:

1. To use the GitHub API without investing much time in OAuth2, you can start with a simple personal access token. To do so, browse to `https://github.com` and access your settings:

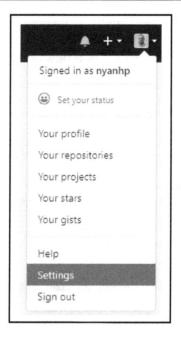

2. Head to **Developer settings** and create a new access token:

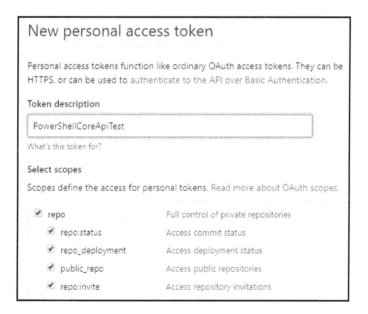

3. The access token is good enough to create new public repositories and generally read from the API. For this, we use `Invoke-RestMethod` in PowerShell. But, can we simply access GitHub's API? Try it now, as follows:

```
# The Invoke-RestMethod cmdlets are useful for interacting with
REST APIs
Get-Command -Name Invoke-RestMethod -Syntax

# Usually, REST APIs require authentication. This can be an API key
to restrict access, or it can be credentials.
# Try accessing github's API without authentication
Invoke-RestMethod -Method Get -Uri
'https://api.github.com/user/repos' -ErrorVariable octoError

# Good thing we store our errors, right?
$errorResponse = $octoError.Message | ConvertFrom-Json

# Read up on that API ;)
start $errorResponse.documentation_url
```

4. With the personal access token from *Step 2*, we can try that again:

```
...
$tokenString =
[Convert]::ToBase64String([Text.Encoding]::ASCII.GetBytes(("{0}:{1}
" -f $credential.UserName,
$credential.GetNetworkCredential().Password)))

# The header is simply a hashtable with whatever headers you need
$header = @{
    Authorization = 'Basic {0}' -f $tokenString
}

$repositories = Invoke-RestMethod -Method Get -Uri
'https://api.github.com/user/repos' -Headers $header -ErrorVariable
octoError
```

5. Brilliant. Have a look at the result that `Invoke-RestMethod` has returned. We can use this to our hearts' content and filter, select, sort, and group the data:

```
# Let's see what we have here
$repositories[0]

# Ever needed a quick way to see your forks?
$repositories | Where fork
```

6. But, wouldn't it be great to create repositories as well? You can prepare the repository data in a hashtable:

```
# Let's start with the properties that
https://developer.github.com/v3/repos/#create has outlined
$repoData = @{
    name = 'NyanHP_Is_Awesome'
    description = 'This is so much better than opening a browser'
    has_wiki = $false
    license_template = 'mit'
}
```

7. `Invoke-RestMethod` can submit a body with each request. For API calls, this is usually JSON:

```
$jsonBody = $repoData | ConvertTo-Json

# With the proper body, this API call will create a new project
$newRepo = Invoke-RestMethod -Method Post -Uri
'https://api.github.com/user/repos' -Authentication Basic -
Credential $credential -Body $jsonBody -ContentType
application/json
```

8. Reap the fruits of your labor by accessing all properties of the freshly created repository:

```
# Ready to get started?
New-Item -ItemType Directory -Path .\MyNewRepo
git clone $newRepo.clone_url MyNewRepo

# Want to see how it looks like?
start $newRepo.html_url
```

9. Using a different method, but the same URI, try to update the repository description with the PATCH method:

```
# Change the description with a simple update
$newRepoJson = @{
    name = 'NyanHP_Is_Awesome'
    description = 'This works like a charm :)'
    has_wiki = $false
    license_template = 'mit'
} | ConvertTo-Json

Invoke-RestMethod -Method Patch -Uri
"https://api.github.com/repos/$($newRepo.full_name)" -
Authentication Basic -Credential $credential -Body $jsonBody -
ContentType application/json
```

How it works...

Like all RESTful APIs, the GitHub API has multiple paths, such as `user/repos`. By accessing those paths, we access different parts of the API—our requests are simply routed to a different endpoint.

Each endpoint will implement typical CRUD methods – **Create, Read, Update, and Delete**. With the GitHub API, this could be **Create a new repository**, **Read one or all repositories**, **Change a repository**, and **Delete a repository**. When translated to request methods, this would be **Post to create**, **Get to read**, **Patch to change**, and **Delete** to delete a repository.

The same principles apply to other APIs as well. In `Chapter 10`, *Using PowerShell with Azure and Google Cloud*, we will see both the Google Cloud API and Microsoft Azure as examples for cloud service infrastructures that can be automated with RESTful APIs as well.

Interacting with MS SQL

There are many ways of interacting with Microsoft SQL Server from within PowerShell. While there is the old SQLPS module as well as the new and improved SqlServer module, neither are fully compatible with PowerShell Core.

Instead, we can turn to .NET and to the much more convenient dbatools module from the community.

Getting ready

Install and start PowerShell Core. If you want to follow along with lab SQL Servers instead of your own infrastructure, you can use AutomatedLab and the lab recipe found at `https:/ /github.com/AutomatedLab/DscWorkshop/blob/master/Lab/03. 10%20Full%20Lab%20with%20DSC%20and%20TFS.ps1`.

How to do it...

Let's perform the following steps:

1. With Windows PowerShell, you could have used both SQLPS, the old module, as well as `SqlServer`, the newer module:

```
Install-Module -Name SqlServer -Scope CurrentUser
```

2. However, the `SqlServer` module is not yet fully ported to PowerShell Core. Most notably, cmdlets such as `Invoke-SqlCmd` are missing:

```
# This module is the official module to manage SQL
Get-Command -Module SqlServer
```

3. Through implicit remoting, you can still interact with SQL:

```
Export-PSSession -Session (New-PSSession DSCCASQL01) -OutputModule
ImplicitSql -Module SqlServer
```

4. While accessing data is, fortunately, easy, this is not really what we wanted:

```
$projects = Invoke-Sqlcmd -ServerInstance DSCCASQL1\NamedInstance -
Database Tfs_AutomatedLab -Credential contoso\install -Query
'SELECT project_name,state from dbo.tbl_projects'

# Your query will contain an array of DataRow objects containing
column names as properties
$projects.Where(
    {
        $_.state -ne 'WellFormed'
    }
).ForEach(
    {
        Write-Host "Your project $($_.project_name) is not well
formed! It reports status $($_.state)"
    }
)
```

5. Using .NET we can bridge that gap and connect to SQL. For this, start with a connection object, as follows:

```
$connection = New-Object -TypeName
System.Data.SqlClient.SqlConnection
```

6. The connection object will need a connection string or database and credential settings:

```
$connection.ConnectionString = 'Data Source=DSCCASQL01;Initial
Catalog=Tfs_AutomatedLab;Trusted_Connection=yes'
```

7. A `SqlCommand` object is used to contain your query or stored procedure and can use parameters and more:

```
$command.CommandText = 'SELECT project_name,state from
dbo.tbl_projects'
$command.CommandType = 'Text'
```

8. A command can be used with a connection to, for example, query data from a remote system:

```
# A reader can be used to advance row by row through your results
$command.Connection = $connection
$connection.Open()
$reader = $command.ExecuteReader()

while ($reader.Read())
{
    Write-Host ("Project {0} is {1}" -f $reader['project_name'],
$reader['state'])
}

# If you are done querying, close the connection to the server.
$connection.Close()
```

9. Fortunately, independent module developers are very quick to port their modules to PowerShell Core, so the famous dbatools (http://dbatools.io) can be used instead of complicated .NET statements:

```
# Are you missing Invoke-SqlCommand from PowerShell Core? Invoke-
DbaQuery has you covered.
$result = Invoke-DbaQuery -SqlInstance dsccasql01 -Query 'SELECT
project_name,state from dbo.tbl_projects' -Database
tfs_automatedlab

# Luckily, the result is an array of DataRows, just like Invoke-
SqlCmd
$result.Where(
    {
        $_.state -eq 'WellFormed'
    }
).ForEach(
    {
        Write-Host "Congratulations. Your project
$($_.project_name) is well formed."
    }
)
```

10. While the simple query in *Step 8* produced the same result as the native cmdlet, there are also highly useful cmdlets such as `Copy-DbaTable`:

```
# A good example is migrating entries from one table to another
# Here, projects from TFS are migrated to Azure DevOps Server.
Get-DbaDbTable -SqlInstance DSCCASQL01 -SqlCredential
contoso\Install -Database Tfs_AutomatedLab -Table dbo.tbl_projects
|
Copy-DbaDbTableData -Destination DSCCASQL02 -DestinationDatabase
AzDevOps_AutomatedLab -DestinationSqlCredential contoso\install -
Table az.tbl_projects
```

11. Even migrations are pretty easy with the `Start-DbaMigration` cmdlet:

```
Start-DbaMigration -Source dsccasql01 -Destination dsccasql02 -
BackupRestore
```

How it works...

The SQL SQLPS and SqlServer modules, as well as dbatools, are using .NET classes from the `System.Data.SqlClient` namespace (and other .NET namespaces) to connect to your SQL instances.

While SQLPS and SqlServer mount a new provider drive to manage your instance, dbatools more than make up for the lack of a drive by providing uniquely useful cmdlets for everything from instance management to queries.

See also

- Read everything on dbatools at `https://docs.dbatools.io/`.

Interacting with PostgreSQL and other database engines

Popular database engines, such as PostgreSQL or MariaDB, often do not have dedicated, well-maintained PowerShell modules. In those cases, we usually need to revert to .NET on PowerShell Core.

Luckily, we can at least use standardized ways of accessing those engines. This recipe examines PostgreSQL, but the learning can be applied to any database engine that offers up a .NET library to handle connections.

Getting ready

Install and start PowerShell Core. To interact with a PostgreSQL database, you can use your favorite hosting or cloud provider. Azure has a PostgreSQL offering to create a full-fledged PostgreSQL server. Most hosting providers will offer you some managed databases, just make sure you have a connection string to use.

How to do it...

Let's perform the following steps:

1. As with MS SQL, you might need a connector to interact with PostgreSQL:

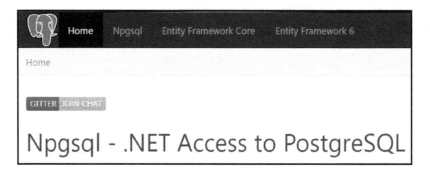

2. Luckily, the package can be downloaded from `https://www.nuget.org/`:

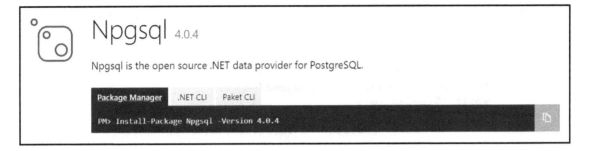

Npgsql 4.0.4

Npgsql is the open source .NET data provider for PostgreSQL.

Package Manager	.NET CLI	Paket CLI

```
PM> Install-Package Npgsql -Version 4.0.4
```

3. Through package management, the package can simply be installed. However, this does not help you yet. You would use this technique with .NET development:

```
# First of all, we can use NuGet to pull the required libraries for
us
# at the time of writing, Save-Package npgsql -path . only worked
with Windows PowerShell
Invoke-WebRequest -Uri
https://www.nuget.org/api/v2/package/Npgsql/4.0.4 -OutFile
.\postgres.zip
Expand-Archive .\postgres.zip
```

4. After adding a reference to the assembly by either using Add-Type or the using statement, the entire assembly can be used like any other .NET assembly:

```
Add-Type -Path .\postgres\lib\netstandard2.0\Npgsql.dll
```

5. Creating a new connection looks very similar; try it out now:

```
# Create a new connection - and the rest stays the same
$connection =
[Npgsql.NpgsqlConnection]::new('host=postgreshost.domain.com
dbname=pgDb user=john password=Somepass1')
```

6. Creating a SQL command also looks very similar:

```
# A new NpgsqlCommand works just like your SqlCommand
$command = [Npgsql.NpgsqlCommand]::new($connection)

# Command text of course might be slightly different with different
SQL dialects
$command.CommandText = 'SELECT * FROM distributors ORDER BY name'
$command.CommandType = 'Text'
$connection.Open()
```

7. Since this model provides uniform access to data from different sources, you can simply use the same methods as you would with MS SQL:

```
# This model provides uniform access to data, regardless of the
source
$reader = $command.ExecuteReader()
while ($reader.Read())
{
    Write-Host "Distributor-ID $($reader.did), Name:
$($reader.Name)"
}
```

8. Regardless of the database, close up once you are done:

```
# As with MSSQL, Postgre connections should also be properly closed
$connection.Close()
```

How it works...

Like .NET application development, where NuGet packages are used to add references to a project, you can use the same distribution method to download the connector packages for different database management systems from within PowerShell.

The rest is pretty standard .NET development that you could wrap in some convenient functions to use later on.

Encrypting data

Nothing is worse than finding your credentials or other confidential information in plain text on the network. While PowerShell cannot protect you against insecure web services, it can protect your credentials, connections strings, and so on as long as possible by supporting the **Cryptographic Message Syntax** (**CMS**).

Currently only supported on the Windows operating system due to the certificate stores that are being used, the CMS allows you to securely pass information to other users or computers. The security of this is based on mathematical problems such as the prime factorization of large (4096 bit) numbers, or calculating coordinates on an elliptic curve. Or, in friendlier terms, public key cryptography.

Getting ready

Install and start PowerShell Core on a Windows system.

How to do it...

Let's perform the following steps:

1. To do anything with the CMS, you will need some certificates. Create the certificates for your recipient node first:

```
Import-WinModule -Name Pki
New-SelfSignedCertificate -Subject 'CN=Node01' -FriendlyName 'DSC
MOF Encryption Cert for machine Node01' -Type
DocumentEncryptionCert -CertStoreLocation Cert:\CurrentUser\my
```

2. The certificates you just created are only good for development purposes. Self-signed certificates should not be used in a production environment—for this, we usually require a public key infrastructure with certificate authorities. Let's explore the certificate a bit:

```
# Let's explore the certificate a bit:
$certificate = Get-ChildItem -Path Cert:\CurrentUser\my | Where-
Object -Property Subject -eq 'CN=Node01'
$certificate | Get-Member -MemberType Methods

# One important method will be Verify. You can execute this method
to verify the certificate chain
$certificate.Verify()

# Other useful methods
$certificate.GetPublicKeyString()
$certificate.GetCertHashString()

# You can always check if you are in possession of the private key
$certificate.HasPrivateKey
```

3. With your document encryption certificate, you can now use the CMS cmdlets:

```
Get-Command -Noun *CmsMessage
```

4. To protect data, you can specify one or more recipients of whom you have the public key:

```
# Encrypting something is simple - as long as you have the public
key of the recipient
# In order to encrypt, document encryption certificates are needed
$protectedMessage = Read-Host -Prompt 'Enter your connection
string' | Protect-CmsMessage -To "CN=Node01"
$protectedMessage
```

5. This message can be sent over an insecure connection and later reconstructed. But, let's examine the message first:

```
# Have a look at the details of the message - there is much you can
read
$protectedMessage | Get-CmsMessage
($protectedMessage | Get-
CmsMessage).ContentEncryptionAlgorithm.Oid.FriendlyName # e.g.
AES256
```

6. If you are in possession of your private key, go ahead and decrypt the message:

```
# To decrypt the message, you need to be in possession of the
private key
$protectedMessage | Unprotect-CmsMessage
```

How it works...

Without diving too much into the mathematics behind public key algorithms such as **Rivest-Shamir-Adleman (RSA)** or **Elliptic-Curve Diffie Hellman (ECDH)**, the security of the encryption hinges on certificates. These certificates, or the private and public keys, are used to encrypt or digitally sign data.

In order to encrypt data, you must know the public key of your recipients. On a Windows system, for example, this is achieved by importing a base64 encoded *.cer file into your personal certificate store. The recipient must be in possession of their private key in order to decrypt the data that was meant for them. Only entities in the possession of the private key can decrypt the data.

A digital signature, on the other hand, works by signing a document with your private key. To verify a signature, the recipient only has to look up your public key and use the public key to validate the signature. If the combination of public and private key is correct and the contents of the signed document are unchanged, the signature will be validated.

6

Windows and Linux Administration

Administrators use PowerShell on Windows quite naturally to manage the operating system. However, PowerShell is also a useful tool on Linux to manage the operating system. While not every function on Linux is implemented in dedicated PowerShell modules, we can still use the powerful processing capabilities of PowerShell to manage the OS.

This chapter might look like a biased comparison in favor of Windows, but that is not the case. It merely illustrates the necessity of more PowerShell cmdlets that work with Linux as well as Windows operating systems.

In this chapter, we will cover the following recipes:

- Enabling a Windows feature
- Installing a Linux package group
- Creating Windows accounts
- Creating Linux accounts
- Modifying the Windows Registry
- Modifying Linux configuration files
- Registering a new Windows service
- Enabling a new Linux daemon
- Planning a Windows scheduled task
- Creating a Linux Cron Job
- Creating a Windows storage pool
- Creating a Linux software RAID device
- Accessing the Windows event log
- Working with the system logs in Linux

Technical requirements

To follow all recipes, you will need access to one Windows system and one Linux system. All recipes on Linux have been done on CentOS 7.4. To install both in one fell swoop, check out one of AutomatedLab's recipes called *ALLovesLinux* to create a domain environment with Windows Server 2016 and CentOS.

Code files for this chapter can be found at the following link : `https://github.com/ PacktPublishing/Powershell-Core-6.2-Cookbook/tree/master/Chapter06`.

Enabling a Windows feature

One of the most basic tasks on a Windows server is enabling a Windows feature. Unfortunately, the `ServerManager` module is not supported in PowerShell Core. There are dependencies to the full .NET Framework that would lead to issues even with the Windows Compatibility Pack installed.

There are, of course, ways around this.

Getting ready

Install and start PowerShell Core on a Windows server.

How to do it...

Please perform the following steps:

1. In PowerShell Core, install the module `WindowsCompatibility`, as shown in the following example:

   ```
   # Now, this comes up empty
   Get-Module -ListAvailable -SkipEditionCheck -Name ServerManager

   # However, dedicated people like Bruce Payette, Steve Lee and Mark
   Kraus made this possible
   Install-Module -Name WindowsCompatibility -Scope CurrentUser -Force
   -AllowClobber
   ```

2. In order for it to work, you will need to import the desired module. In our case, `ServerManager`, as shown in the following example:

```
# With this module, implicit remoting is used for incompatible
modules
# One of those being ServerManager
Import-WinModule -Name ServerManager
```

3. Discover the exported cmdlets by traditional methods, as shown in the following example:

```
# Now, the discovery cmdlets work as well
Get-Command -Module ServerManager
```

4. The cmdlets now work and behave just fine, as shown in the following example:

```
# Suddenly, it all works out just fine
Get-WindowsFeature
Get-WindowsFeature -Name powershell-v2
```

5. Removing a security hole is now easy again, as can be seen in the following example:

```
# of course, with implicit remoting, pipelining is hit and miss
# In this case however, it works beautifully
Get-WindowsFeature -Name powershell-v2 | Remove-WindowsFeature
```

6. As is installing management tools or enabling other features, as can be seen in the following example:

```
# of course, adding features is also a breeze
Get-WindowsFeature -Name RSAT-AD-Tools | Install-WindowsFeature
```

How it works...

Even though it looks like a script module, if you examine `ServerManager` in the module path, it requires additional assemblies that are so far not compatible.

The `WindowsCompatibility` module is essential when it comes to easy server administration. While many modules are so-called **Cmdlet Definition XML (CDXML)** modules that work out of the box, some important ones are not, and never will be. CDXML modules essentially wrap cmdlets around CIM interactions and thus simply work as intended.

See also

- *Learn PowerShell Core 6.0* by *David das Neves* and *Jan-Hendrik Peters* on remoting.
- For documentation on the `WindowsCompatibility` module, visit `https://github.com/PowerShell/WindowsCompatibility`.

Installing a Linux package group

Many Linux package management tools support installing package groups of related packages. This is not really comparable with a Windows feature. For example, a package group might be a basic web server and will include a collection of packages such as Apache2, Perl, and Python.

Getting ready

Install and start PowerShell Core.

How to do it...

Please perform the following steps:

1. First of all, we will need to familiarize ourselves with the system, and examine the installed package groups, as shown in the following code:

    ```
    # Let's get a lay of the land first
    yum groups list
    ```

2. Filtering Linux command output in PowerShell is very easy, even for administrators coming from Windows, as can be seen in the following example:

    ```
    # Since OS commands always return text, we can use PowerShell to get to
    # the information we want
    yum groups list | Select-String 'Web Server'
    (yum groups list) -match 'Web Server'
    ```

3. Notice that the output is not entirely filtered; the yum command appears to be writing warnings to the error stream. We can get rid of them easily with the following redirection operators:

```
# Suppress the error stream
(yum groups list 2>$null) -match 'Web Server'
```

4. Now that we have what we need, we can use further yum commands and react to their status with some built-in variables, as per the following example:

```
$groupname = ((yum groups list 2>$null) -match 'Web Server').Trim()
yum groups install $groupname -y

# Without using Start-Process, all we have is the last exit code
if ($LASTEXITCODE -ne 0)
{
    Write-Warning "Installing $groupname failed"
}
```

5. Using Start-Process, while not as natural as just running a command, offers more control and insight, as can be seen in the following example:

```
# Try it again with a process - be careful to use double quotation
marks
$process = Start-Process -FilePath yum -ArgumentList
groups,install, "`"$groupname`"", '-y' -Wait -PassThru

if ($process.ExitCode -ne 0)
{
    Write-Warning "Installation with the following command line
failed: $($process.StartInfo.FileName)
$($process.StartInfo.Arguments)"
}
```

6. To list the installed packages, we can again rely on PowerShell to properly process the text information that is returned, as shown in the following example:

```
# Now our tools show up properly
# With the awesome features of PowerShell, grabbing the correct
string in a text is easy
(yum groups list 2>$null | Out-String) -match "Installed
Environment Groups:\s+(?<PackageName>[\w\s]+)`n"
$Matches.PackageName
```

How it works...

This is just plain Linux—we are using package management cmdlets for the RPM interface YUM. Instead of using Linux commands such as `grep`, `sed`, and `awk` to process the string data returned, we instead use PowerShell's helpful cmdlets, such as `Select-String`, and operators such as the match operator.

Creating Windows accounts

One of the typical tasks that system administrators have to do, even with a directory service such as **Active Directory Domain Services** (**AD DS**), is creating and managing local users and groups. On a Windows system with PowerShell Core, this is still easily possible. In this recipe, you will create and modify local accounts on a Windows system.

Getting ready

Install and start PowerShell Core.

How to do it...

Please perform the following steps:

1. We are dealing with a Windows PowerShell module, which fortunately can be fully utilized in PowerShell Core. In recent versions of Windows, the module in question is marked as compatible with PowerShell Core, removing *Step 1*. Get started by enabling Windows modules, as shown in the following code:

   ```
   Add-WindowsPSModulePath
   ```

2. Now we can discover the necessary module and make use of it, as follows:

   ```
   Import-Module Microsoft.PowerShell.LocalAccounts -SkipEditionCheck
   ```

3. With the `New-LocalUser` cmdlet, you can simply create a local account, as follows:

   ```
   New-LocalUser -AccountExpires (Get-Date -Year 2020 -Month 1) -
   Description 'A test user' -Name JHP -Password (Read-Host -
   AsSecureString)
   ```

4. Adding the user to a local group is also not a problem, as shown in the following example:

```
Add-LocalGroupMember -Group Administrators -Member JHP
```

5. Besides local accounts, you can add domain accounts (including Azure AD) as well as Microsoft accounts to local groups, as shown in the following example:

```
Add-LocalGroupMember -Group users -Member
"MicrosoftAccount\username@Outlook.com"
```

6. Removing a user is again just a cmdlet call away, as can be seen in the following code:

```
Get-LocalUser -Name *JHP* | Remove-LocalUser
```

How it works...

The `LocalAccounts` module is a typical binary module that consists of a library `'Microsoft.Powershell.LocalAccounts.dll'` and a module manifest. After having been examined for compatibility with .NET Standard, the property `CompatiblePSEditions` has been adjusted, as shown in the following code:

```
CompatiblePSEditions = @('Desktop', 'Core')
```

In this recipe, you used operating system methods wrapped in cmdlets to create new users, modify local groups, and, finally, remove users. Using the pipeline, these tasks are very easy to do. PowerShell's verbose syntax makes this code pretty self-documenting.

Creating Linux accounts

On Linux there are, again, no native PowerShell cmdlets available to create and manage local accounts. However, PowerShell can still be used to securely pass credentials to OS commands, generate hashed user passwords, and so on. In this recipe, you will use PowerShell Core to help create user accounts in Linux as well, to get you started with cmdlet development when no cmdlets exist.

Getting ready

Install and start PowerShell Core.

How to do it...

Please perform the following steps:

1. First of all, let's see if there already is a command available, as follows:

```
# Search for appropriate commands - all of them are external
Get-Command -Name *user*
```

2. `useradd` and `adduser` are typically used on Linux systems to create local accounts on the fly, as shown in the following example:

```
# With useradd we can pass a password - but it has to be hashed
man useradd
```

3. These commands, however, expect a password hashed in a certain way. So let's start by getting a credential in a secure way, as shown in the following example:

```
$credential = Get-Credential -UserName notImportant
```

4. While the current user can still access the plaintext password that the Linux command needs, the credential is still protected, as shown in the following example:

```
$credential.GetNetworkCredential().Password
```

5. Since the format for a password in Linux is rather special, we use other automation tools such as Perl or Python to help us out, as shown in the following example:

```
$hashedPassword = python -c ('import crypt;
print(crypt.crypt(\"{0}\", crypt.mksalt(crypt.METHOD_SHA512)))' -f
$credential.GetNetworkCredential().Password)
```

6. Now it is easy to create a user account with a proper password, as follows:

```
useradd -G wheel -p $hashedPassword john
```

7. Without an alternative way of generating password hashes for Linux, you could have created the user and set the password later on, as shown in the following example:

```
# This would have been the ugly alternative
useradd jim
$credential.GetNetworkCredential().Password | passwd --stdin jim
```

How it works...

Working with PowerShell Core in this context might not feel natural, but, again, PowerShell makes it possible to work a bit more easily with data input and variables. Its more verbose style might not be what Linux administrators are accustomed to, but there are clear benefits when it comes to readability.

In this recipe, you created a user and added him to a group. The way that credentials were handled is far from ideal, demonstrating that there is still a lot to be done with PowerShell Core on Linux. Both the Python command to generate a password hash as well as using the `passwd` command used the plaintext password of your user. This is never a good idea.

Modifying the Windows Registry

The Windows Registry stores a lot of configuration settings for the operating system. Through multiple stores, so-called hives, user and machine-related settings can be stored and quickly retrieved. Usually the registry is not touched manually that often, but is modified through group policies instead.

It might still be necessary to modify registry settings on the fly to change settings for the operating system as well as for applications.

Getting ready

Install and start PowerShell Core.

How to do it...

Please perform the following steps:

1. The registry is made accessible through the `Registry` provider, as follows:

```
Get-PSProvider -PSProvider Registry
Get-PSDrive -PSProvider Registry
```

2. So, in order to browse the registry, you can simply use the Item, Location, and Content cmdlets, as shown in the following example:

```
Get-ChildItem -Path HKCU:\Software
Set-Location -path HKCU:\Software
Get-ItemProperty -Path HKCU:\Software\Classes -name EditFlags
```

3. Modifying a value is very easy to do locally, as can be seen in the following example:

```
# Modifying the local registry is easy enough
# e.g. to disable the Server manager UI at logon
Set-ItemProperty -Path "HKLM:\SOFTWARE\Microsoft\ServerManager" -
name "DoNotOpenServerManagerAtLogon" -Value 1
```

4. Recall the output of *Step 1*—the Registry provider is not capable of mounting remote registry hives. So how can we access a remote machines registry from the local host? Let's look at the following code:

```
# Working with a remote registry is not possible with the built-in
cmdlets
(Get-PSProvider -PSProvider Registry).Capabilities
# However, with .NET, anything is possible
$remoteHive =
[Microsoft.Win32.RegistryKey]::OpenRemoteBaseKey('LocalMachine',
'DSCCASQL01')
```

5. With the hive opened, we can open a sub key with write access, as follows:

```
# To open a key with write access, use the boolean value
$key = $remotehive.OpenSubKey('SoFTWarE\microsoft\servermanager',
$true)
```

6. Now we can read data, as follows:

```
# Now the remote key can be used as well
$key.GetValue('DoNotopenServerManagerAtLogon')
```

7. We can also change data, as follows:

```
# And with write access, we can write to it as well
$key.SetValue('DoNotopenServerManagerAtLogon', 0)
```

How it works...

While we can simply work locally with the providers that we saw in the previous chapters, not all providers can work remotely. The registry is one of them. So, in order to interact with remote registries we can use either PowerShell remoting or .NET.

This recipe enabled you to create and change local registry keys and values with the registry provider, which is comfortable to do. On the other hand, you saw how complicated it was to access the registry remotely; it is considerably more difficult.

When using .NET to access the registry, we are using Distributed COM and **Remote Procedure Calls** (**RPCs**)—in other words, native OS remoting. With PowerShell remoting we, of course, use WSMan and the TCP port 5985. However, in the case of remote registry manipulation, this is not possible unless you wrap your local code in an Invoke-Command call.

Modifying Linux configuration files

What the registry is for Windows, configuration files are still for Linux. Many components of the operating system can be managed through configuration files.

While there aren't any Linux management cmdlets out there for PowerShell Core, we can still reap the benefits of the flexible type system as well as powerful language elements and cmdlets.

Getting ready

Install and start PowerShell Core.

How to do it...

Please perform the following steps:

1. The following example shows the most common point of entry, /etc:

```
# It all starts here
Get-ChildItem -Path /etc -File
```

2. In order to modify system settings such as the maximum amount of shells per user group, we might want to modify /etc/security/limits.conf, as per the following example:

```
# To control the limits of pam, have a look at limits.conf
Get-Content -Path /etc/security/limits.conf

# Try filtering for the important parts
Get-Content -Path /etc/security/limits.conf | Where-Object {-not
$_.StartsWith('#')}
```

3. The entries in the PAM-related limits.conf and the configuration files in limits.d all follow the same syntax, that could very well be parsed with PowerShell, as demonstrated in the following example:

```
# With these bits, a certain pattern emerges... Values, separated
by whitespace
man limits.conf

# And sure enough, looking at the man page reveals <domain> <type>
<item> <value>
$limits = Get-Content -Path /etc/security/limits.conf | Where-
Object {-not $_.StartsWith('#')} |
    ForEach-Object {
    $null = $_ -match "(?<Domain>[\w@]+)\s+(?<Type>hard|soft|-
)\s+(?<Item>\w+)\s+(?<Value>\d+)"

        # Remove the entire match - we don't really need this
        $Matches.Remove(0)

        # Matches is a dictionary. Incidentally what PSCustomObject can
use
        [pscustomobject]$Matches
}

# Normal variables that can be modified and stored again
$limits[0].Type = 'Soft'
$limits[0].Item = 'nproc'
$limits[0].Value = 10
```

4. Writing new values back is as easy as Add-Content, as shown in the following example:

```
# Add a new limit like this, e.g. to limit the user MyUser to 20
processes
Add-Content -Value 'MyUser hard nproc 20' -Path
/etc/security/limits.conf
```

5. PowerShell has some serious RegEx capabilities, so we can simply replace content in files as well, as the following example demonstrates:

```
# PowerShell is also excellent to quickly change a value in a
configuration
# Linux admins can still use illegible Regular Expressions - with
PowerShell's
# verbose language, beginners tend to understand at least the
purpose better
$newPort = 4729
(Get-Content -Path /etc/ssh/sshd_config) -replace "^Port\s+\d+" |
Set-Content -Path /etc/ssh/sshd_config -Whatif
```

How it works...

Again, we only use PowerShell as a better text processing engine. The nice thing about PowerShell Core is the verbose language. While you can surely obfuscate PowerShell scripts to resemble some of the famously ugly Perl scripts—any developer determined enough can turn even the most beautiful language ugly—PowerShell encourages a readable scripting style.

This recipe started you off with typical text processing in PowerShell Core on Linux. Because many configuration items are stored in configuration files, text processing is a necessity.

To work with text in PowerShell, regular expressions are often used. They are very versatile, but can be hard to comprehend. The pattern we have used in *Step 3* combines multiple elements:

- Character classes:
  - \w meaning any word character, a-z, A-Z, 0-9 and _
  - \d meaning any decimal number
  - \s meaning any whitespace character, such as a single tabulator
- Quantifiers:
  - + meaning 1 - n results
  - * meaning 0 - n results
  - {n, m} meaning n - m results, where m can be empty if it should be indefinite
- Groups:
  - (?<Name>) meaning a so-called named capturing group, with the name specified in angle brackets

- Logical operators:
    - | meaning a logical OR
- Escape character:
    - \ to escape any special character

Our port replacement pattern in the last step, `^Port\s+\d+`, replaces a line beginning with `P` followed by `ort`, at least one white space and at least one number. So, the following are examples that would be replaced: `Port 80`, `Port 7`.

Registering a new Windows service

Whether you are a developer or an operations person, registering a new service is one of those things you don't do very often. PowerShell, again, makes it very easy to create a new service, with or without parameters, using different credentials if necessary.

Getting ready

Install and start PowerShell Core.

How to do it...

Please perform the following steps:

1. For a new service, we first of all need a binary that interacts with the service controller—the application you interact with when executing the venerable `sc.exe`, as per the following example:

```
# Build the dummy service template
dotnet build .\project1
```

2. This simple dummy service accepts requests from the service control manager, for example `Start-Service` and `Stop-Service`, as shown in the following example:

```
# This simple service just reacts to requests and does nothing
.\project1\bin\debug\project1.exe
```

3. With the `New-Service` cmdlet, you can register your service as follows:

```
# With our dummy the service even reacts to the other service
cmdlets
# Resolve path is necessary since New-Service does not resolve the
relative path
New-Service -Name Dummy1 -BinaryPathName (Resolve-Path -Path
.\project1\bin\debug\project1.exe).Path
Start-Service Dummy1
Stop-Service Dummy1
```

4. Of course `New-Service` as well as `Set-Service` allow different credentials, as can be seen in the following example:

```
$credential = [pscredential]::new('LocalUserJohn', ('Somepass1!' |
ConvertTo-SecureString -AsPlainText -Force))
New-LocalUser -Name $credential.UserName -Password
$credential.Password
Set-Service -Name Dummy1 -Credential $credential -StartupType
AutomaticDelayedStart
```

5. A cmdlet that is sorely missed in Windows PowerShell, even after all those years in service, is `Remove-Service`. PowerShell Core fortunately has it, as shown in the following example:

```
# One cmdlet that is still missing even today from Windows
PowerShell
Remove-Service -Name dummy1 -Verbose
```

How it works...

The Service cmdlets use .NET and the `ServiceController` class to provide access to Windows services. Whether or not you can interact with them depends on the rights you have on the service control manager or individual services. This is usually specified in group policies.

While the `Get-` and `Set-Service` cmdlets support a `ComputerName` parameter, and thus are capable of remoting, they will use DCOM and RPC instead of **Windows Remote Management** (**WinRM**).

This recipe enabled you to create a new service with a binary that can react to the Windows service control manager. You also saw how to modify existing services with the `Set-Service` cmdlet. With cmdlets such as `Get-Credential` or `Read-Host -AsSecureString` you can safely query a user for credentials that are used with `Set-Service`.

To remove existing services with PowerShell Core, the `Remove-Service` cmdlet is used. This is comparatively new, as Windows PowerShell never supported removing a service.

There's more...

You could also use CIM remoting and the `Win32_Service` class to properly modify a remote service, as shown in the following example:

```
$cimsession = New-CimSession somehost
$service = Get-CimInstance -Query 'SELECT * FROM Win32_Service WHERE Name =
"wuauserv"' -CimSession $cimsession
$service | Invoke-CimMethod -MethodName StopService
```

Enabling a new Linux daemon

The service cmdlets that exist in Windows do not exist at all in Linux. The main reason for this is the fragmentation of init systems available. This chapter will focus on `systemd`, which is enabled by default on CentOS, for example.

Getting ready

Boot a Linux distribution using `systemd`, install and start PowerShell Core.

How to do it...

Please perform the following steps:

1. Start by searching for the available cmdlets—at the time of writing there are none. This is shown in the following example:

   ```
   # No service cmdlets yet
   Get-Command -Noun Service
   ```

2. On CentOS, Fedora, and Red Hat among others, `systemd` is used as the init
   system, as shown in the following example:

   ```
   # The main reason is that there are different systems like systemd
   man systemctl
   ```

3. While it can be used for entities other than services, we will concentrate on the
   service part, as shown in the following example:

   ```
   # Systemd is an init system that is of course used for more than
   just services (daemons)
   systemctl status sshd
   service sshd status # deprecated with systemd
   ```

4. First of all, we can use PowerShell to create a nice function around `systemd`,
   which we will call `Get-Service`. To do that, notice the pattern in the output of
   `systemctl` in the following example:

   ```
   # We can still use PowerShell though
   systemctl list-units --type service --no-pager
   ```

5. We can use that to improve the output by creating new objects that can be
   formatted. Start with an empty function and the default parameters first, as
   shown in the following code:

   ```
   function Get-Service
   {
       [CmdletBinding()]
       param
       (
           [string[]]
           $Name,

           [string]
           $ComputerName
       )
   }
   ```

6. Of course, `Get-Service` is capable of running remotely. Or better: `systemctl` is
   able to query remote hosts via SSH. The command to execute thus changes to
   that which follows:

   ```
   $results = if ($ComputerName)
   {
       systemctl list-units --type service --no-pager -H $ComputerName
   }
   else
   ```

```
    {
        systemctl list-units --all --type service --no-pager
    }
```

7. Now, we can apply a simple regular expression to create new objects, as shown in the following example:

```
$services = foreach ($result in $results)
    {
        #UNIT LOAD ACTIVE SUB DESCRIPTION
        if ($result -match
'(?<Name>\w+)\.service\s+(?<LoadedState>\w+)\s+(?<UnitStatus>\w+)\s
+(?<Status>\w+)\s+(?<Description>\w[\w\s]*)')
        {
            $tmp = $Matches.Clone()
            $tmp.Remove(0)
            [pscustomobject]$tmp
        }
    }
```

8. Afterwards, we need to filter if the user decided to use the Name parameter, as follows:

```
if ($Name)
{
    Write-Verbose -Message "Applying like-filter for $Name"
    return $services | Where-Object -Property Name -like $Name
}

$services
```

9. Now, we can use all kinds of useful cmdlets, as shown in the following example:

```
# For example for formatting purposes
Get-Service | Format-Table -Property Status, Name, Description
Get-Service | Where-Object -Property Status -eq 'Running'

# Or sorting
Get-Service | Sort-Object -Property Name

# Or Grouping
Get-Service | Group-Object -Property Status
```

10. New services can also be created very easily, as demonstrated in the following example:

```
# Creating a new daemon requires the same basic components as a
Windows service:
# Something to execute.
# Let's take the Polaris script from "Learn PowerShell Core"!
Get-Content ./LinuxDaemon/polaris.ps1

# We can create the service definition in PowerShell as well
# A here-string is perfect for that.
@"
[Unit]
Description=File storage web service

[Service]
ExecStart=$((Get-Process -Id $pid).Path) $((Resolve-Path -Path
./startpolaris.ps1).Path)

[Install]
WantedBy=multi-user.target
"@ | Set-Content /etc/systemd/system/polaris.service -Force

systemctl daemon-reload
systemctl start polaris
```

11. Instead of creating files, we can also create a new cmdlet called `New-Service`, as follows:

```
function New-Service
{
    param
    (
        [Parameter(Mandatory)]
        [string]
        $BinaryPathName,

        [Parameter(Mandatory)]
        [string]
        $Name,

        [string]
        $Description,

        [string]
        $User = 'root',

        # one of systemctl list-units --type target --no-pager
```

```
            [string]
            $Target = 'multi-user'
        )
    }
```

12. `New-Service` simply adds the parameter values to the service definition file, as shown in the following example:

```
@"
[Unit]
Description=$Description

[Service]
ExecStart=$BinaryPathName
User=$User

[Install]
WantedBy=$Target.target
"@ | Set-Content "/etc/systemd/system/$Name.service" -Force

# Execute daemon-reload to pick up new service file
systemctl daemon-reload

Get-Service -Name $Name
```

13. After registering your new service, you could create another new cmdlet or use:
`systemctl start polaris`

How it works...

Unfortunately, the `System.Service.ServiceController` class that the `Service` cmdlets use is Windows-only. However, PowerShell Core still makes your life a lot easier, and the migration from Windows to Linux a lot more bearable, by allowing you to create your own custom cmdlets.

Again, as Linux is predominantly string-based, we are using regular expressions to parse the output of the Linux commands and simply convert them to proper objects. Observe how the match operator is used here—the `$Matches` variable is cloned, group 0 is removed and the resulting hash table is used as the parameter for your new object.

This recipe showed you how to use functions to create reusable code that wraps around operating system functionality. It is often necessary to extend existing functions, or create new ones in PowerShell, if nothing suitable exists. Reusable code such as `Get-Service` and `New-Service` can help you be productive on Windows and Linux.

Planning a Windows scheduled task

Scheduled tasks are a staple in the Windows world. Again, cmdlets simplify everything related to scheduled tasks. Since Windows PowerShell 3, the task scheduler can be used for scheduled jobs as well as proper tasks.

While a scheduled job is essentially a PowerShell background job that is executed by the task scheduler, a scheduled task can be anything. Scheduled jobs retain their results and can be retrieved with the job cmdlets, while a scheduled task cannot.

Getting ready

Install and start PowerShell Core.

How to do it...

Please perform the following steps:

1. Discover the `ScheduledTask` cmdlets, as follows:

   ```
   Get-ScheduledTask
   ```

2. First of all we would like to list registered tasks on a system, as follows:

   ```
   Get-ScheduledTask -TaskName *Cache*
   Get-ScheduledTask -TaskPath \Microsoft\Windows\Wininet\
   ```

3. Remoting can be achieved using CIM remoting, as shown in the following example:

   ```
   Get-ScheduledTask -TaskName *Cache* -CimSession (New-CimSession -ComputerName host1)
   ```

4. To register a new task, some components should be used. First of all, the action to execute, as per the following example:

   ```
   $action = New-ScheduledTaskAction -Execute pwsh -Argument '-Command " & {"It is now $(Get-Date) in task land"}'
   ```

5. Next, a trigger is useful as well, as follows:

   ```
   $trigger = New-ScheduledTaskTrigger -At (Get-Date).AddMinutes(5) -Once
   ```

6. Lastly, and entirely optional, are the task settings, as shown in the following example:

```
$settings = New-ScheduledTaskSettingsSet -AllowStartIfOnBatteries
-RunOnlyIfNetworkAvailable
```

7. With the `New-ScheduledTask` cmdlet, a task object is created. This object is still not functional, as the following example demonstrates:

```
$task = New-ScheduledTask -Action $action -Description "Says hello"
-Trigger $trigger -Settings $settings
```

8. Registering the task object does the trick, as shown in the following code:

```
$registeredTask = $task | Register-ScheduledTask -TaskName MyTask -
TaskPath \MyTasks\
```

9. We can now interact with the task as necessary. This is shown in the following example:

```
# The task cmdlets can be used to interact with the task
$registeredTask | Start-ScheduledTask
$registeredTask | Stop-ScheduledTask

# Finally, to unregister a task
$registeredTask | Unregister-ScheduledTask
```

How it works...

The `ScheduledTask` cmdlets are used to interact via CIM with the Windows task scheduler. With CIM and CIM remoting the authentication is very flexible. You can register the same task on multiple remote machines with CIM remoting, query a bunch of machines, and so on.

By using the different building blocks of a task, you can create everything that is necessary and export the task definition to CliXML, for example. The entire object can be used with the `Register-ScheduledTask` cmdlet to register the task in the system.

Planning a Linux Cron Job

Linux has a scheduling service, called cron, which is used for recurring jobs. The scheduler service, crond, works with files called `CronTab`, to schedule tasks.

As you might imagine, this is, again, very text-based. Luckily, the PowerShell team created a demo module that is very helpful. It is called `CronTab`.

Getting ready

Install and start PowerShell Core.

How to do it...

Please perform the following steps:

1. Start by discovering any existing cmdlets, as follows:

   ```
   # Again - no native cmdlets
   Get-Command *ScheduledTask*
   ```

2. Again, we need to work around missing code. However, the PowerShell team has something in store for this occasion, as shown in the following example:

   ```
   # Download the CronTab module from GitHub
   $null = New-Item -ItemType Directory -Path
   /usr/local/share/powershell/Modules/CronTab -ErrorAction
   SilentlyContinue
   Invoke-WebRequest -Uri
   https://raw.githubusercontent.com/PowerShell/PowerShell/master/demo
   s/crontab/CronTab/CronTab.psm1 -OutFile
   /usr/local/share/powershell/Modules/CronTab/CronTab.psm1
   ```

3. The newly downloaded module can be imported automatically as we stored it in the `PSModulePath`. However, it is a great idea to examine the module contents first, as shown in the following example:

   ```
   cat /usr/local/share/powershell/Modules/CronTab/CronTab.psm1
   ```

4. Now that there is a module, cmdlet discovery works as follows:

```
# Discover the contents
Get-Command -Module CronTab
```

5. Try examining the existing `CronTab` first, as per the following example:

```
# Let's see if there are existing jobs
Get-CronTab

# Get-Crontab displays the contents, Get-CronJob is a bit
friendlier:
Get-CronJob
```

6. To add a new entry (register a new task) we can use the `New-CronJob` cmdlet, as shown in the following example:

```
# Creating a new job is very easy
New-CronJob -Minute 5 -Hour * -DayOfMonth * -Command "$((Get-
Process -Id $pid).Path) -Command '& {Add-Content -Value awesome -
Path ~/taskfile}'"
```

7. Finding existing jobs is a bit tricky as they don't have names or paths like the Windows scheduled tasks had. This is demonstrated by the following code:

```
# Since cron jobs don't have names like scheduled tasks, finding
them might be a bit tricky
Get-CronJob | Where-Object -Property Command -like '*awesome*'
Get-CronJob | Where-Object -Property Minute -eq 5
```

8. Be sure to locate the correct job before you remove anything, as per the following example:

```
# This is especially important when trying to remove a job
Get-CronJob | Where-Object -Property Command -like '*awesome*' |
Remove-CronJob -WhatIf
Get-CronJob | Where-Object -Property Command -like '*awesome*' |
Remove-CronJob -Confirm:$false
```

How it works...

Again, the cmdlets that the module exposes are very simple. Using the humble split operator, the contents of a `CronTab` are separated into their field and converted to custom `CronJob` objects that serve as property bags.

You could easily extend the module to allow creating entries for other users, for example.

Creating a Windows storage pool

Windows storage pools are, essentially, software RAID devices that are used with Storage Spaces and **Storage Spaces Direct** (**S2D**) to provide virtual disks for different purposes. Much like a traditional RAID device, resiliency can be configured flexibly. Any storage connected to a server running Windows Server 2012, and more recent, can be used to create a storage pool.

As you might imagine, a single disk can only be part of one storage pool.

Getting ready

To get ready for this recipe, a lab environment is highly recommended. To create a lab environment on a Hyper-V machine, you can use the following code snippet:

```
New-LabDefinition -Name PoolParty -DefaultVirtualizationEngine HyperV

$disks = foreach ($count in 1..10)
{
    Add-LabDiskDefinition -Name d$count -DiskSizeInGb 5 -SkipInitialize -
PassThru
}

Add-LabMachineDefinition -Name PoolNoodle -DiskName $disks.Name -Memory 8GB
-OperatingSystem 'Windows Server 2016 Datacenter (Desktop Experience)'

Install-Lab
```

This snippet will create a basic virtual machine with some empty disks attached. AutomatedLab requires downloading at least a trial version of Windows Server or an active Azure subscription to create the VM.

How to do it...

Please perform the following steps:

1. Start by having a look at the storage pool that always exists—the primordial pool—as shown in the following code:

   ```
   Get-StoragePool
   ```

2. Like the primordial soup, the primordial pool simply contains the elements for all new storage pools. Disks that can be added to a pool are indicated by the property `CanPool`, as shown in the following example:

```
Get-StoragePool -IsPrimordial $true | Get-PhysicalDisk | Where-
Object -Property CanPool
```

3. Try adding the first half of the disks to one pool, as shown in the following example:

```
$disks = Get-StoragePool -IsPrimordial $true | Get-PhysicalDisk |
Where-Object -Property CanPool | Select -First 5

# Now we can create a new virtual disk and ultimately a new volume
Get-StorageSubSystem
New-StoragePool -PhysicalDisks $disks -FriendlyName 'Splish splash'
-StorageSubSystemFriendlyName 'Windows Storage*'
```

4. Now we can create a new virtual disk and, ultimately, a new volume, as per the following example:

```
Get-StoragePool -FriendlyName 'Splish Splash' |
    New-VirtualDisk -FriendlyName Accounting -UseMaximumSize

$volume = Get-VirtualDisk -FriendlyName Accounting | Get-Disk |
Initialize-Disk -Passthru | New-Partition -AssignDriveLetter
-UseMaximumSize | Format-Volume
$largefile =
[System.IO.File]::Create("$($Volume.DriveLetter):\largefile")
$largefile.SetLength($volume.SizeRemaining - 1kB)
$largefile.Close()
```

5. You will notice that the available storage is getting less and less. To expand a storage pool you can simply add another set of poolable disks to it, as shown in the following example:

```
Get-StoragePool -FriendlyName 'Splish Splash' |
    Add-PhysicalDisk -PhysicalDisks (Get-StoragePool -IsPrimordial
$true | Get-PhysicalDisk | Where-Object -Property CanPool)
```

6. Now that the pool has grown, the virtual disk and volume can grow as well, as can be seen in the following example:

```
Get-VirtualDisk -FriendlyName Accounting | Resize-VirtualDisk -Size
16GB
$volume | Get-Partition | Resize-Partition -Size 15GB
```

How it works...

Storage Spaces is a feature of Windows Server 2012, and more recent, and allows you to create so-called storage pools or software RAID devices. With simple PowerShell cmdlets that are available in PowerShell Core as well, pools can be created.

Virtual disks can be carved out of pools and used as storage for applications, divisions, and so on. Like other software RAIDs, storage pools can be extended and shrunk at runtime.

See also

- Read more about storage pools at https://docs.microsoft.com/en-us/
  windows-server/storage/storage-spaces/deploy-standalone-storage-spaces

Creating a Linux software RAID device

Linux provides many different ways of creating software RAIDs, none of which, of course, come with dedicated PowerShell cmdlets. In this recipe, we will look at mdadm to create a very simple RAID.

Getting ready

To get ready for this recipe, a lab environment is highly recommended. To create a lab environment on a Hyper-V machine, you can use the following code snippet:

```
New-LabDefinition -Name PoolParty -DefaultVirtualizationEngine HyperV
Add-LabVirtualNetworkDefinition -Name 'Default Switch' -HyperVProperties @{
SwitchType = 'External'; AdapterName = 'Ethernet' }

$disks = foreach ($count in 1..10)
{
 Add-LabDiskDefinition -Name linuxd$count -DiskSizeInGb 5 -SkipInitialize -
PassThru
}

Add-LabMachineDefinition -Name PoolNoodle -DiskName $disks.Name -Memory 8GB
-OperatingSystem 'CentOS 7.4' -Network 'Default switch'

Install-Lab
```

This snippet requires you to download CentOS. If you are using another Linux distribution, please install it as you normally would and attach additional storage to the virtual machine.

How to do it...

Please perform the following steps:

1. It all starts with examining the available volumes. Since cmdlets such as `Get-PhysicalDisk` are Windows-only, we have to take to the text-based CLI again, as per the following example:

```
lsblk -io KNAME,TYPE,SIZE,MODEL
```

2. Like the `Get-Disk` cmdlet, `lsblk` will list block devices that we can use for our software RAID. Creating a RAID device is no more complicated than creating a storage pool. Let's polish our data with PowerShell a little bit though. First of all, we can create a very simple property bag, as shown in the following example:

```
class BlockDevice
{
    [string] $Name
    [string] $Type
    [int64] $Size
}
```

3. Now, we need to create a function to have some reusable code, as shown in the following example:

```
function Get-Disk
{
    lsblk -ibo KNAME,TYPE,SIZE,MODEL | Select-Object -Skip 1 |
ForEach-Object {
        if ($_ -match
'(?<Name>\w+)\s+(?<Type>\w+)\s+(?<Size>[\w\d.]+)\s')
        {
            $tmp = $Matches.Clone()
            $tmp.Remove(0)
            [BlockDevice]$tmp
        }
    }
}
```

4. We can now filter on our disks, as per the following example—we could've used the `Get-ChildItem` cmdlet as well, provided we know how our disk devices are called:

```
Get-Disk | Where-object -Property Type -ne 'part'
```

5. The `mdadm` command in Linux can create a RAID device—but we want to use PowerShell to our advantage. A new function springs to mind. Start with an enumeration and a new class, as follows:

```
enum RaidLevel
{
    RAID0 = 0
    RAID1 = 1
    RAID4 = 4
    RAID5 = 5
    RAID6 = 6
    RAID10 = 10
}

class RaidDevice
{
    [string] $DeviceName
    [string[]] $MemberDevice
    [RaidLevel] $Level
}
```

6. Now, we can use our new data types in a new function called `Get-SoftwareRaid` before starting to create a new one, as shown in the following example:

```
function Get-SoftwareRaid
{
[CmdletBinding()]
param
(
$DeviceName
)

    $devices = foreach ($line in (Get-Content -Path /proc/mdstat))
    {
        if ($line -match
'(?<DeviceName>[\w\d]+)\s+:\s+active\s+raid(?<Level>[\d])\s+')
        {
            $tmp = $Matches.Clone()
            $tmp.Remove(0)
            $device = [RaidDevice]$tmp
```

```
                $deviceString = $line -replace ".*raid\d{1,2}\s+"
                $device.MemberDevice += $deviceString -split "\s" -
replace "\[\d+\]"
                $device
            }
        }

        if ($DeviceName)
        {
            $devices = $devices | Where-Object -Property DeviceName -eq
$DeviceName
        }

        $devices
    }
```

7. Now that we can get existing RAID configurations, why not create a cmdlet that uses mdadm in an orderly fashion? An example of this is as follows:

```
function New-SoftwareRaid
{
    ...

    process
    {
        if (($MemberDevice | Test-Path) -contains $false)
        {
            Write-Error -Message "One or more member devices not
found."
            return
        }

        $devices += $MemberDevice.FullName
        $deviceCount += $MemberDevice.Count
    }
    end
    {
        ...
        Start-Process -FilePath (Get-Command mdadm).Path -
ArgumentList $arguments -Wait -NoNewWindow
    }
}
```

8. Beautiful. Try your new cmdlet in the pipeline, as shown in the following code:

```
Get-ChildItem -Path /dev/sd[cd] | New-SoftwareRaid -DeviceName md0
-Level Raid0 -Verbose
```

9. Now for the clean-up. Create the new `Remove-SoftwareRaid` function by combining the necessary OS commands with PowerShell, as shown in the following example:

```
function Remove-SoftwareRaid
{
    . . .

    begin
    {
        $memberDisks = @()
    }

    process
    {
        . . .
        $raid = Get-SoftwareRaid -DeviceName $DeviceName.BaseName
        umount $DeviceName.FullName
        mdadm --stop $DeviceName.FullName
        mdadm --zero-superblock /dev/$memberDisk
    }
}
```

10. Try the new cmdlet as well, as follows:

```
Get-Item -Path /dev/md0 | Remove-SoftwareRaid -WhatIf
Get-Item -Path /dev/md0 | Remove-SoftwareRaid -Confirm:$false
```

How it works...

How `mdadm` works is well documented in man `mdadm`. What we did in this recipe was to slowly add new cmdlets to manage otherwise text-based commands. With proper data types and enumerations we can control the data our cmdlets work with. Moreover, we can enable tab completion and IntelliSense easily.

By using the `CmdletBinding` attribute, we can add important functionality, such as risk mitigation. The cmdlet binding attribute property `SupportsShouldProcess` indicates that we would like to get the additional parameters `WhatIf` and `Confirm`. The `ConfirmImpact` property tells the caller that our cmdlet has a high impact on the operating system—we are removing a RAID device.

By adopting PowerShell best practices for scripting and reusable functions, you can slowly start building your Linux cmdlet arsenal. Better yet: you can bundle your cmdlets into a module and publish it on the PowerShell Gallery for fame and glory!

Accessing the Windows event log

Whenever things go sideways, or the operating system behaves in a way that was neither planned nor foreseeable, Windows administrators have grown accustomed to accessing the event log. Regrettably, many administrators are still using the graphical user interface for that.

The trade-off of a colorful UI, of course, is that it does not scale. How are you going to consolidate the event you are looking for on hundreds of servers? How can you efficiently parse the event log for that one piece of information hidden in some event? Why, by using PowerShell Core, of course.

This recipe will introduce you to the `Get-WinEvent` cmdlet and its filtering capabilities with a very typical task: parsing the security logs for one specific user logon.

Getting ready

Install and start PowerShell Core on a Windows operating system.

How to do it...

Please perform the following steps:

1. Like in most recipes, get familiar with your surroundings first, as per the following example:

   ```
   # Let's get familiar with the cmdlet first - brace for impact!
   Get-WinEvent -ListLog * -ErrorAction SilentlyContinue | Format-Wide
   -Property LogName -Column 4
   ```

2. The **Event Tracing for Windows (ETW)** channels are a wealth of information. Let's look at the following command:

   ```
   Get-WinEvent -ListProvider *Security* | Format-Wide -Property Name
   -Column 4
   ```

3. However, we are interested in the `Security` log; specifically failed logins, as shown in the following example:

   ```
   Get-WinEvent -LogName Security -MaxEvents 1
   ```

4. We can generate the event we need by failing to log in, as per the following example:

```
# Be sure to use the wrong password for it to work ;)
runas /user:$($env:COMPUTERNAME)\$($env:USERNAME) pwsh
```

5. There are two ways to get to the event. The efficient and the inefficient way. Start with the inefficient one to see the improvement more easily, as shown in the following example:

```
# We can get to this event rather inefficiently. Doing so prompts
Get-WinEvent to comb through the
# ENTIRE security log - and you know how big those get.
Get-WinEvent -LogName Security | Where-Object -Property ID -eq 4625
```

6. The better way is to use one of the filter parameters—remember: filter as early as possible—as shown in the following example:

```
# There is a better way
Get-Command Get-WinEvent -Syntax

# Let's start with FilterHashtable because of its simplicity -
blazingly fast
$failedLogin = Get-WinEvent -FilterHashtable @{LogName =
'Security'; ID = 4625} -MaxEvents 1
```

7. With that event retrieved, we can examine it a bit more, as shown in the following example:

```
# Now we can examine it - a lot of information
$failedLogin | Get-Member -MemberType Properties

# One piece of information is particularly useful - the properties.
But alas, they have no names
# But we'll see about that
$failedLogin.Properties
```

8. Since we don't want to work with unstructured information, such as an array of strings, we can have a look at the XML structure of the event. An example of this can be seen in the following code:

```
# As we know, every event in its natural form is an XML structure
$failedLogin.ToXml()

# We can use XML
$xmlEvent = [xml]$failedLogin.ToXml()
```

```
# There we go :)
$xmlEvent.Event.EventData.Data

# More importantly, we can now filter out exactly what we need
($xmlEvent.Event.EventData.Data | Where Name -eq
TargetUserName).InnerText
```

9. The great feature of `Get-WinEvent` is that we can filter the events even further—for example by the `TargetUserName` we were interested in—as shown in the following example:

```
# Enter the XPATH filter.
$filter = '*[System[EventID=4625]] and *[EventData[Data[@Name =
"TargetUserName"] = "japete"]]'
Get-WinEvent -FilterXPath $filter -LogName Security
```

10. And if `XPATH` is not something you can easily remember, try `FilterHashtable` again. There is one key called `'*'`, maybe we can use it, as shown in the following example:

```
Get-Help Get-WinEvent -Parameter FilterHashtable
Get-WinEvent -FilterHashtable @{LogName = 'Security'; ID = 4625;
TargetUserName = 'japete'}
```

11. Be aware that remoting with the `ComputerName` parameter is highly inefficient. Only one machine at a time can be used. Instead, make use of PowerShell remoting, as shown in the following example:

```
# Of course, everything we did here, we can do remotely to dozens
of machines.
$filterTable = @{LogName = 'Security'; ID = 4625; TargetUserName =
'japete'}

Invoke-Command -ComputerName (Get-Content
.\thousandsOfMachines.txt) -ScriptBlock {
    Get-WinEvent -FilterHashtable $using:filterTable
}
```

How it works...

The Windows event logs and event channels can be filtered much more efficiently than the UI lets on. Especially when filtering the more hidden parts of the event that you usually don't readily see in the UI, such as the `EventData` section entries.

To generate XPATH queries with a little help, you can try designing a custom view in the event viewer. This view will always have an **XML** tab that you can use for your filtering needs, as demonstrated by the following screenshot:

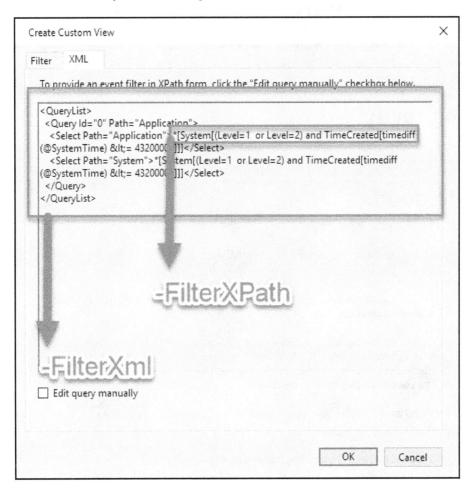

See also

- For details on ETW please visit the following link: https://docs.microsoft.com/en-us/windows/desktop/etw/event-tracing-portal

Working with the system logs in Linux

Linux also works with events, of course. However, unlike the Windows event log, Linux systems usually use syslog to log messages. Syslog is documented in RFC 5424 and is a well-structured, easy to automate protocol. The great thing with PowerShell is that we can get structured data into objects with very little work. And, of course, we only do the work once and then offload the functionality in a module.

Getting ready

Install and start PowerShell Core on a Linux system.

How to do it...

Please perform the following steps:

1. First things first, we need to get familiar with the very basics. Let's look at the following commands:

   ```
   # Linux does not work with event logs like Windows does
   Get-ChildItem /var/log

   # To make matters worse, the default log files are all in a
   different format
   Get-ChildItem -Path /var/log -File | foreach {$_ | Get-Content |
   Select -First 1 -Skip 5 }
   ```

2. Let's have a look at one very generic log, /var/log/messages, which is shown in the following command:

   ```
   Get-Content /var/log/messages
   ```

3. Depending on your distribution, a daemon such as rsyslogd will take care of logging and can be configured to log different syslog facilities and priorities to different log files, as per the following example:

   ```
   cat /etc/rsyslog.conf
   ```

4. Tools such as logger can write to the various logs, as shown in the following example:

```
# Now, to log, there is no need for a cmdlet. We should use logger
instead.
# The configuration of e.g. rsyslogd will govern how the SYSLOG
messages are written
# when logger logs them
logger -p local0.emergency "Oh god, it buuuurns"
```

5. To easily read a log file, we can, again, create our own functions, beginning with a class to store logging entries, as shown in the following example:

```
class LogEntry
{
    [string] $Message
    [datetime] $TimeWritten
    [string] $ComputerName
    [string] $Source
    [uint32] $ProcessId
}
```

6. We can, again, use regular expressions to parse the text. Refer *Modifying Linux configuration files* recipe, in this chapter to learn more. Let's look at the following code:

```
# \d matches decimals, \w alphanumeric characters
# The quantifiers + and {n,m} are used to specify the amount of
characters
$logpattern =
"(?<TimeWritten>\w{3}\s+\d{1,2}\s+\d{2}:\d{2}:\d{2})\s+"

# The quantifier ? means 0 or 1 occurrence. This should match our
ProcessID just fine
$logpattern +=
"(?<ComputerName>\w+)\s+(?<Source>\w+)(\[(?<ProcessId>)\d+\])?:.*"

# So, what to do about the useless date format? For example: Mar 6
20:30:01
# We can easily convert that as well with a DateTime static method
ParseExact
[datetime]::ParseExact('Mar 6 20:30:01', 'MMM d HH:mm:ss',
[cultureinfo]::InvariantCulture)
```

7. Wrapping this code in a small function and adding some logic makes your code reusable and flexible, as shown in the following example:

```
function Import-SystemLog
{
    . . .
    Get-Content -Path $PAth | ForEach-Object {
        if ($_ -match $logpattern)
        {
            $logEntry = [LogEntry]::new()
            $logEntry.TimeWritten =
[datetime]::ParseExact(($Matches.TimeWritten -replace '\s+',' '),
'MMM d HH:mm:ss', [cultureinfo]::InvariantCulture)
            $logEntry.Message = $Matches.Message
            $logEntry.Source= $Matches.Source
            $logEntry.ComputerName = $Matches.ComputerName
            $logEntry
        }
    }
}

Import-SystemLog -Path /var/log/messages
Import-SystemLog -Path /var/log/cron
```

8. Fortunately, to write syslog messages, the module `Posh-SYSLOG` is already there. While this module contains just one cmdlet, it is very useful to convey messages from within PowerShell scripts, as demonstrated in the following example:

```
Install-Module Posh-SYSLOG

# While this cmdlet is meant to be used with a SYSLOG sink, using
# it with the Verbose switch shows you which message is being sent
Send-SyslogMessage -Server localhost -Message hello -Severity
Emergency -Hostname localhost -Facility local0 -Verbose
```

How it works...

Messages from the kernel, spool, mail, and other facilities are processed by various logging daemons. For example, emergency messages, regardless of the facility, will, by default, be displayed on screen, as soon as the console is refreshed. The mail facility will, by default, be stored in `/var/log/maillog`.

With PowerShell, logs regardless of the format can be parsed using regular expressions. With PowerShell classes, log messages can be cast into a more useful format that can, again, be processed at your leisure.

Windows Server Administration 7

This chapter will show you some Windows administrative tasks that naturally occur. While the **Internet Information Services** (**IIS**) or **Desired State Configuration** (**DSC**) cannot be fully used with PowerShell Core at the time of writing, it is nevertheless important to know how to access these features from within PowerShell Core.

Expect to see a lot of the `WindowsCompatibility` module in this chapter, as this is your anchor to the legacy world running Windows PowerShell.

In this chapter, we will cover the following recipes:

- File services management
- Domain services management
- IIS management – deploying and configuring
- IIS management – creating a website
- Configuring Storage Spaces Direct (S2D)
- Using Docker with Hyper-V containers
- Remote Desktop Services (RDS) deployment
- Integrating DSC configuration into a Windows Server image

Technical requirements

To follow all of the recipes in this chapter, you will need to have access to some Windows virtual machines that can be generated with the PowerShell module, AutomatedLab, if you do not have the time to build everything from scratch. See the technical requirements in `Chapter 1`, *Introduction to PowerShell Core*, for details.

File services management

The humble file server is a staple of many companies. While you can (and should) start using services such as Azure File Sync, there are always instances where an on-premises file server may be necessary.

This recipe demonstrates how you can use the **Distributed File System (DFS)** to replicate folder contents between multiple file servers. We will use a hub and spoke topology with read-only connections.

Getting ready

The cmdlets that are used here are not compatible with PowerShell Core. You may want to use the `WindowsCompatibility` module or remoting.

How to do it...

Perform the following steps:

1. Execute the following lines to view the file and storage services status:

```
Import-WinModule ServerManager
Get-WindowsFeature -Name FileAndStorage-Services
```

2. Simulate the feature installation by executing the following code:

```
Install-WindowsFeature -Name FileAndStorage-Services -WhatIf
```

3. Add another parameter and run the following code:

```
Install-WindowsFeature -Name FileAndStorage-Services -
IncludeManagementTools -WhatIf
```

4. Now, install two required features, including management tools:

```
Install-WindowsFeature -Name FileAndStorage-Services,FS-DFS-
Replication -IncludeManagementTools
```

5. You can start the **Distributed File System Replication (DFSR)** setup by preparing some variables first:

```
$hubComputer = 'DFS-FS-A'
$spokeComputer = 'DFS-FS-B','DFS-FS-C'
$allComputers = $hubComputer + $spokeComputer
$replicationGroupName = 'MyReplicationGroup'
$folderName = 'MyFolderTarget'
$contentPath = 'C:\DfsReplicatedFolder'

if (Get-DfsReplicationGroup -GroupName $replicationGroupName -
ErrorAction SilentlyContinue) { return }
```

6. Then, create some files and enable this feature throughout all participating clients:

```
$root = New-Item -ItemType Directory -Path $contentPath
$null = 1..1000 | % {New-Item -Path $root.FullName -Name "File$_"}

Invoke-Command -ComputerName $spokeComputer -ScriptBlock {
    Install-WindowsFeature -Name FS-DFS-Replication -
IncludeManagementTools
}

# Finally - we can start
$replicationGroup = New-DfsReplicationGroup -GroupName
$replicationGroupName -Description 'A simple hub and spoke group' -
DomainName contoso.com
```

7. Add a new replicated folder:

```
$replicatedFolder = $replicationGroup | New-DfsReplicatedFolder -
FolderName $folderName -Description 'Some folder' -DomainName
contoso.com
```

8. Add the members:

```
$replicationGroup | Add-DfsrMember -ComputerName $allComputers
```

9. Add some connections as well:

```
foreach ($spokeComputerName in $spokeComputer)
{
    $connection = Add-DfsrConnection -GroupName
$replicationGroupName -SourceComputerName $HubComputer -
DestinationComputerName $spokeComputerName -CreateOneWay
}
```

10. Set the replication group memberships:

```
$memberships = Set-DfsrMembership -GroupName $replicationGroupName
-FolderName $folderName -ComputerName ($hubComputer +
$spokeComputer) -ContentPath $ContentPath -Force

# Declare this server as primary
$primaryMember = Set-DfsrMembership -GroupName
$replicationGroupName -FolderName $folderName -ComputerName
$hubComputer -PrimaryMember $true -Force
```

11. Initiate the replication by executing the following lines of code:

```
Update-DfsrConfigurationFromAD -ComputerName $allComputers

# This should not take long. Have a look at the folder contents:
foreach ($spoke in $spokeComputer)
{
    Get-ChildItem "\\$spoke\c$\$(Split-Path $contentPath -Leaf )"
}
```

How it works...

DFSR is a technology that's used to replicate data reliably over a possibly bad connection. A replication group describes a group of servers that are participating in the replication of data. DFSR is able to work with a schedule per replication group.

In a replication group, you can replicate one or more folders. This can be done in a full mesh, where changes are replicated back and forth. Alternatively, this can be done in a hub and spoke topology where changes are replicated down through a hierarchy.

The DFSR PowerShell module is Windows PowerShell only, but can be used with implicit remoting.

You started by using the Get-WindowsFeature cmdlet to see whether DFSR was already enabled. In *Steps 2* to *4*, you gradually enabled the file and storage services, including all management tools.

Step 5 began the DFSR deployment by having you check whether a replication group already exists. Using remoting, you enabled the DFSR feature on multiple machines so that you could get started with the replication group. You then added a replicated folder, replication group members, and the member connections to be able to replicate data.

In *Step 10*, you declared one server as the primary member, which is the source for the initial replication only. *Step 11* showed you how to update the DFS configuration from Active Directory.

Domain services management

Countless day-to-day tasks revolve around a directory service in some shape or form. In a Microsoft environment, this will usually be the Active Directory Domain Services.

In this recipe, you will deploy a new Active Directory forest and its first domain controller. After that, you will establish trust to your existing forest.

Getting ready

Connect to the domain controller, PACKT-DC2.

How to do it...

Perform the following steps:

1. First of all, the domain services need to be installed. Note that, when using PowerShell Core, you either need to run Windows PowerShell or use the WindowsCompatibility module:

   ```
   powershell -Command "& {Install-WindowsFeature -Name AD-Domain-
   Services,DNS,RSAT-AD-PowerShell}"
   ```

2. You can discover the necessary cmdlets from within the new module, ADDSDeployment:

   ```
   Get-Command -Module ADDSDeployment
   ```

3. Start a deployment—the configuration settings are very straightforward. Try using your own data to understand what is happening better:

   ```
   $parameters = @{
       DomainName = 'partsunlimited.com'
       SafeModeAdministratorPassword = Read-Host -AsSecureString -
   Prompt 'Safemode admin password'
       InstallDNS = $true
       DomainMode = 'WinThreshold'
   ```

```
        Force = $true
        ForestMode = 'WinThreshold'
        DomainNetbiosName = 'partsunlimited'
        Verbose = $true
}

Install-ADDSForest @parameters
```

4. Execute the following command:

```
Get-Command -Noun ADTrust
```

5. Since there is no existing cmdlet, we need to use .NET. Discover the necessary type, DirectoryContext, first:

```
[System.DirectoryServices.ActiveDirectory.DirectoryContext]::new
[enum]::GetValues([System.DirectoryServices.ActiveDirectory.Directo
ryContextType])
```

6. First of all, we create a context to retrieve the remote forest:

```
$targetForestCtx=
[System.DirectoryServices.ActiveDirectory.DirectoryContext]::new('F
orest','contoso.com','contoso\Install','Somepass1')
```

7. Next, we retrieve the remote forest object that we will use later:

```
$targetForest =
[System.DirectoryServices.ActiveDirectory.Forest]::GetForest($targe
tForestCtx)
```

8. The second ingredient will be our current forest:

```
$currentForest =
[System.DirectoryServices.ActiveDirectory.Forest]::GetCurrentForest
()
```

9. Building the actual trust now is very easy:

```
$Forest.CreateTrustRelationship($TargetForest,"Bidirectional")
```

10. You can verify whether it worked on both domains by running the following commands:

```
# Verify
Get-ADTrust -Filter *

# Verify again
```

```
Get-ADTrust -Filter * -Server contoso.com -Credential
contoso\install
```

How it works...

With this recipe, you deployed a new forest with a new domain. The same cmdlets can be used to deploy a new domain controller to an existing domain environment. The `InstallDNS` parameter configures the domain controller as a DNS server, providing name resolution for your environment.

Make note of *Step 1*, which showed you a different way of using Windows PowerShell modules that does not require the `WindowsCompatibility` module.

Using the domain and forest functional level parameters, you can configure the functionality that is available in your deployment. Please make sure to read the documentation first. With the newer domain and forest functional levels, legacy systems that are long out of support, such as Server 2003, will be forced out.

See also

- You can learn more about Active Directory deployment at `https://docs.microsoft.com/en-us/windows-server/identity/ad-ds/deploy/ad-ds-deployment`.

IIS management – deploying and configuring

Web servers are essentially everywhere. Many applications offer RESTful APIs or web interfaces instead of separate GUI applications. On Windows, the web server of choice is the IIS. Much like Apache, Tomcat, and other web servers, IIS can be configured in detail.

This recipe shows you how to deploy a simple web server and enroll for an SSL certificate.

Getting ready

Install and start PowerShell Core.

How to do it...

Perform the following steps:

1. Start by examining the necessary features to install:

```
Import-WinModule ServerManager
Get-WindowsFeature -Name Web*
```

2. This installation requires that we mount the installation sources. Do so now:

```
$isoLocation = throw "Fill this in before continuing!"
Add-VMDvdDrive -VMName PACKT-WB1 -Path $isoLocation
```

3. The installation of IIS is straightforward and will also enable the PowerShell module, WebAdministration:

```
Install-WindowsFeature -Name Web-Server -IncludeAllSubFeature -
IncludeManagementTools -Source D:\sources\sxs -Verbose

# If the installation was successful, you should be able to find
the WebAdministration module
Get-Module -ListAvailable -Name WebAdministration
Get-Command -Module WebAdministration
```

4. Every web server should be configured to use SSL! Request a certificate from your lab's certificate authority:

```
$certParam = @{
        Url = 'ldap:'
        SubjectName = "CN=$env:COMPUTERNAME"
        Template = 'ContosoWebServer'
        DnsName = $env:COMPUTERNAME,
([System.Net.Dns]::GetHostByName($env:COMPUTERNAME))
        CertStoreLocation = 'Cert:\LocalMachine\my'
    }
$null = Get-Certificate @certParam
```

5. You can verify this with Windows PowerShell:

```
powershell.exe -Command "& {Get-ChildItem -Path
Cert:\LocalMachine\My -SSLServerAuthentication}"
```

6. Usually, web servers handle CGI scripts. To make IIS to do the same, we need to do some configuration. But first, we need to download PHP:

```
Invoke-WebRequest -Uri
https://windows.php.net/downloads/releases/php-7.3.3-nts-Win32-VC15
-x64.zip -OutFile php.zip
Expand-Archive -Path .\php.zip -DestinationPath C:\php

# We can already make some adjustments to the configuration
# ConvertFrom-StringData works with key=value entries -
unfortunately it does not work yet
Get-Content c:\php\php.ini-production | ConvertFrom-StringData #
Fails

# Filtering the content a little bit looks better already
Get-Content c:\php\php.ini-production |
    Where {-not [string]::IsNullOrWhiteSpace($_) -and -not
$_.StartsWith(';') -and -not $_.StartsWith('[')} |
    ConvertFrom-StringData
```

7. We can set some PHP configuration items in the php.ini file:

```
(Get-Content c:\php\php.ini-production) `
    -replace 'upload_max_filesize.*', 'upload_max_filesize = 1G' `
    -replace 'max_execution_time.*', 'max_execution_time = 300' |
Set-Content C:\php\php.ini
```

8. The IIS side of things consists of registering a new handler and adding a new FastCgi application:

```
New-WebHandler -Name PHPCGI -Path *.php -Verb * -Modules
FastCgiModule -ScriptProcessor C:\php\php-cgi.exe -ResourceType
File
Add-WebConfiguration -Filter 'system.webserver/fastcgi' -Value
@{'fullPath' = 'C:\php\php-cgi.exe' }
```

9. With the correct handler permissions in place, we can add our index.php as a new default document:

```
Get-WebHandler -Location 'IIS:\Sites\Default Web Site' -Name PHPCGI
| Set-WebHandler -RequiredAccess Execute

# Add e.g. index.php to the default site
Add-WebConfigurationProperty //defaultDocument/files
"IIS:\sites\Default Web Site" -AtIndex 0 -Name collection -Value
index.php
```

10. After restarting IIS, we can try it out with a very simple example site:

```
# Restart IIS and give it a go
iisreset

# Try it!
@'
<html>
 <head>
  <title>PHP Test</title>
 </head>
 <body>
 <?php echo '<p>Hello World</p>'; ?>
 <?php phpinfo(); ?>
 </body>
</html>
'@ | Set-Content C:\inetpub\wwwroot\index.php

start http://localhost/index.php
```

How it works...

IIS is enabled by enabling Windows features, just like any other feature. Selecting the correct modules, however, requires a bit more knowledge. This recipe had you install the full IIS feature, along with all of its sub-features. Be aware that, in production, you should choose the amount of features you use a bit more carefully. Only install what you need to provide, for example, less attack surface.

To use SSL, you had to request a certificate with the help of the PKI module. A web server certificate allows your server to prove its identity and encrypt the communication channel between your server and its clients. This is very important, and there is really no good reason not to encrypt your traffic.

This recipe had you use the certificate template, ContosoWebServer, which is based on an integrated template in your lab PKI called WebServer. Duplicating existing templates before modifying them is a best practice. Since auto-enrollment is configured and all domain computes are allowed to enroll in a web server certificate, the Get-Certificate cmdlet does not require any more input or different permissions.

Configuring the web server itself is done easily through PowerShell. Configuring PHP, however, requires some Linux-style configuration file editing. With PowerShell, setting these configurations is easy as well. As an example, this recipe had you increase the maximum script execution time and increase the maximum upload file size.

IIS management – creating a website

Aa typical task for web server administrators is creating a new website and adding content to it. This recipe will show you how to create HTML code in PowerShell and how to register your SSL certificate on your website.

Getting ready

Install and start PowerShell Core.

How to do it...

Perform the following steps:

1. First of all, we will clean up the default website we don't need:

```
Import-WinModule WebAdministration
Get-WebSite | Remove-WebSite
```

2. To create a new website, we can generate some HTML content with the ConvertTo-Html cmdlet:

```
Get-Service | Select Name, Status | ConvertTo-Html | ForEach-Object
{
    if ($_ -match 'Running')
    {
        $_ -replace '<tr>', '<tr color="Green">'
    }
    elseif ($_ -match 'Stopped')
    {
        $_ -replace '<tr>', '<tr color="Red">'
    }
    else
    {
        $_
    }
} | Set-Content -Path (Join-Path -Path $webDirectory.FullName -
ChildPath 'index.html')
```

3. The `ConvertTo-Html` cmdlet is also able to generate fragments instead of entire pages. This way, you can create your site dynamically:

```
$svcFragment = Get-Service ...
$prcFragment = Get-Process | Where WS -gt 150MB | Select
ProcessName,@{Name='WS in MB';Expression={[math]::Round(($_.WS /
1MB),2)}} | ConvertTo-Html -Fragment
@"
<html>
<head><title>PowerShell is AWESOME</title></head>
<body>
<p>Service status on $($env:COMPUTERNAME)</p>
$($svcFragment)
<p>Running processes gt 150MB RAM<p>
$($prcFragment)
</html>
"@ | Set-Content -Path (Join-Path -Path $webDirectory.FullName -
ChildPath 'overview.html')
```

4. IIS needs to get the information about your new website as well, so create a new site now:

```
New-Website -Name 'HostOverview' -Port 443 -PhysicalPath
$webDirectory.FullName -Ssl
```

5. The previous command created a website and registered an SSL binding. However, we need to set the certificate as well:

```
$binding = Get-WebSite -Name HostOverview | Get-WebBinding
$certificate = Get-ChildItem Cert:\LocalMachine\my | Where-Object
{$_.Subject -eq "CN=$env:COMPUTERNAME" -and $_.Issuer -like
'*LabRootCA1*'}
$binding.AddSslCertificate($certificate.Thumbprint, 'My')
```

6. Browse to your encrypted website now:

```
start https://packt-wb1/overview.html
```

How it works...

Creating a new website in IIS does not require manually editing configuration files. Through the `WebAdministration` module, you can script the entire website's deployment. If your website is getting too complicated, you can look into the `WebConfigurationProperty` cmdlet, which allows you to set anything in your `web.config` XML file.

With PowerShell's `ConvertTo-Html` cmdlet, you can generate simple static websites in a dynamic fashion. This recipe had you query the services and processes and convert them into simple HTML tables. With a simple parameter, you can now add your own CSS style sheets as well.

Configuring Storage Spaces Direct (S2D)

Storage Spaces Direct (S2D) is a new feature of Windows Server 2016 that extends Storage Spaces from previous server versions. S2D is excellent for software-defined storage solutions and is well-suited for your hyper-converged infrastructure.

This recipe will show you how to create a S2D cluster that serves as a **Scale-Out File Server (SOFS)**.

Getting ready

Install and start PowerShell Core.

How to do it...

Perform the following steps:

1. To get started, we need to enable a few features on all participating file servers through WinRM:

```
$fileServers = 'PACKT-FS-A','PACKT-FS-B','PACKT-FS-C'

# The list of features to deploy S2D is a bit longer
$features = @(
    'Failover-Clustering',
    'Data-Center-Bridging',
    'RSAT-Clustering-PowerShell',
    'Hyper-V-PowerShell',
    'FS-FileServer'
)

Invoke-Command -ComputerName $fileServers -ScriptBlock {
    Install-WindowsFeature -Name $using:features
}
```

2. The storage module is quintessential to your S2D efforts. As a **Cmdlet Definition XML (CDXML)** module, it is compatible with PowerShell Core and can be easily used. Here, we are making use of **Common Information Model (CIM)** sessions to work remotely:

```
$cimsessions = New-CimSession -ComputerName $fileServers
```

3. As a preparation task, refresh the storage provider cache to list any newly added disks:

```
Update-StorageProviderCache -CimSession $cimsessions
```

4. All disks that are not yet part of a pool and that aren't system disks can be used with our cluster:

```
Get-Disk -CimSession $cimsessions | Where-Object {
    -not $_.IsBoot -and -not $_.IsSystem -and $_.PartitionStyle -eq
'RAW'
}
```

5. Before creating a cluster, you can first run a cluster validation test:

```
Import-WinModule FailoverClusters
$clusterTest = Test-Cluster -Node $fileServers -Include 'Storage
Spaces Direct', Inventory, Network, 'System Configuration'
start $clusterTest.FullName
```

6. With the test done, you can deploy your cluster:

```
$cluster = New-Cluster -Name S2DCluster -Node $fileServers -
NoStorage -StaticAddress 192.168.56.99
```

7. While the cluster has been automatically configured, you can and should configure things such as the cluster quorum yourself:

```
# Next, we add a cluster witness to help build a quorum. If you
want to, try the Azure Cloud Witness
$null = New-AzResourceGroup -Name witnesses -Location 'West Europe'
$account = New-AzStorageAccount -ResourceGroupName witnesses -Name
packtwitnesses -Location 'West Europe' -SkuName Standard_LRS
$keys = $account | Get-AzStorageAccountKey
$cluster | Set-ClusterQuorum -CloudWitness -AccountName
$account.StorageAccountName -AccessKey $keys[0].Value

# If your environment is not connected, a node majority will be
enough
$cluster | Set-ClusterQuorum -NodeMajority
```

8. To enable S2D, you only need the `Enable-ClusterStorageSpacesDirect` cmdlet:

```
Enable-ClusterStorageSpacesDirect -Confirm:$false
```

9. Create some **Cluster Shared Volumes** (**CSV**) in the storage pool that the previous cmdlet just created:

```
New-Volume -FriendlyName FirstVolume -FileSystem CSVFS_ReFS -
StoragePoolFriendlyName S2D* -Size 10GB
```

10. From here on out, you can go in different directions. One could be enabling SOFS:

```
Add-ClusterScaleOutFileServerRole -Name FiletMignon -Cluster
S2DCluster
```

How it works...

This recipe showed you how to use CDXML cmdlets, which you can find in many modules such as storage and NetTCPIP. We can use CIM sessions for remote configuration management, which makes tasks like the one that was performed in this recipe a lot easier.

The using scope you used in *Step 1* helps with remote scripts. Prepending this scope to your local variables allows you to read them from within remote sessions and background jobs.

In this recipe, you looked at two different types of cluster witnesses to build the quorum. Server 2016 added the Azure Cloud Witness, which is an Azure Storage Blob instead of, for example, a file share witness.

Using Docker with Hyper-V containers

Containerized applications are commonly used nowadays. Since Server 2016, containers can be used on Windows Server as well, due to its new containers feature. With container engines such as Docker and clustered container services such as Docker Swarm or Kubernetes, you can provide your developers with a great infrastructure that they can deploy their containerized application on.

This recipe, however, will show you how to get started with Docker so that you can create your own containers. While this example will host a simple web service, you could also use containers to host the DSC Pull Server, among others.

Getting ready

Install and start PowerShell Core on a Hyper-V enabled host.

How to do it...

Perform the following steps:

1. To be able to use containers, we need to enable the actual feature:

```
powershell -command "& {Install-WindowsFeature Containers}"
```

2. Deploying Docker has gotten a lot easier since PackageManagement and PowerShellGet have been around:

```
Install-Module -Name Docker -Force
# With the module installed, we can use it to install docker
Install-Docker
```

3. To make use of Docker, you need to download a container image at some point. These can come from a private or public container registry, for example, Docker Hub:

```
docker pull mcr.microsoft.com/powershell:6.2.0-nanoserver-1809
```

4. Docker pulls the container image data to ProgramData on Windows. This directory can be configured, though:

```
Get-ChildItem -Path (Join-Path -Path $env:ProgramData -ChildPath Docker) -File -Recurse
```

5. To list your existing images, you can use the Docker CLI with Docker images:

```
docker images
```

6. Start your first container with docker run. This command will place you in an interactive prompt:

```
docker run -it mcr.microsoft.com/powershell:6.2.0-nanoserver-1809

# After a few seconds, you are running PowerShell Core on a Nano
Server image
$PSVersionTable # 6.2.0, Core
# Exit the container
exit
```

7. By using `docker ps`, you can list your running and stopped containers:

```
# To list running containers you use
docker ps

# An in our special case to see stopped containers
docker ps -a
```

8. A container is a container image with customization merged into it. You can do this with a `DockerFile`:

```
Save-Module -Name Polaris -Path .\polaris
@"
# The image our container is based on
FROM mcr.microsoft.com/powershell:6.2.0-nanoserver-1809

# Our image requires a port to be opened
EXPOSE 8080

# Copy the Polaris module
COPY ["Polaris/", "C:/Program Files/PowerShell/Modules/Polaris/"]

# Copy the script
COPY startpolaris.ps1 startpolaris.ps1

# We want to run something
CMD ["pwsh.exe", "-File", "./startpolaris.ps1"]
"@ | Set-Content .\polaris\Dockerfile
```

9. In this container, we want to run Polaris each time the container starts. This script defines a new Get route for our little RESTful API:

```
@'
New-PolarisGetRoute -Path /containerizedapi -Scriptblock
{$response.Send("Your lucky number is $(Get-Random -min 0 -max
9999)");}
Start-Polaris -Port 8080
while ($true)
{ sleep 1 }
'@ | Set-Content .\polaris\startpolaris.ps1
```

10. To merge your customizations onto the container image, you can use `docker build`:

```
docker build .\polaris -t myrepo:mypolaris
```

11. We don't need interactivity now—you can run your container in the background with the -d (daemon) switch:

```
$containerId = docker run -d -p 8080:8080 myrepo:mypolaris
```

12. Your code is now working, and you can immediately browse your API:

```
$result = docker inspect $containerId
$ip = ($result | ConvertFrom-
Json).networksettings.networks.nat.ipaddress
Invoke-RestMethod -Uri "http://$($ip):8080" -Method Get
```

13. Have a look at the processes running in your container:

```
docker top $containerId
```

14. Finally, kill your container once you are done:

```
docker kill $containerId
```

How it works...

When you are running containers, you are using shared infrastructure components such as the OS kernel and private infrastructure components such as the container's contents. We refer to the nucleus of your container, that is, the required container operating system, as the container image. An image, combined with a layer that is referred to as a sandbox layer, makes a container.

As an enterprise, you would create your own container images based on official images, build them with your own customizations, and host them in a container repository. This could be made publicly available on Docker Hub, whereas a private one could be made available on the Azure Container Registry.

This recipe had you create your own little container so that you can host a fast-starting RESTful API endpoint using PowerShell Core.

Remote Desktop Services (RDS) deployment

RDS is a popular choice for many enterprises. Whether **virtual desktops** should be provided or virtual applications should be hosted, RDS is a good choice.

Fortunately, they are also configurable with PowerShell with the usual constraints. This recipe will have you create your own Remote Desktop deployment, including the new Remote Desktop web client.

Getting ready

Install and start PowerShell Core.

How to do it...

Perform the following steps:

1. First of all, import the necessary Windows modules and have a look at the available cmdlets:

```
Import-WinModule RemoteDesktop, PKI

# Without enabling any role or feature yet, we have the module
Get-Command -Module RemoteDesktop
```

2. You need to request a new SSL certificate if you haven't done it in *IIS management – deploying and configuring* recipe:

```
if (-not (Get-ChildItem Cert:\LocalMachine\my | Where-Object
{$_.Subject -eq "CN=$env:COMPUTERNAME" -and $_.Issuer -like
'*LabRootCA1*'}))
{
    $certParam = @{
        Url = 'ldap:'
        SubjectName = "CN=$env:COMPUTERNAME"
        Template = 'ContosoWebServer'
        DnsName = $env:COMPUTERNAME,
([System.Net.Dns]::GetHostByName($env:COMPUTERNAME)).HostName
        CertStoreLocation = 'Cert:\LocalMachine\my'
    }
    $null = Get-Certificate @certParam
}
```

3. With that out of the way, you can start by initiating a new session deployment:

```
Invoke-Command -ComputerName PACKT-DC1 -ScriptBlock {
 New-RDSessionDeployment -ConnectionBroker PACKT-WB1.contoso.com -
SessionHost PACKT-WB1.contoso.com -WebAccessServer PACKT-
WB1.contoso.com -Verbose
 }
```

4. Your deployment should look like this:

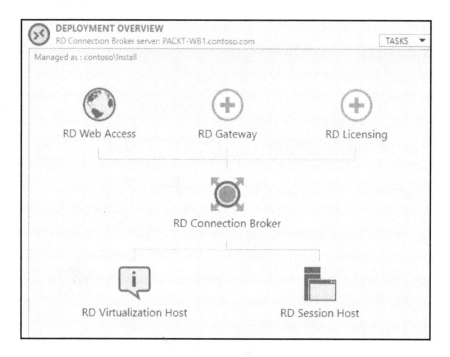

5. As soon as the session host has been restarted, you can continue by adding two additional servers to the deployment, the Gateway and the License Server:

```
# the gateway with the correct external FQDN for our certificate
Add-RDServer -Server PACKT-WB1.contoso.com -Role RDS-GATEWAY -
ConnectionBroker PACKT-WB1.contoso.com -GatewayExternalFqdn PACKT-
WB1.contoso.com -Verbose

# as well as the licensing server
Add-RDServer -Server PACKT-WB1.contoso.com -Role RDS-LICENSING -
ConnectionBroker PACKT-WB1.contoso.com -Verbose
```

6. Your Remote Desktop infrastructure should also be using SSL. To do this, we need to export the certificate first, since the management cmdlets at the time of writing did not support supplying either an X509 Certificate nor a thumbprint:

```
Export-PfxCertificate -Cert (Get-ChildItem Cert:\LocalMachine\my |
Where-Object {$_.Subject -eq "CN=$env:COMPUTERNAME" -and $_.Issuer
-like '*LabRootCA1*'} | Select-Object -First 1) -Force -ChainOption
BuildChain -FilePath C:\cert.pfx -ProtectTo contoso\install

Set-RDCertificate -ConnectionBroker PACKT-WB1.contoso.com -
ImportPath C:\cert.pfx -Role RDGateway -Force
Set-RDCertificate -ConnectionBroker PACKT-WB1.contoso.com -
ImportPath C:\cert.pfx -Role RDPublishing -Force
Set-RDCertificate -ConnectionBroker PACKT-WB1.contoso.com -
ImportPath C:\cert.pfx -Role RDWebAccess -Force
Set-RDCertificate -ConnectionBroker PACKT-WB1.contoso.com -
ImportPath C:\cert.pfx -Role RDRedirector -Force
```

7. Lastly, we can create the session collection that our users can connect to so that they can get their own virtual desktop environment:

```
New-RDSessionCollection -CollectionName PACKT -
CollectionDescription "Get more great books at packt.com!" -
SessionHost PACKT-WB1.contoso.com -COnnectionBroker PACKT-
WB1.contoso.com -PersonalUnmanaged
```

8. If you want to add the HTML 5 web client as well, you need to update PowerShellGet first so that the AcceptLicense parameter is available:

```
Install-Module -Name PowerShellGet -Force
exit # Restart PowerShell to reload the module
```

9. Next, the RDWebClientManagement module can be downloaded:

```
Install-Module -Name RDWebClientManagement -Force -AcceptLicense
```

10. First, you need to install the client itself:

```
Install-RDWebClientPackage
```

11. Then, you need to import the SSL certificate:

```
Import-RDWebClientBrokerCert C:\cert.pfx
```

12. Last but not least, you need to publish the client and browse to it:

```
Publish-RDWebClientPackage -Type Production -Latest

# Now the URL is accessible!
start https://PACKT-WB1.contoso.com/RDWeb/WebClient
```

How it works...

A remote desktop deployment is usually not a very complicated step, as you can see with the New-RDSessionDeployment cmdlet. You should, however, give a bit more thought to your session host deployment and service configuration. While this recipe had you deploy every component on one single server, you would usually deploy to multiple servers in an enterprise environment.

In this recipe, you can also see the different requirements that modules and setup guides might have. The Remote Desktop web client, for example, can be installed through the PowerShell Gallery, but only if you are able to accept the license. The necessary parameter to do that has been added in an updated version of the PowerShellGet module.

Integrating DSC configuration into a Windows Server image

DSC is a great feature of Windows PowerShell. By using PowerShell Core, we can prepare our DSC configurations and **Local Configuration Manager** (**LCM**) configurations so that they are applied during a VM deployment.

This recipe shows you how to customize disk images that have been created from a Windows image so that you can set the meta configuration, as well as apply an initial configuration, for a domain join.

Getting ready

Install and start PowerShell core on PACKT-HV1.

How to do it...

Perform the following steps:

1. To configure a VM with DSC, we need the actual configuration. For this recipe, we will start with the meta configuration for the LCM:

```
[DscLocalConfigurationManager()]
configuration LcmSettings
{
    Settings
    {
        RebootNodeIfNeeded = $true
        ConfigurationMode = 'ApplyAndAutoCorrect'
        StatusRetentionTimeInDays = 5
    }
}

$configurationPath = Join-Path -Path $env:TEMP -ChildPath
'PacktDscConfigs'
$metaConfig = LcmSettings -OutputPath $configurationPath
```

2. Additionally, we would like to configure a domain join with DSC. This is done in a normal configuration element:

```
configuration InitialSystemConfig
{
    Import-DscResource -ModuleName PSDesiredStateConfiguration
    Import-DscResource -ModuleName ComputerManagementDsc

    node $AllNodes.NodeName
    {
        Computer $Node.NodeName
        {
            DomainName = $Node.DomainName
            Name = $Node.NodeName
            Credential = $Node.DomainJoinCredential
            Description = 'Automation is THE BEST ♥'
        }
    }
}
```

Please note that this step requires the ComputerManagementDsc module, which is part of the lab deployment.

3. With `ConfigurationData`, we can ensure that the **Managed Object Format** (**MOF**) file contains the necessary credentials for the domain join. In a production environment, these credentials should be encrypted with a certificate:

```
$configData = @{
    AllNodes = @(
        @{
            NodeName = '*'
            PSDSCAllowPlaintextPassword = $true
            PSDSCAllowDomainUser = $true
        }
        ...
    )
}

# Compile the config
$dscConfig = InitialSystemConfig -ConfigurationData $configData -
OutputPath $configurationPath
```

4. Next, we need to mount the disk image file:

```
Import-Module Storage -SkipEditionCheck
$disk = Mount-DiskImage -ImagePath
'D:\BASE_WindowsServer2016Datacenter_10.0.14393.0.vhdx' -Access
ReadWrite -StorageType VHDX -PassThru | Get-DiskImage
```

5. With both configurations compiled, it is a simple matter of `Copy-Item`:

```
# Copy the meta config
Copy-Item $metaConfig.FullName -Destination
E:\Windows\System32\configuration\metaconfig.mof

# Copy the pending config
Copy-Item $dscConfig.FullName -Destination
E:\Windows\System32\configuration\pending.mof

# And the module
Copy-Item "C:\Program
Files\WindowsPowerShell\Modules\ComputerManagementDsc" -Destination
"E:\Program Files\WindowsPowerShell\Modules"
```

6. Once done, dismount the image again:

```
$disk | Dismount-DiskImage
```

7. Now, create a simple VM from it:

```
$null = New-VmSwitch -Name DomainEnv -SwitchType External
$vm = New-Vm -Name DscConfiguredThisVm -MemoryStartupBytes 2GB -
VHDPath 'D:\BASE_WindowsServer2016Datacenter_10.0.14393.0.vhdx' -
SwitchName DomainEnv -Generation 2
```

8. That's all—after starting the VM, it will automatically configure itself as necessary:

```
$vm | Start-Vm
```

How it works...

DSC uses configuration files with the MOF extension, in conjunction with the LCM, to enact a configuration. In this recipe, you created two configurations: one for the LCM itself, making settings such as the node's reboot behavior, and another that contains the actual configuration code in order to successfully join a machine to a domain.

With the meta configuration and the machine configuration in place, you then mounted the virtual hard disk containing the operating system and copied both MOF files to the appropriate locations. From the disk, you created your virtual machine, which configured itself correctly and joined the domain automatically.

Remoting and Just Enough Administration

This chapter will show you how to configure and use remoting with PowerShell Core to securely connect to Windows and Linux systems on a large scale. We will also look at **Just Enough Administration (JEA)**, a feature of Windows PowerShell that we can use with PowerShell Core, as well.

In this chapter, we will cover the following recipes:

- Enabling PowerShell remoting on Windows
- Enabling PowerShell remoting on Linux
- Configuring PowerShell remoting
- Securely connecting to remote endpoints
- Remotely retrieving data
- Remote script debugging
- Creating a JEA role
- Creating JEA session configuration
- Connecting to endpoints using different session configuration
- Using the Common Information Model (CIM)
- Using PowerShell Direct and PowerShell Core

Technical requirements

To follow the recipes in this chapter, you need a machine that's capable of running PowerShell Core and that is connected to the internet.

The code for this chapter can be found in the following GitHub repository: `https://github.com/PacktPublishing/Powershell-Core-6.2-Cookbook/tree/master/Chapter08`.

Enabling PowerShell remoting on Windows

Remote management is one of the very basic features that every administrator needs. While Windows PowerShell enables remote management by default on Windows Server 2012 and newer, we still need to enable it for PowerShell Core.

This very short and simple recipe shows you how to enable remote management.

Getting ready

Install and start PowerShell Core.

How to do it...

Let's perform the following steps:

1. Enable remote management using the `Enable-PSRemoting` cmdlet:

   ```
   Enable-PSRemoting -Force -Verbose
   ```

2. Should you be on a public network and really want to enable remoting, you would need to use the following command:

   ```
   Enable-PSRemoting -Force -Verbose -SkipNetworkProfileCheck
   Get-NetFirewallRule -Name WINRM-HTTP-In-TCP | Set-NetFirewallRule -
   Profile Public
   ```

3. Have a look at the output of the following cmdlet. It shows you so-called session configurations, which govern what you can and cannot do in a remote session:

   ```
   Get-PSSessionConfiguration
   ```

4. You could, for example, examine the **Access Control List** (**ACL**) behind a configuration:

   ```
   (Get-PSSessionConfiguration -Name PowerShell.6).Permission
   ```

5. Try the following line of code to change the default ACL, for example, to make it more restrictive or permissive:

   ```
   Get-PSSessionConfiguration -Name PowerShell.6 | Set-
   PSSessionConfiguration -ShowSecurityDescriptorUI
   ```

After executing the preceding command, you will be presented with the Permissions dialog window, as shown in the following screenshot:

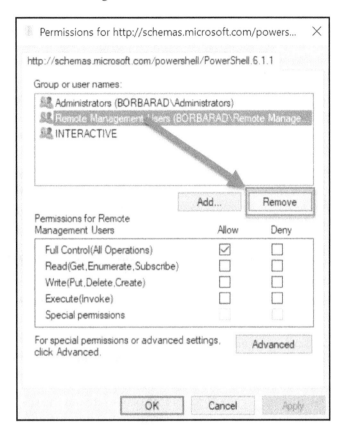

How it works...

The `Enable-PSRemoting` cmdlet serves multiple purposes in this recipe. First of all, it will enable and start the WinRM service, which is quite essential for Windows Remote Management. Then, it will configure listeners, specifically one listener behind TCP port `5985`. Lastly, incoming firewall rules for the WinRM port will be configured.

Setting the ACL on a session configuration is a first, very simple way of restricting remote access. The groups that are allowed to connect by default are administrators and remote management users.

Enabling PowerShell remoting on Linux

With the advent of PowerShell on Linux came the desire to remote into and from Linux systems as well. This recipe will show you how to enable PowerShell Remoting with the **Open Management Infrastructure PowerShell Remoting Protocol (OMI PSRP)** server, as well as using PowerShell Core as a subsystem for **Secure Shell (SSH)**.

Getting ready

Install and start PowerShell Core.

How to do it...

Let's perform the following steps:

1. The easiest choice by far that is still very secure is SSH remoting. To do this, configure PowerShell Core as a subsystem:

```
if (-not (Get-Content -Path /etc/ssh/sshd_config | Select-String -
Pattern"Subsystem.*/usr/bin/pwsh"))
{
    Add-Content -Path /etc/ssh/sshd_config -Value 'Subsystem
powershell /usr/bin/pwsh -sshs -NoLogo -NoProfile'
}
```

2. Another way to enable remoting on Linux is to install the OMI PSRP server, which is available from the same repository that you installed PowerShell Core from:

```
# OMI-PSRP-Server
yum install omi-psrp-server
```

3. Different to Windows, OMI PSRP uses HTTPS on TCP port 5986 by default. Carefully review the other settings that you can modify in omiserver.conf:

```
Get-Content -Path /etc/opt/omi/conf/omiserver.conf
```

4. Regardless, you will need to enable an incoming firewall rule for either SSH or PSRemoting. On CentOS, you can use `firewall-cmd` to accomplish this:

```
firewall-cmd --zone=public --permanent --add-port=5985/tcp
```

5. Lastly, take care of SELinux and add the incoming port:

```
semanage port -a -t ssh_port_t -p tcp 5985
```

How it works...

PowerShell remoting on Linux is quite flexible. With PowerShell Core, you not only can connect the secure shell protocol via WinRM, but also via SSH. For Linux administrators who already have their public keys distributed to remote targets, this is the easiest way to enable remoting.

This recipe started with configuring SSH remoting by adding the PowerShell subsystem to the SSH daemon configuration file. A subsystem is simply a binary that gives the user a remote shell. In our case, the shell is PowerShell.

As an alternative, you configured the OMI server in *Steps 2* and *3*, which required that you install a package from a distributions package management system (DEB, RPM, and so on) and then configured it with the necessary configuration file.

In *Steps 4* and *5*, you added a firewall rule with `firewall-cmd` and added the incoming port to the SELinux configuration of your system. Adapt this if you configured SSH instead of OMI, as the ports are different. Of course, *Steps 4* and *5* are only applicable if your distribution uses `firewall-cmd` and SELinux. Please refer to the man pages of iptables if your distribution only uses iptables.

If you don't have a public/private key pair to securely connect to your Linux machines already, you might as well have a look into OMI PSRP, which is installed by default on the `PACKT-CN1` lab node.

Configuring PowerShell remoting

Even though remoting is enabled out of the box on all Windows server systems since 2012, you may still want to configure some settings.

This recipe shows you both the WSMan provider as well as the Group Policy settings that concern remoting.

Getting ready

Install and start PowerShell Core.

How to do it...

Let's perform the following steps:

1. All of the settings that you need are neatly located in one location: the WSMan drive, which is exposed by the WSMan provider:

   ```
   Get-ChildItem -Path WSMan:\localhost
   ```

2. The client-specific settings govern the capabilities of your client, for example, the normally untrusted and unauthenticated hosts your client is allowed to connect to:

   ```
   Get-ChildItem -Path WSMan:\localhost\Client
   ```

3. By default, unencrypted traffic is prohibited, and the list of unauthenticated remote systems (for example systems, that aren't part of a domain) is empty:

   ```
   Get-Item -Path
   WSMan:\localhost\Client\AllowUnencrypted,WSMan:\localhost\Client\Tr
   ustedHosts
   ```

4. Notice the authentication options in this step. Basic authentication is disabled for security reasons since your credentials would be transferred in plain text:

   ```
   Get-ChildItem -Path WSMan:\localhost\Client\Auth
   ```

5. Now, use the `Set-Item` cmdlet to set some limits for your users:

```
# The IdleTimeout specifies the default timeout for a remote
session and is 2 hours
$newTimeout = New-TimeSpan -Hours 8
Set-Item WSMan:\localhost\Shell\IdleTimeout -Value
$newTimeout.TotalMilliseconds

# MaxConcurrentUsers specifies how many users may connect at the
same time
# and MaxShellsPerUser the number of shells they may start.
Set-Item WSMan:\localhost\Shell\MaxConcurrentUsers -Value 10
Set-Item WSMan:\localhost\Shell\MaxShellsPerUser -Value 2
Set-Item WSMan:\localhost\Shell\MaxMemoryPerShellMB -Value 50
```

6. On a Windows system in an Enterprise environment, a Group Policy is usually best suited for settings on a large scale. Open `gpedit.msc` and then navigate to **Computer Configuration** | **Administrative Templates** | **Windows Components** | **Windows Remote Shell** to modify the shell settings from the previous step:

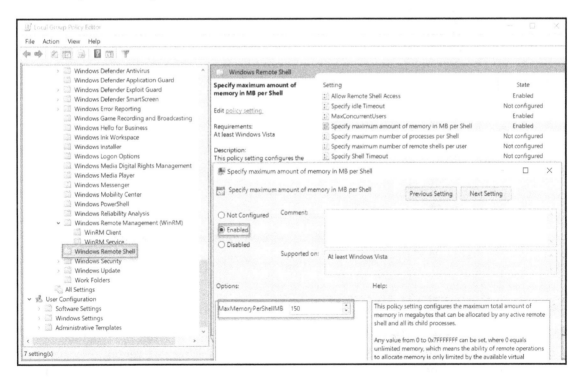

7. In addition to the connection-specific settings, you may also want to configure the WinRM listeners, as opposed to the first recipe, where you configured them manually. To do this, open `gpedit.msc` and navigate to **Computer Configuration** |**Administrative Templates** | **Windows Components** | **Windows Remote Management (WinRM)** | **WinRM Service**. Use the following screenshot as a reference:

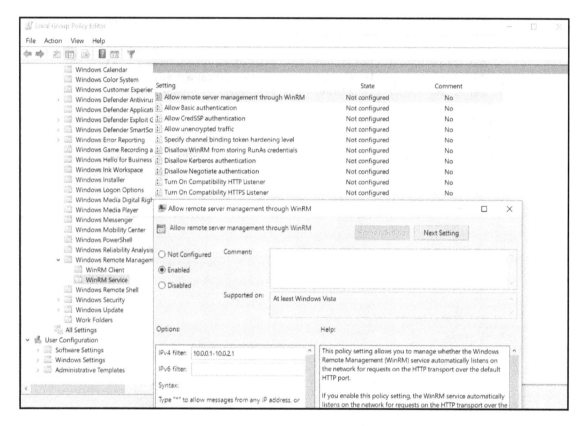

The compatibility listeners for older WinRM versions (for example, PowerShell 2.0) do not need to be enabled.

How it works...

The configuration in its entirety is documented in an old standard from 2008 that has been adapted for Windows in MS-WSMAN and MS-WSMV. By setting different options for client, shell, service, and listeners, you can customize your remoting experience for your enterprise.

This recipe showed you some important settings, such as the idle timeout that you likely want to configure for your own business needs. Be aware though that modifying these settings is usually not required and can lead to issues if you don't know what you are doing.

See also

- WSMan technical documentation (Windows): `https://docs.microsoft.com/en-us/openspecs/windows_protocols/ms-wsman/70912fec-c815-44ef-97c7-fc7f2ec7cda5`
- WSMan technical documentation (DMTF): `https://www.dmtf.org/sites/default/files/standards/documents/DSP0226_1.0.0.pdf`
- WSMan configuration: `https://docs.microsoft.com/de-de/windows/desktop/WinRM/installation-and-configuration-for-windows-remote-management`

Securely connecting to remote endpoints

Securely connecting to remote nodes is the bread and butter of PowerShell scripting. Whether you do this for remote data retrieval or for bulk changes on many resources, a secure connection is paramount.

This recipe shows you how to use different authentication methods with PowerShell core, such as the new SSH authentication, as well as stored credentials.

Getting ready

Install and start PowerShell Core. This recipe requires the lab environment.

How to do it...

Let's perform the following steps:

1. When administrators perform remoting for the first time, many run into trouble and immediately resort to old (and insecure) tools such as PSExec or remote WMI:

```
Enter-PSSession -ComputerName PACKT-DC1
```

2. Just by specifying credentials, PowerShell will try to negotiate the authentication mechanism so that either Kerberos or NTLM is used:

```
Enter-PSSession –ComputerName PACKT-DC1 –Credential contoso\Install
```

3. Notice how your prompt has changed—you are now working on the remote machine. Be sure to exit the session once you're done:

```
Exit-PSSession
```

4. You can easily test whether a remote can be connected to as well:

```
Test-WSMan –ComputerName PACKT-DC1 –Credential contoso\Install –
Authentication Negotiate
```

5. Of course, you can also used stored credentials in your scripts:

```
$credential = Get-Credential
Connect-WSMan –ComputerName PACKT-DC1 –Credential $credential –
Authentication Negotiate
```

6. When connecting to a Linux system, things might be slightly different. Try connecting via SSH in this step:

```
Enter-PSSession –HostName PACKT-CN1 –UserName root
```

7. When using SSH for a connection, you can beef up security by using a key pair:

```
Enter-PSSession –HostName PACKT-CN1 –UserName root –KeyFilePath
$home/.ssh/myPubKey
```

How it works...

With remoting enabled, the WinRM service (or the OMI PSRP server) will listen on port 5985 (or 5986) for incoming WSMan requests and serve them. Depending on other factors, such as the session configuration or RBAC role assignments from JEA, your connection will simply work as you saw in *Step 1*.

Authentication is handled by Kerberos in a domain environment and NTLM in a work group environment. You saw this happen in *Step 2*. This is often a source of confusion, but it is really rather simple. Any system that is a domain member and not localhost or one of the loopback addresses (127.0.0.1 and ::1) will be authenticated to use Kerberos.

In *Step 4*, you saw how a remote endpoint can be tested for availability using different authentication methods and credentials. In comparison to Windows, you also saw how SSH remoting would be used by using the `HostName` and `UserName` parameters of the `Enter-PSSession` cmdlet.

See also

- For good and concise information on resource-based constrained delegation when authenticating to resources from within a remote session, see `https://blogs.technet.microsoft.com/ashleymcglone/2016/08/30/powershell-remoting-kerberos-double-hop-solved-securely/`

Remotely retrieving data

One extremely common task is to retrieve data remotely with PowerShell. Whether you are just checking some configuration settings or you want to see the current system state, you most likely use WinRM.

This recipe shows you how to retrieve and work with data from remote systems.

Getting ready

Install and start PowerShell Core.

How to do it...

Let's perform the following steps:

1. Most data retrieval will start with one command to rule them all: `Invoke-Command`. Try to find out which process we are using remotely:

```
$remoteProcess = Invoke-Command -ComputerName PACKT-DC1 -Credential
contoso\Install -ScriptBlock {
    Get-Process -Id $pid
}
```

2. From the output, everything looks fine. Notice the process name! To make your life easier, the PSComputerName property has appeared:

```
# On the output stream, everything looks fine
$remoteProcess

# In case you did not notice it - the remote host process is the
WSMan provider host, wsmprovhost.exe
$remoteProcess | Format-Table Name, Id, PSComputerName
```

3. Try accessing normal .NET methods on your remote object, such as the Kill() method of a process:

```
$remoteProcess.Kill()
```

4. That didn't work out too well. During deserialization (see Chapter 5, *Importing, Using, and Exporting Data*), the remote object was reconstructed. You can verify this with one extremely important cmdlet, Get-Member:

```
$remoteProcess | Get-Member
```

5. With persistent sessions, you can reuse an existing sessions multiple times, saving the time it takes to authenticate you to your remote systems:

```
$sessions = New-PSSession -ComputerName PACKT-FS-A,PACKT-FS-
B,PACKT-FS-C -Credential contoso\Install
```

6. Invoke-Command tries to use up to 32 parallel connections by default, regardless of whether you are using sessions or computer names. Create some data in all of your sessions:

```
Invoke-Command -Session $sessions -ScriptBlock {
    $eventEntries = Get-WinEvent -FilterHashtable @{
        LogName = 'System'
        ID = 6005,6006
    }
}
```

7. Now, every time you reconnect while the session has not been torn down, you can access your data:

```
Invoke-Command -Session $sessions -ScriptBlock { $eventEntries }
```

8. With the automatic `PSComputerName`, filtering and grouping your data is really easy:

```
Invoke-Command -Session $sessions -ScriptBlock { $eventEntries } |
Where-Object PSCOmputerName -eq 'PACKT-FS-B'

$groupedResult = Invoke-Command -Session $sessions -ScriptBlock {
$eventEntries } | Group-Object PSCOmputerName -AsHashTable -
AsString
$groupedResult.'PACKT-FS-B' # Events on PACKT-FS-B
```

9. You can do even more with sessions. For instance, you can import them entirely:

```
$module = Import-PSSession -Session $sessions[0]
Get-Command -Module $module
```

10. To persist your remote module, you can use `Export-PSSession`. Importing the module later on only requires the credentials you used when creating the session:

```
Export-PSSession -Session $sessions[0] -OutputModule
.\MyReusableSession -Module Storage
```

How it works...

Every time you work remotely with `Invoke-Command`, your commands or scripts will be executed locally on the remote hosts. Any processing that you do later will be done with a remnant of the original data. During a process called serialization, objects are deconstructed so that they can be sent over your connection. On your end, the objects will be reconstructed, or deserialized.

During this process, most .NET types will lose some fidelity, most notably their methods. Be careful when working remotely: Only if you are working within the confines of Invoke-Command will object methods be executable. As soon as the data is transferred to your local session, you will lose many if not all methods.

Remote script debugging

Remote debugging is a feature that found its way into PowerShell, starting with Windows PowerShell 5. Being able to debug scripts remotely is a game-changer. There is probably nothing worse than an inadvertent colleague who kicks off a *short* script on Friday, 4:55 p.m. and then hurriedly leaves to an undisclosed location without cell reception.

This recipe shows you how you, as an administrator, can debug and cancel the scripts of other users.

Getting ready

Install and start PowerShell Core. This recipe is intended to be used in this book's lab environment. If you have another lab environment, please adjust the computer names accordingly.

How to do it...

Let's perform the following steps:

1. First of all, you need targets for the long-running script:

```
$unsuspectingHosts = Get-ADComputer -Filter * | Select -Expand
DnsHostName

Write-Host -Fore Red "Doing some 'quick' tasks on
$($unsuspectingHosts.Count) hosts - generating nooo tickets ♥"
```

2. The next ingredient is an infinite loop:

```
$someCondition = $true
while ($someCondition)
{
    Start-Sleep -Seconds 1

    if ((Get-Date).DayOfWeek -eq 'Sunday')
    {
        $someCondition = $false
    }
    ...
}
```

3. Lastly, start the script and then walk away:

```
Invoke-Command -ComputerName PACKT-HV1 -Credential contoso\Install
-ScriptBlock $remotescript -InDisconnectedSession
```

4. To be able to debug the script, you need to open a second channel to your machine:

```
Enter-PSSession -ComputerName PACKT-HV1 -Credential contoso\Install
```

5. So far, so good. With the next cmdlet, you can actually see all PowerShell processes running on the remote, including other users' processes:

```
Get-PSHostProcessInfo -Name wsmprovhost
```

6. We have an easy way to find out which process is not our own. It will be harder to find the correct process where the offending script is running:

```
$foreignProcess = Get-PSHostProcessInfo -Name wsmprovhost | Where-
Object ProcessId -ne $pid
```

7. Now, the magic starts: enter the host process of the other user. Notice how your prompt changes:

```
Enter-PSHostProcess -Id $foreignProcess.ProcessId
```

8. Execute the following code in order to list all existing runspaces:

```
Get-Runspace

# The runspace that is busy is yours - it was executing Get-
Runspace
$foreignRunspace = Get-Runspace | Where-Object -Property
RunspaceAvailability -ne 'Busy'
Get-RunspaceDebug -RunspaceId $foreignRunspace.Id
```

9. Lastly, step into the debugger. Notice another prompt change:

```
Debug-Runspace -Runspace $foreignRunspace
```

After executing Debug-Runspace, you should see a similar prompt to the following:

```
[PACKT-HV1]: [DBG]: [Process:888]: [RemoteHost]: PS C:\Users\Install\Documents>> ?
```

10. When you're done debugging, either quit or detach the debugger:

```
quit

Exit-PSHostProcess
Exit-PSSession
```

How it works...

In *Steps 1* to *3*, you started the remote script, simulating a colleague leaving for the weekend. *Step 4* started remote debugging by opening a second channel to your machine. In *Steps 5* through *7* you listed, identified, and connected to the remote PowerShell host process that the script from *Step 1* was running in.

Step 8 had you locate the runspace that the script was running in. PowerShell executes code in runspaces, where a runspace contains all relevant data, such as functions, variable definitions, and the session state. In *Step 9*, you actually started debugging the runspace.

Debugging a foreign process is, of course, only possible for system administrators. This is by no means a security hole—this is a system working as it was designed to. Any account holding the debug privilege (**SeDebugPrivilege**) can do this. By default, it should only be members of the local administrators group holding this privilege.

When debugging in VS Code, you don't have to use the command-line debugger. VS Code will actually display the entire script block that was executed with `Invoke-Command` and allow you to use all of the debugging capabilities you would normally use locally:

```
 05 - Remote script debugging.ps1      [PACKT-HV1] Script Listing.ps1  ×
 1
 2      # The typical Friday afternoon scripter kicks off a "quick script" on "some servers"
 3      # at 4:55 pm and then leaves like the Road Runner
 4      $unsuspectingHosts = Get-ADComputer -Filter * | Select -Expand DnsHostName
 5
 6      Write-Host -Fore Red "Doing some 'quick' tasks on $($unsuspectingHosts.Count) hosts - generating nooo tickets ♥
 7
 8      # Why, I need a loop
 9      $someCondition = $true
10      while ($someCondition)
11      {
12          Start-Sleep -Seconds 1
13
14          if ((Get-Date).DayOfWeek -eq 'Sunday')
15          {
16              $someCondition = $false
17          }
18
19          # not Sunday yet? Time for scripting
20          $someData = Get-CimInstance Win32_OperatingSystem
21
22          # Whoops... We are now looping for a very long time - unless you are reading this on Sundays
23      }
24
```

In *Step 10*, you closed your debugging session properly. Using the `quit` command, you not only exited the debugger, but also stopped the remote script from running.

See also

- For more information on the debug privilege, visit `https://support.microsoft.com/en-us/help/131065/how-to-obtain-a-handle-to-any-process-with-sedebugprivilege`.

Creating a JEA role

JEA is a rather new feature of PowerShell that allows administrators to tightly lock down PowerShell remote access to servers with the ultimate goal to ban users from connecting via Remote Desktop.

JEA allows you to apply role-based access control to your remote sessions. This way, you can limit user capabilities rather elegantly.

Getting ready

Install and start PowerShell Core. You may want to use the lab environment.

How to do it...

Let's perform the following steps:

1. Every time you connect to a remote system via WSMan, you use a session configuration in the background:

   ```
   Get-PSSessionConfiguration
   ```

2. The important components in a JEA session configuration are the roles. Designing these can get complicated very fast. Let's start by identifying some cmdlets that an administrative user might need:

   ```
   $cmdlets = @(
       'Storage\Get-*'
       'Microsoft.PowerShell.Management\Get-Item*'
   )
   ```

3. Other than being able to select which cmdlets are available, you can also lock down access to the cmdlet parameters:

```
$cmdlets += @{ Name = 'Stop-Process'; Parameters = @{ Name =
'Name'; ValidateSet = 'msiexec', 'CoreServicesShell' }, @{Name =
'Force'; ValidateSet = $true, $false}}
$cmdlets += @{ Name = 'Restart-Service'; Parameters = @{Name =
'Name'; ValidatePattern = 'Spoo\w+'}}
```

4. By default, in a JEA session, you won't have access to any provider. You can, however, add single providers:

```
$providers = 'FileSystem', 'Registry'
```

5. To import and execute code to which the user does not have access, for example, to set some settings, you can import scripts:

```
Set-Content .\somescript.ps1 -Value 'Write-Host "Hello
$env:USERNAME!`r`nWith great power comes great responsibility @_@"'
-Encoding utf8
$scriptsToProcess = (Resolve-Path .\somescript.ps1).Path
```

6. For WinRM to automatically pick up roles and check the role assignment in the next recipe, your roles need to be part of a module:

```
$modulePath = New-Item -ItemType Directory -Path
"$PSHOME\Modules\MyJeaModule\RoleCapabilities" -Force
$null = New-Item -Path $modulePath.Parent -Name MyJeaModule.psm1
$null = New-ModuleManifest -Path
"$($modulePath.Parent)\MyJeaModule.psd1" -CompatiblePSEditions Core
-ModuleVersion 1.0.0
```

7. With one single cmdlet call, create your new role description:

```
New-PSRoleCapabilityFile -Path (Join-Path $modulePath -ChildPath
LocalServiceAdmin.psrc) -VisibleCmdlets $cmdlets -VisibleProviders
$providers -ScriptsToProcess $scriptsToProcess

# Review the contents
psedit (Join-Path $modulePath -ChildPath LocalServiceAdmin.psrc)
```

How it works...

A session configuration consists of many parts, such as cmdlets, modules to import, assemblies needed, the account that should be used, and so on. JEA allows you to set these settings on a per-user or per-group basis. This way, you can apply fine-grained policies to your users' sessions.

This recipe showed you the basic steps for creating a role that will be used in the following recipe. In an Enterprise environment, the organizational effort to define your roles will likely be much higher than the actual implementation with PowerShell.

Creating a JEA session configuration

The session configuration is the component that collects a bunch of role capability files and links them to groups, such as Active Directory groups. It governs the use of a service account or a virtual administrative account for new sessions. The role assignments are responsible for building the ACL of a session configuration.

This recipe shows you how to create a configuration, link up your roles, and register the session configuration.

Getting ready

Install and start PowerShell Core. Use the same environment you used for the previous recipe.

How to do it...

Let's perform the following steps:

1. All of your session configurations should contain at least a valid session type. For JEA, `RestrictedRemoteServer` is preferred:

   ```
   SessionType = 'RestrictedRemoteServer'
   ```

2. To find out what your users are doing and which errors they encounter, you can configure logging. To do so, you can enable transcription on a session configuration:

   ```
   TranscriptDirectory = 'C:\PSTranscript'
   ```

3. To allow users to transfer data to and from a session, you can mount a user drive. This is just a plain filesystem directory:

```
MountUserDrive = $true
UserDriveMaximumSize = 10MB
```

4. Using a virtual account, you can have PowerShell create a local administrative account to manage the local machine:

```
RunAsVirtualAccount = $true
```

5. The language mode controls how PowerShell will behave, whether .NET can be used, and more. The preferred language mode is either NoLanguage or ConstrainedLanguage for these sessions:

```
LanguageMode = 'ConstrainedLanguage'
```

6. Lastly, and most importantly, you need to link local or domain groups to your roles:

```
RoleDefinitions = @{
        # RoleCapability: The name of your role capability file
without extension
        'contoso\Domain Admins' = @{RoleCapabilities =
'LocalServiceAdmin'}

    # Adding multiple groups might result in a merging of
capabilities!
        }
```

7. Now, you can create the session configuration and register it as a way of connecting:

```
New-PSSessionConfigurationFile @sessionConfigParameters -Path
.\MySessionConfig.pssc
Register-PSSessionConfiguration -Path .\MySessionConfig.pssc -Name
SupportSession
```

How it works...

This recipe had you create a session configuration bit by bit. While there are plenty more settings, most of the important settings, such as cmdlet restrictions, actually come from the roles you created. The session configuration should set the proper language mode, configure a virtual account or service account, and set up transcription if necessary.

By registering a session configuration, it becomes available for all users that are part of the groups in your role assignments. Be aware that multiple role assignments will mean that settings are merged. This will usually result in a user gaining more privileges, and can even lead to a dangerous combination of cmdlets. If role A allows filesystem access and role B allows unconstrained access to Set-Content, your administrator can simply change their own role capability at any time.

Connecting to endpoints using different session configuration

Bringing together the previous two recipes, this recipe will show you how to connect to different session configurations easily with PowerShell Core.

Getting ready

Install and start PowerShell Core.

How to do it...

Let's perform the following steps:

1. Connecting to a different session configuration is extremely simple, if you know the session configuration name. You can test your user's effective session capabilities with the following command:

   ```
   $configurationName = 'SupportSession'

   # If your user can be matched to any role, you will be admitted
   # You can test this before
   # Run this command directly on e.g. PACKT-DC1
   Get-PSSessionCapability -ConfigurationName SupportSession -Username
   contoso\Install
   ```

2. Once you are confident that you can do what you need, you can connect:

   ```
   $session = New-PSSession -ComputerName PACKT-DC1 -ConfigurationName
   SupportSession -Credential contoso\Install
   ```

3. You can simply enter the session. As soon as you execute Get-Command, you will know what you are up against:

```
Enter-PSSession $session

# Try to find out what you can do
Get-Command
```

4. Try some commands in the remote session:

```
Restart-Computer -Force # Nope
Enable-Privileges # Nope
Get-Item HKLM:\SOFTWARE # No we are getting somewhere
Get-Item cert:\localmachine # :(
```

5. With certain cmdlets, you can only use very specific parameters and parameter values:

```
Restart-Service -Name Spooler
Exit-PSSession
```

6. The same permissions, of course, apply to Invoke-Command as well:

```
Invoke-Command -Session $session -ScriptBlock {
    Get-Item C:\Windows # Yes!
}

Invoke-Command -Session $session -ScriptBlock {
    Restart-Computer -Force # Nope.
}
```

7. The restricted sessions can also be imported and exported:

```
Import-PSSession -Session $session -Prefix Restricted
Get-RestrictedItem -Path C:\Windows # How cool is that...
```

8. To make it easier for your users to support help desk scenarios where agents don't want to bother learning all of your fancy session configuration names, you can use a built-in variable:

```
$PSSessionConfigurationName = 'SupportSession'

# Ideal: Add this to a profile
Add-Content -Path $profile.AllUsersAllHosts -Value
'$PSSessionConfigurationName = "SupportSession"'
```

How it works...

By simply using the `ConfigurationName` parameter, you can connect to restricted sessions. It is usually a good idea to host very few restricted configurations and use a proper RBAC concept on these configurations so that you don't confuse your users too much.

Changes to role capabilities are applied immediately for new connections, whereas session configurations need to be registered.

This recipe had you connect to the session configuration you registered in the *Creating a JEA session configuration* recipe automatically by using the role capabilities that were assigned from the *Creating a JEA role* recipe. In *Steps 3 to 7*, you saw that restricted sessions can still be used like any other session type.

Step 8 then showed you how to configure the correct remote configuration name so that you can connect to a bunch of users by means of the system-wide PowerShell Core profile script.

Using the Common Information Model (CIM)

The CIM is an open standard that was developed by the **Distributed Management Task Force** (**DMTF**), and defines the structure and relationship of IT elements. On Windows, the **Windows Management Instrumentation** (**WMI**) implements CIM. To work with these data structures remotely in PowerShell, you can use CIM remoting. This recipe shows you some common use cases for CIM remoting.

Getting ready

Install and start PowerShell Core.

How to do it...

Let's perform the following steps:

1. Technically, CIM sessions don't require either PowerShell or Windows:

   ```
   Get-Help about_CimSession
   ```

   ```
   # CIM sessions do not require PowerShell nor do they require
   Windows
   $cimSessions = New-CimSession -ComputerName PACKT-HV1, PACKT-DC1 -
   Credential Contoso\Install
   ```

2. Like WinRM, CIM uses port 5985 by default. However, these sessions cannot be used interactively:

   ```
   Enter-PSSession -Session $cimSessions[0]
   Invoke-Command -Session $cimSessions -ScriptBlock {Get-CimInstance
   Win32_Process}
   ```

3. You can use these sessions with all cmdlets that accept CimSessions, though:

   ```
   Get-CimClass -ClassName Win32*System -CimSession $cimSessions
   ```

4. CIM classes can be discovered comfortably with the Get-CimClass cmdlet:

   ```
   # By property
   Get-CimClass -PropertyName LastBootUpTime -CimSession
   $cimSessions[0]
   ```

   ```
   # By method
   Get-CimClass -MethodName Change -CimSession $cimSessions[0]
   ```

5. To request data from CIM, you usually specify the CIM class, for example, Win32_OperatingSystem:

   ```
   Get-CimInstance -ClassName Win32_OperatingSystem -CimSession
   $cimSessions | Format-Table PSComputerName, LastBootUpTime
   ```

6. The Query parameter makes for a very efficient filter:

   ```
   Get-CimInstance -Query 'SELECT * FROM Win32_Process WHERE
   CommandLine like "%ExecutionPolicy%"' | Select-Object -Property
   Name, ProcessId, CommandLine
   ```

7. **Desired State Configuration (DSC)** also uses CIM sessions for everything (but is currently only accessible in Windows PowerShell):

```
Get-DscLocalConfigurationManager -CimSession $cimSessions[0]
```

8. CIM classes also have methods that can be called. Instead of the old dot notation, you can use the `Invoke-CimMethod` cmdlet:

```
$result = Get-CimInstance -Query 'SELECT * FROM Win32_Service WHERE
Name = "Spooler"' |
    Invoke-CimMethod -MethodName ChangeStartMode -Arguments
@{StartMode = 'Automatic'}

$result.ReturnValue
```

9. The **Cmdlet Data XML (CDXML)** cmdlets also work with one or more CIM sessions, making bulk changes unbelievably easy:

```
Get-NetAdapter -CimSession $cimSessions # Brilliant.
```

How it works...

Windows operating systems come with a variety of CIM classes (Win32, CIM, and MSFT) that you can use at your leisure. While many PowerShell cmdlets don't require you to use CIM, there are some tasks that you simply cannot do with a cmdlet.

This recipe had you use CIM sessions for CIM remoting, but you can, of course, also query local CIM classes. Many CIM and CDXML cmdlets support multiple sessions and will throttle automatically. You can use the `ThrottleLimit` parameter to tell PowerShell how many parallel connections are used.

Using PowerShell Direct in PowerShell Core

PowerShell Direct is a Windows-only technology that allows you to connect to VMs, even when the VMs themselves are offline or have disabled remoting.

This recipe shows you when and how to use PowerShell Direct.

Getting ready

Install and start PowerShell Core on a Hyper-V host.

How to do it...

Let's perform the following steps:

1. Disconnect all network adapters from one of the lab machines, for example, PACKT-FS-A:

```
Get-Vm -Name PACKT-FS-A | Get-VMNetworkAdapter | Disconnect-
VMNetworkAdapter
```

2. Try to connect to the machine using PowerShell remoting:

```
Enter-PSSession -ComputerName PACKT-FS-A -Credential
Contoso\Install
```

3. Without network access, there would normally be no way to remote into a machine. Now, let's try a different parameter:

```
$directSession = New-PSSession -VMName PACKT-FS-A -Credential
Contoso\Install
```

4. Verify the type of connection by using Invoke-Command and Get-Process remotely:

```
Invoke-Command -Session $directSession -ScriptBlock {
    Get-Process -id $pid
}
```

5. You can even use these kinds of sessions with remoting entirely disabled:

```
Invoke-Command -Session $directSession -ScriptBlock {
    Disable-PSRemoting -Force
}
```

6. Try to reconnect again:

```
Invoke-Command -Session $directSession -ScriptBlock {
 Write-Host "Remoting on $env:COMPUTERNAME is still working like a
charm"
}
```

How it works...

PowerShell Direct is reserved for Hyper-V and guest operating systems of Windows Server 2016 and newer. Since PowerShell does not use PowerShell remoting at all, this can be your last way into a machine that is otherwise not responsive.

If you want to use PowerShell Direct, you still need to know the credentials of a local or domain account that is allowed to log on to the machine. Additionally, you need to be a member of the Hyper-V administrators on the Hyper-V host itself.

Using PowerShell for Hyper-V and Azure Stack Management

9

This chapter is all about the private cloud. Through very simple recipes, you will see how to automate an on-premises Hyper-V environment as well as an on-premises Azure Stack that may or may not be integrated into Azure.

We will cover the following topics:

- Setting up Hyper-V
- Setting up Azure Stack
- Virtual networks in Hyper-V
- Virtual networks in Azure Stack
- Provisioning storage in Hyper-V
- Provisioning storage in Azure Stack
- Provisioning compute resources in Hyper-V
- Provisioning compute resources in Azure Stack
- Creating a compute cluster with DSC
- Configuring guests with DSC on Hyper-V
- Configuring guests with DSC on Azure Stack

Technical requirements

The code used in this chapter is available at `https://github.com/PacktPublishing/Powershell-Core-6.2-Cookbook/tree/master/Chapter09`.

In order to go through the Azure Stack examples, you need a physical or virtual machine that complies with the requirements outlined here: `https://docs.microsoft.com/en-us/azure/azure-stack/asdk/asdk-deploy-considerations`.

Setting up Hyper-V

The Hyper-V role on Windows Server has been available since Server 2008 R2 and has evolved a lot since then. The release of Windows Server 2016 saw the release of important features such as shielded virtual machines and generation 2 virtual machines capable of using the trusted platform module.

This recipe will guide you through setting up Hyper-V with PowerShell Core.

Getting ready

Install and start PowerShell Core.

How to do it...

Let's perform the following steps:

1. Let's start with importing the following packages:

```
Import-WinModule Dism
Import-WinModule ServerManager
```

2. Once you have done this, execute the following command:

```
Enable-WindowsOptionalFeature -FeatureName Microsoft-Hyper-V-All -
Online
```

3. After a reboot, run the following command:

```
Get-Command -Module Hyper-V
```

4. Execute the following command:

```
Get-VMHost
```

5. Now, let's run the following command:

```
$parameters = @{
    EnableEnhancedSessionMode = $true
    NumaSpanningEnabled = $true
    VirtualHardDiskPath = 'D:\Other-VMs'
    VirtualMachinePath = 'D:\Other-VMs'
}

Set-VMHost @parameters
```

How it works...

Enabling the Hyper-V feature is usually all that it takes to make use of virtualization. While there are licensed products such as the **System Center Virtual Machine Manager** (**SCVMM**) as part of the System Center Suite, you can also do it without them. This recipe showed you how to configure your virtual machine host.

While there are some settings that you can configure with PowerShell Core, there is really only one cmdlet, Set-VMHost, to apply those changes.

In *Step 1*, you started by importing the Windows-only modules, DISM (the module to interact with the Deployment Image Servicing and Management (DISM)) and ServerManager. Next, you enabled the Hyper-V optional feature to deploy all necessary binaries. After the restart, Get-Command in *Step 3* showed you the available cmdlets. In *Step 4*, you discovered that to configure your compute host, there really only are two cmdlets.

In the last step, you used the Set-VMHost cmdlet to enable the enhanced session mode and modify the default paths for new virtual machines and virtual disk files.

There's more...

When it comes to a secure configuration, there are many more things to take into consideration, such as adding users that need to manage the Hyper-V host to the Hyper-V administrators group but not granting them any rights at all on the Hyper-V guests. The opposite is also true, as virtual machine administrators should never have permissions on the Hyper-V host.

For more information on securing your deployment, see https://docs.microsoft.com/en-us/windows-server/virtualization/hyper-v/plan/plan-hyper-v-security-in-windows-server.

Setting up Azure Stack

Setting up Azure Stack is a lot more complicated than setting up Hyper-V. This recipe will show you how to do a trial installation of Azure Stack with the Azure Stack **Software Development Kit (SDK)**. Be aware that this recipe has many moving parts, and it even failed on me multiple times. It seems impossible to catch all possible exceptions as you will likely notice.

Using Azure Stack, on the other hand, is no different than using Azure, with a few limitations that we will explore in the upcoming recipes.

Getting ready

Prepare to spend up to $100 on Azure, depending on the total execution time of your deployment. Install and start PowerShell Core. To successfully execute this recipe to the end, you also need an administrative account in your Azure Active Directory tenant.

How to do it...

Let's perform the following steps:

1. Start by creating a new resource group:

   ```
   New-AzResourceGroup -Name BlauerStapel -Location 'West Europe'
   ```

2. Deploy the virtual machine from a template:

   ```
   $param = @{
       TemplateParameterFile = '.\ch09\Template\parameters.json'
       TemplateFile = '.\ch09\Template\template.json'
       ResourceGroupName = 'BlauerStapel'
       adminUserName = 'PACKT'
       adminPassword = 'M3g4Secure!' | ConvertTo-SecureString -
   AsPlainText -Force
   }
   New-AzResourceGroupDeployment @param
   ```

3. Connect via Remote Desktop by using the next line of code:

   ```
   Get-AzRemoteDesktopFile -ResourceGroupName BlauerStapel -Name
   AZSTACK -LocalPath "$env:TEMP\AZStack.rdp" -Launch
   ```

4. Initialize all additional disks first:

```
Get-Disk | Where-Object PartitionStyle -eq raw | Initialize-Disk -
PartitionStyle GPT
```

5. Then, resize the OS partition to accommodate Azure Stack:

```
Get-Partition -DriveLetter C | Resize-Partition -Size 255GB
```

6. Download and start the extractor:

```
Invoke-WebRequest -Uri
https://azurestack.azureedge.net/masdownloader-preview/1.0.3.1090/A
zureStackDownloader.exe -OutFile D:\az.exe
Start-Process d:\az.exe
```

7. While the SDK is downloaded and extracted, you can prepare some features to save time:

```
Add-WindowsFeature Hyper-V, Failover-Clustering, Web-Server,
NetworkController, RemoteAccess -IncludeManagementTools
Add-WindowsFeature RSAT-AD-PowerShell, RSAT-ADDS -
IncludeAllSubFeature
Install-PackageProvider nuget -Verbose
Rename-LocalUser -Name $env:USERNAME -NewName Administrator #
yuuuup...
Set-Item wsman:localhost\client\trustedhosts -Value * -Force
Enable-WSManCredSSP -Role Client -DelegateComputer * -Force
```

8. When your extraction is finished, reboot the server and reconnect.

9. Next, mount `CloudBuilder.vhdx` and copy the `CloudDeployment`, fwupdate, and `tools` folders:

```
$azureStackCloudBuilder =
'D:\AzureStackDevelopmentKit\CloudBuilder.vhdx'
$vhDisk = Mount-VHD -Path $azureStackCloudBuilder -Passthru
$pw = 'M3g4Secure!' | ConvertTo-SecureString -AsPlainText -Force
Robocopy.exe G:\CloudDeployment C:\CloudDeployment /MIR
Robocopy.exe G:\fwupdate C:\fwupdate /MIR
Robocopy.exe G:\tools C:\tools /MIR
$vhDisk | Dismount-VHD
```

10. Bootstrap the code as well as the necessary packages:

```
C:\CloudDeployment\Setup\BootstrapAzureStackDeployment.ps1
```

11. The fail gives us the opportunity to make some necessary modifications to the code. By *some*, I mean *too many*. Modify the `BareMetal.Tests.ps1` file as well as `Helpers.psm1`:

```
$replaceCpu = '\(\$physicalMachine.Processors.NumberOfEnabledCores
\| Measure-Object -Sum\)\.Sum'
$replaceVirt = "\(\`$Parameters.OEMModel -eq 'Hyper-V'\)"
$content = (Get-Content -Path
"C:\CloudDeployment\Roles\PhysicalMachines\Tests\BareMetal.Tests.ps
1") -replace $replaceCpu, 1000 -replace $replaceVirt, '$true'
$content | Set-Content -path
"C:\CloudDeployment\Roles\PhysicalMachines\Tests\BareMetal.Tests.ps
1" -encoding utf8
$content = Get-Content -Path
'C:\CloudDeployment\Common\Helpers.psm1'
$content = $content | ForEach-Object {if ($_ -like
'*packagesavemode "nuspec"*'){$_ + " -ExcludeVersion"}}
$content | Set-Content -Path
'C:\CloudDeployment\Common\Helpers.psm1' -encoding utf8
```

12. Now, finally, you can run the deployment. Once again, this will take a long time—a very long time:

```
$param = @{
    AdminPassword = $pw
    DNSForwarder = '8.8.8.8'
    TimeServer = '0.de.pool.ntp.org'
    InfraAzureDirectoryTenantName = 'M365x027443.onmicrosoft.com' #
Generated by demos.microsoft.com
}
C:\CloudDeployment\Setup\InstallAzureStackPOC.ps1 @param
```

13. If the deployment is done and the portal is accessible, you can register your deployment with Azure. To do this, start by installing the necessary modules:

```
invoke-webrequest -Uri
https://github.com/Azure/AzureStack-Tools/archive/master.zip -
OutFile master.zip

# Expand the downloaded files.
Expand-Archive master.zip -DestinationPath . -Force
cd AzureStack-Tools-master

# Install AzureStack module
Install-Module AzureRM -RequiredVersion 2.4.0
Install-Module -Name AzureStack -RequiredVersion 1.7.0
Import-Module .\Registration\RegisterWithAzure.psm1
```

14. Now, connect your own Azure account that you are using to access Azure:

```
Add-AzureRmAccount
Register-AzureRmResourceProvider -ProviderNamespace
Microsoft.AzureStack
```

15. With the resource provider registered, you can register Azure Stack with the next command that will access the privileged endpoint:

```
$CloudAdminCred = [pscredential]::New('AzureStack\CloudAdmin', $pw)
$RegistrationName = "<unique-registration-name>" # Fill this in
yourself!
$param = @{
    PrivilegedEndpointCredential = $CloudAdminCred
    PrivilegedEndpoint = 'AzS-ERCS01'
    BillingModel = 'Development'
    RegistrationName = $RegistrationName
}

Set-AzsRegistration @param
```

How it works...

The Azure Stack SDK deploys Azure Stack as a single-node **Proof of Concept** (**PoC**) that is useful to test how the real Azure Stack would look and feel. This recipe had you create a potent Hyper-V host in the cloud by deploying an **Azure Resource Manager** (**ARM**) template. You used the Azure Stack installer and the accompanying PowerShell scripts to download the necessary bits and run the PoC setup.

Most of this recipe, incidentally, is on troubleshooting. Each new version of the Azure Stack SDK brought new little errors that arise sometime in the five to eight hour deployment. This recipe should show you all of the errors you can encounter with Azure Stack 1901.

The installer itself is pretty interesting to look at. **Pester** is heavily used to validate the entire environment. **Desired State Configuration** (**DSC**) is used to configure everything from the Hyper-V host to each virtual machine. The resources used to do this are mostly customized and are not available on the PowerShell Gallery.

If everything worked, you should see the following in Hyper-V Manager:

AzS-ACS01	Running	0 %	8192 MB
AzS-ADFS01	Running	0 %	3072 MB
AzS-CA01	Running	0 %	1024 MB
AzS-DC01	Running	0 %	4096 MB
AzS-ERCS01	Running	0 %	4096 MB
AzS-Gwy01	Running	0 %	2048 MB
AzS-NC01	Running	0 %	4096 MB
AzS-SLB01	Running	0 %	2048 MB
AzS-Sql01	Running	0 %	4096 MB
AzS-WAS01	Running	0 %	4096 MB
AzS-WASP01	Running	1 %	8192 MB
AzS-Xrp01	Running	0 %	8192 MB

After a successful setup, you should also be able to open the portal from a browser on the Azure Stack SDK host at `https://adminportal.local.azurestack.external/`:

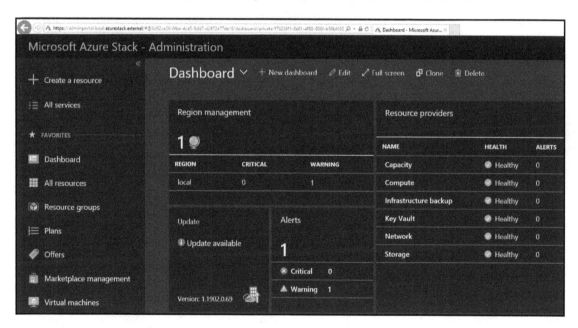

In the next recipe, we will have a look at network switches.

Virtual networks in Hyper-V

Networking on Hyper-V depends highly on your own network infrastructure. This very simple recipe shows you how to deploy different types of network switches and manage them as much as possible.

Out of scope are technologies such as software-defined networking with the network controller that has been introduced in Windows Server 2016.

Getting ready

Install and start PowerShell Core.

How to do it...

Let's perform the following steps:

1. Discover the necessary commands by executing the following:

   ```
   Get-Command -Noun VMSwitch*
   ```

2. Create a new private switch first:

   ```
   New-VMSwitch -Name ClusterHeartbeat -SwitchType Private
   ```

3. Now add an internal switch called `Management`:

   ```
   New-VMSwitch -Name Management -SwitchType Internal
   ```

4. Next, create an external switch that is bound to an existing network adapter:

   ```
   New-VMSwitch -Name Domain -NetAdapterName Wi-Fi
   ```

5. Try to list the switch extensions by executing the following:

   ```
   Get-VMSwitch -Name Management | Get-VMSwitchExtension
   ```

6. Now, disable the capturing extension by executing the next line of code:

   ```
   Get-VMSwitch -Name Management | Disable-VMSwitchExtension -Name
   'Microsoft NDIS Capture'
   ```

7. Try to remove an existing switch called `ClusterHeartbeat`:

```
Get-VMSwitch -Name ClusterHeartbeat | Remove-VMSwitch -Force
```

8. Find all online network adapters and try to add them to a switch team. Adapt this to your own network adapter names:

```
Get-NetAdapter | ? Status -eq Up
New-VMSwitch -Name DoubleTeam -NetAdapterName 'eth0','eth1'
```

9. Now modify the switch team with different network adapter names:

```
Set-VMSwitchTeam -Name DoubleTeam -NetAdapterName 'eth0','eth4'
```

How it works...

In this recipe, you saw the three different virtual switch types that Hyper-V is able to use. A private switch would be used for a virtual machine internal network, for example, to provide a customer a set of virtual machines that they can use without being able to connect to any other resource on the network.

An internal switch is often seen in lab environments when you actually need network access from the Hyper-V host to its guests.

The external switch is also a regular with most enterprises, as this allows virtual machines to connect to the outside world, whether this means the internet or your own routed network is up to you.

Step 1 started with exploring the available cmdlets, which is always a good idea. Next, you added a private network that is only used for inter-virtual machine communication on the same Hyper-V host. In *Step 3*, you then added an internal network that is used for inter-virtual machine communication on the same host as well as communication with the Hyper-V host.

Step 4 had you create an external switch that is bound to one or more physical network adapters and is used for communication with the outside world, that is, your own routed network infrastructure. In *Step 5*, you saw the extensible switch interface. This is used to enable extensions—these are usually provided by software vendors to add additional features such as **port mirroring**.

To disable the **Network Driver Interface Specification** (**NDIS**) capture extension on the management switch, you used the commands in *Step 6*. To remove an existing switch, simply use the `Remove-VMSwitch` cmdlet. *Step 7* had you try that as well with the `ClusterHeartbeat` switch.

With Server 2016, you can also use switch teams that can connect to multiple physical **Network Interface Cards** (**NICs**), which you did in *Step 8*. *Step 9* finished the recipe off with modifying team members of a switch team.

Virtual networks in Azure Stack

Virtual networks on Azure Stack work mostly as you are used to them from working on Azure. There are many differences when it comes to capabilities. Azure Stack does not, for example, allow VNet peering, which would allow you to route traffic between virtual networks without additional resources such as VPN Gateways.

This recipe shows you how to connect to Azure Stack and how to work with the `AzureRmVirtualNetwork` cmdlets.

Getting ready

Install Azure Stack and start PowerShell Core.

How to do it...

Let's perform the following steps:

1. Add your new environment:

   ```
   Add-AzureRMEnvironment -Name "Hochstapler" -ArmEndpoint
   "https://management.local.azurestack.external"
   ```

2. Retrieve the ID of your Azure Active Directory tenant:

   ```
   $AuthEndpoint = (Get-AzureRmEnvironment -Name
   "Hochstapler").ActiveDirectoryAuthority.TrimEnd('/')
   $AADTenantName = "M365x027443.onmicrosoft.com"
   $TenantId = (invoke-restmethod
   "$($AuthEndpoint)/$($AADTenantName)/.well-known/openid-
   configuration").issuer.TrimEnd('/').Split('/')[-1]
   ```

3. Now, you can add your account:

```
Add-AzureRmAccount -EnvironmentName "Hochstapler" -TenantId
$TenantId
```

4. Finally, you can start by reviewing the necessary cmdlets first:

```
Get-Command -Noun AzureRmVirtualNetwork*
```

5. Similar to Azure, we will create a resource group first. Do that now, and use the only location available, local:

```
$rg = New-AzureRmResourceGroup -Name DEWESTNetworking -Location
local
```

6. Before creating a virtual network, you should create subnet configurations. Try adding four different subnets now:

```
$sn1 = New-AzureRmVirtualNetworkSubnetConfig -Name management -
AddressPrefix 10.0.0.0/24
$sn2 = New-AzureRmVirtualNetworkSubnetConfig -Name frontend -
AddressPrefix 10.0.1.0/24
$sn3 = New-AzureRmVirtualNetworkSubnetConfig -Name management -
AddressPrefix 10.1.0.0/24
$sn4 = New-AzureRmVirtualNetworkSubnetConfig -Name frontend -
AddressPrefix 10.1.1.0/24
```

7. These subnets with the CIDR 24 fit perfectly into a 23 network. Create the virtual networks now:

```
$param = @{
    Name = 'DEDUEVN01'
    Subnet = $sn1, $sn2
    ResourceGroupName = 'DEWESTNetworking'
    AddressPrefix = '10.0.0.0/23'
    Location = 'local'
}
$param2 = $param.Clone()
$param2.Subet = $sn3, $sn4
$param2.AddressPrefix = '10.1.0.0/23'
$param2.Name = 'DEFRAVN01'
$vNet = New-AzureRmVirtualNetwork @param
$vNet2 = New-AzureRmVirtualNetwork @param2
```

8. In order to grow or shrink a subnet later on, you will have to rewrite the subnet configuration. Try to shrink the management and frontend subnets in DEDUENV01 now:

```
$vnet = Get-AzureRmVirtualNetwork -Name deduevn01 -
ResourceGroupName dewestnetworking
$null = Set-AzureRmVirtualNetworkSubnetConfig -Name management -
VirtualNetwork $vnet -AddressPrefix 10.0.0.0/25
$null = Set-AzureRmVirtualNetworkSubnetConfig -Name frontend -
VirtualNetwork $vnet -AddressPrefix 10.0.1.0/25
```

9. Up until now, you only modified the object reference stored in $vnet. To persist the changes, use Set-AzureRmVirtualNetwork now:

```
$vnet | Set-AzureRmVirtualNetwork
```

10. Finally, to remove a network, pipe the object to Remove-AzureRmVirtualNetwork:

```
$vnet | Remove-AzureRmVirtualNetwork
```

How it works...

In this recipe, you created two virtual networks with different subnet configurations, modified those configurations later, and finally removed one of the virtual networks.

Usually this is not a regular task. Virtual networks are normally created during an ARM template deployment and will require a bit more interaction only where VPN connections are concerned.

As you have seen, Azure Stack is at the time of writing (version 1901) incapable of using the new Az cmdlets. You have to continue using the ARM cmdlets in an older version due to incompatible API versions.

Provisioning storage in Hyper-V

Like networking, storage in Hyper-V can be managed quite easily. However, this depends highly on your own infrastructure. Do you use iSCSI and have to connect to a portal? Or do you use a **Scale-Out File Server** (**SOFS**)? (See the *Configure S2D* recipe in Chapter 7, *Windows Server Administration*.)

Regardless of where your virtual disks could come from, this simple recipe shows you how to create new disks and attach them to a VM. You will also see how to enable resource metering to be able to bill your customers correctly. Also, you will see the difference between dynamic, fixed, and differencing disks.

Getting ready

Install and start PowerShell Core. Execute this recipe on your own host that is running the lab environment, as we will be modifying the disks of PACKT-WB1.

How to do it...

Let's perform the following steps:

1. Discover the necessary cmdlets with Get-Command:

   ```
   Get-Command -Noun VHD*
   ```

2. Create three new dynamic disks, each 5 GiB large:

   ```
   New-VHD -Path D:\Other-VMs\Disks\VM1_DataDisk1.vhdx -Dynamic -
   SizeBytes 5GB
   New-VHD -Path D:\Other-VMs\Disks\VM1_DataDisk2.vhdx -Dynamic -
   SizeBytes 5GB
   New-VHD -Path D:\Other-VMs\Disks\VM1_DataDisk3.vhdx -Dynamic -
   SizeBytes 5GB
   ```

3. Create a fixed disk of 5 GiB in size:

   ```
   New-VHD -Path D:\Other-VMs\Disks\VM1_DataDisk3.vhdx -Fixed -
   SizeBytes 5GB
   ```

4. Add the storage path to a new resource pool:

   ```
   New-VMResourcePool -Name InternalCustomer01_storage -
   ResourcePoolType storage -Paths D:\Other-VMs\Disks
   ```

5. Attach the disks to the virtual machine PACKT-WB1 and assign the resource pool:

   ```
   foreach ($disk in (Get-ChildItem D:\Other-VMs\Disks\*.vhdx))
   {
       Add-VMHardDiskDrive -VMName PACKT-WB1 -Path $disk.FullName -
   ResourcePoolName InternalCustomer01_storage
   }
   ```

6. Enable metering by executing the following:

```
Enable-VMResourceMetering -VMName PACKT-WB1
```

7. Now, create a differencing disk on your lab host by grabbing the OS base disk that `AutomatedLab` created:

```
$param = @{
    Path = 'D:\Other-VMs\OSDisks\VM1_OS.vhdx'
    ParentPath = 'D:\AutomatedLab-
VMs\BASE_WindowsServer2016Datacenter_10.0.14393.0.vhdx'
    Differencing = $true
}
New-VHD @param
```

8. Create a new **Virtual Disk Set** (**VHDS**) next:

```
New-VHD -Path D:\Other-VMs\Disks\ClusterWitness.vhds -SizeBytes
1GB -Dynamic
```

9. Attach the disk set to your file servers and mark it as a shared disk:

```
$param = @{
    VMName = 'PACKT-FS-A', 'PACKT-FS-B', 'PACKT-FS-C'
    Path = 'D:\Other-VMs\Disks\ClusterWitness.vhds'
    ShareVirtualDisk = $true
    ControllerNumber = 0
    ControllerLocation = 4
}
Add-VMHardDiskDrive @param
```

10. Resize the disk while the machines are still running:

```
Resize-VHD -Path D:\Other-VMs\Disks\ClusterWitness.vhds -SizeBytes
5Gb
```

How it works...

This recipe had you not only create disks, but also disk sets. These are particularly useful in a clustered scenario. While you have been able to use shared virtual hard disks since Windows Server 2012 R2, extending those disks required you to shut down all cluster nodes—talk about high availability. With the new sets, you can simply expand them while the machines are running, which is very convenient.

Amid the disks, you saw another Hyper-V component: the **resource pools**. Resource pools are available for other resource types as well and are not only meant for storage. However, storage resource pools need to be created separately from other resource pools. A resource pool on Hyper-V has a different meaning than one on VMware. The resources are not pooled together but are simply used for metering purposes.

In *Step 1*, you discovered the necessary cmdlets with `Get-Command`. *Step 2* directly started with creating multiple disks for your virtual machines. You started with three dynamically expanding **Virtual Hard Disk (VHD)** files. In comparison to the dynamic disks in *Step 2*, you added a static disk in *Step 3*.

Step 4 had you create a resource pool to prepare billing on the `D:\other-vms\disks` directory. You added the created disks to a virtual machine in *Step 5* and enabled metering in *Step 6*.

Another disk type was introduced in *Step 7*. You created a differencing disk that was based on the Windows Server 2016 base disk. *Steps 8* through *10* had you create a virtual disk set to be able to share disks between virtual machines that could still be dynamically resized.

Provisioning storage in Azure Stack

Like networking on Azure Stack, there are some key differences to account for. Azure Stack is incapable of providing file shares and cannot provide blob storage accounts, for example. It is also not possible to set firewall rules or use anything other than locally redundant storage.

That aside, this recipe will show you how to provision storage accounts on Azure Stack and use them to store backups, DSC configurations, and more.

Getting ready

Install Azure Stack, and install and start PowerShell Core.

How to do it...

Let's perform the following steps:

1. Review the relevant cmdlets with `Get-Command`:

```
Get-Command -Noun AzureRmStorage*, AzureStorage*
```

2. Create a resource group as follows:

```
New-AzureRmResourceGroup -Name StorageAccounts -Location 'local'
```

3. Now you can create a new storage account:

```
$saParam = @{
    ResourceGroupName = 'StorageAccounts'
    Name = -join (1..15 | % {Get-Random -min 1 -max 9})
    SkuName = 'Standard_LRS'
    Location = 'local'
    Kind = 'Storage'
}

$sa = New-AzureRmStorageAccount @saParam
```

4. Your storage account can contain multiple resource types such as containers, tables, and queues. Create a blob container now:

```
$container = New-AzureStorageContainer -Name dscmofs -Context
$sa.Context
```

5. These containers are well-suited for classical IaaS workloads, but also to host your DSC configurations and configuration data. Use the Set AzureStorageBlobContent cmdlet to set the file contents:

```
configuration AzSBaseline
{
    node @('vm1', 'vm2', 'vm3')
    {
        File TimeStamp
        {
            DestinationPath = 'C:\DeployedOn'
            Contents = Get-Date -Format yyyy-MM-dd
            Type = 'File'
        }
    }
}

$content = AzSBaseline | ForEach-Object {
    Set-AzureStorageBlobContent -File $_.FullName -
CloudBlobContainer $container.CloudBlobContainer -Blob $_.Name -
Context $account.Context -Force
}
```

6. Try the next lines to get both context as well as the primary and secondary account keys:

```
$sa.Context
$sa | Get-AzureRmStorageAccountKey
```

How it works...

This recipe showed you how to create and use storage accounts on Azure Stack. From an infrastructure point-of-view, storage accounts are very much lagging behind the capabilities of the Azure public cloud. Features such as the Azure File Sync service, premium storage, storage tiering, and more are simply not yet available on Azure Stack.

In *Step 1*, you reviewed the relevant cmdlets with `Get-Command`. You proceeded to *Step 2* and created a resource group to contain your storage accounts. In *Step 3*, you created a new storage account. Different than the public Azure Cloud, Azure Stack storage accounts can only be v1, locally-redundant storage.

In *Step 4*, you added a blob storage container to your storage accounts, only to upload some sample data in *Step 5*. Should your developers need details regarding their storage accounts, you will find most of them in the account's context. *Step 6* showed you how to get both context as well as the primary and secondary account keys.

See also

- Read more about all limitations: https://docs.microsoft.com/en-us/azure/azure-stack/user/azure-stack-acs-differences.

Provisioning compute resources in Hyper-V

In Hyper-V, compute is the central component. After all, what good is a hypervisor if you are not using it to run virtual machines? This recipe will show you the necessary cmdlets to create compute workloads, enable nested virtualization, and provide value to your internal customers.

Getting ready

Install and start PowerShell Core. Finish the *Storage in Hyper-V* recipe.

How to do it...

Let's perform the following steps:

1. First of all, explore the necessary cmdlets using the `Get-Command` code.
2. With one of the disks from *Provisioning Storage on Hyper-V* recipe, simply create a new virtual machine that is connected to the management switch:

   ```
   $vm = New-VM -Name VM1 -MemoryStartupBytes 1GB -VHDPath D:\Other-
   VMs\OSDisks\VM1_OS.vhdx -Generation 2 -SwitchName Management
   ```

3. Since Server 2016, nested virtualization can be used. Enable it now for your newly created virtual machine:

   ```
   $vm | Set-VMProcessor -ExposeVirtualizationExtensions $true
   ```

4. To make management easier, you can create VM groups. Try to create a new virtual machine collection now:

   ```
   New-VMGroup -Name PACKT -GroupType VMCollectionType
   Add-VMGroupMember -Name PACKT -VM $vm
   ```

5. Groups can also be nested. Try to create a management group that can contain other groups now:

   ```
   New-VMGroup -Name PACKT_MGMT -GroupType ManagementCollectionType
   Add-VMGroupMember -Name PACKT_MGMT -VMGroupMember (Get-VMGroup
   Packt)
   ```

6. Now, management is more streamlined. Try to start all machines that are in the Packt group now:

   ```
   $group = Get-VMGroup -Name Packt
   Start-VM -VM $group.VMMembers
   ```

7. In order to connect to the virtual machines (as long as they are not shielded VMs), you can use the `vmconnect` tool:

   ```
   vmconnect.exe localhost $group.VMMembers.Name
   ```

8. To create a snapshot of a running VM, you can use `Checkpoint-VM`. Try it now with `VM1`:

```
Checkpoint-VM -Name $group.VMMembers.Name -SnapshotName BeforeDsc
```

9. Now restore the snapshot:

```
Get-VMSnapshot -VMName $group.VMMembers.Name | Restore-VMSnapshot -
Confirm:$false
```

10. Now remove it:

```
Remove-VMSnapShot -VMName $group.VMMembers.Name
```

11. If you need to retire a virtual machine, you can use the `Remove-Vm` cmdlet. Try it now:

```
$vm | Remove-Vm -Force
Get-VMGroup -Name PACKT | Remove-VMGroup -Force
Get-VMGroup -Name PACKT_MGMT | Remove-VMGroup -Force
```

How it works...

Virtual machines are at the heart of Hyper-V. This recipe had you create a generation 2 virtual machine. These machine types are capable of using the trusted platform module and Secure Boot, for example. Legacy virtual hardware such as IDE controllers are replaced, and their replacements are capable of supporting more resources.

You also saw another feature in action called VM groups. While those groups are not visible in the Hyper-V Manager, they can be used to better automate maintenance tasks and generally help to organize your VMs. You could, for example, create one management group per customer and add nested groups containing that customer's services.

Provisioning compute resources in Azure Stack

Creating compute resources is what Azure Stack is made for. Whether these resources are created in the UI or in PowerShell, you can benefit from a template deployment.

This recipe shows you how to deploy resources using PowerShell Core and the ARM cmdlets. If you already know how to do this, you can skip ahead to the last recipe, *Configuring guests with DSC on Azure Stack*, where you will be using ARM templates.

Getting ready

Install Azure Stack, and install and start PowerShell Core.

How to do it...

Let's perform the following steps:

1. Connect to your Azure Stack VM and open the Azure portal. Navigate to the **Marketplace management** and download the **Windows Server 2016 Datacenter Pay-as-you-use** item:

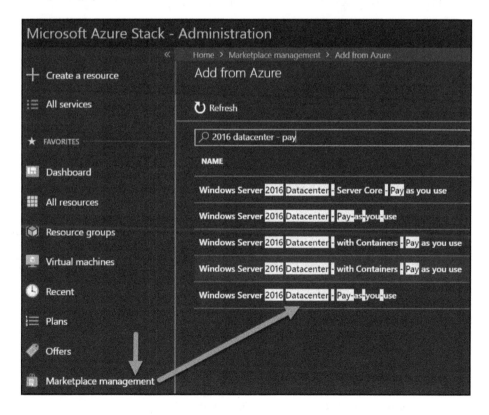

2. Next, download the DSC item from the same page.

3. As soon as the marketplace items are downloaded, you can create your first VM. To do it, create a resource group and make use of the quick create functionality of `New-AzureRmVm`:

```
New-AzureRmResourceGroup -Name VM -Location local
$adminCredential = [pscredential]::new('VmAdmin', ('M3g4Secure!' |
ConvertTo-SecureString -AsPlainText -Force))
New-AzureRmVM -ResourceGroupName VM -Location local -Name myVM01 -
ImageName Win2016Datacenter -Credential $adminCredential
```

4. The VM should be ready fairly quickly. If Azure Stack is configured properly, you can directly download the RDP file and connect to your VM:

```
Get-AzureRmVm -Name myVM01 -ResourceGroupName VM |
    Get-AzureRmRemoteDesktopFile -LocalPath .\myvm.rdp -Launch
```

5. In productive environments, you often require more control over the parameters. Start by declaring some variables for the next deployment:

```
$resourceGroupName = 'VM'
$storageAccountName = "s$((1..8 | ForEach-Object {
[char[]](97..122) | Get-Random }) -join '')"
$location = 'local'
$vmName = 'MyFirstVm'
$roleSize = 'Standard_DS2'
$cred = Get-Credential
```

6. In your resource group, create a new storage account. This is not necessary if you can use managed disks:

```
New-AzureRmStorageAccount -ResourceGroupName $resourceGroupName -
Name $storageAccountName -SkuName Standard_LRS -Location $location
$storageContext = (Get-AzureRmStorageAccount -Name
$storageAccountName -ResourceGroupName $resourceGroupName).Context
```

7. To configure networking properly, you would use network security groups. Create the first security rule now:

```
$paramRule1 = @{
    Name = 'rdp-in'
    Description = 'Allow Remote Desktop'
    Access = 'Allow'
    Protocol = 'Tcp'
    Direction = 'Inbound'
    Priority = 100
    SourceAddressPrefix = 'Internet'
```

```
        SourcePortRange = '*'
        DestinationAddressPrefix = '*'
        DestinationPortRange = 3389
}
$rule1 = New-AzureRmNetworkSecurityRuleConfig @paramRule1
```

8. Now create the second rule:

```
$paramRule2 = $paramRule1.Clone()
$paramRule2.Name = 'WinRM TCP in'
$paramRule2.Description = 'Allow WinRM'
$paramRule2.Priority = 101
$paramRule2.DestinationPortRange = 5985
$rule2 = New-AzureRmNetworkSecurityRuleConfig @paramRule2
```

9. With both rule configurations, you can create the resource. Try it now:

```
$nsgParam = @{
    ResourceGroupName = $resourceGroupName
    Location = $location
    Name = "NSG-FrontEnd"
    SecurityRules = $rule1, $rule2
}
$nsg = New-AzureRmNetworkSecurityGroup @nsgParam
```

10. With the security group in place, you can create the virtual network and subnet. Assign the security group to the subnet configuration and apply the whole configuration:

```
New-AzureRmVirtualNetwork -Name $resourceGroupName -
ResourceGroupName $resourceGroupName -Location $location -
AddressPrefix "10.0.0.0 / 16"
Get-AzureRmVirtualNetwork -Name $resourceGroupName -
ResourceGroupName $resourceGroupName |
Add-AzureRmVirtualNetworkSubnetConfig -Name someSubnet -
AddressPrefix '10.0.0.0/24' -NetworkSecurityGroup $nsg |
Set-AzureRmVirtualNetwork

$subnet = Get-AzureRmVirtualNetwork -Name $resourceGroupName -
ResourceGroupName $resourceGroupName | Get-
AzureRmVirtualNetworkSubnetConfig
```

11. Next, add the VM configuration itself. Configure the role size and the operating system SKU as well as remoting:

```
$vm = New-AzureRmVMConfig -VMName $vmName -VMSize $RoleSize
$vm = Set-AzureRmVMOperatingSystem -VM $vm -Windows -ComputerName
$vmName -Credential $cred -ProvisionVMAgent -EnableAutoUpdate -
```

```
WinRMHttp
$vm = Set-AzureRmVMSourceImage -VM $vm -PublisherName
'MicrosoftWindowsServer' -Offer WindowsServer -Skus 2016-Datacenter
-Version "latest"
```

12. Add a network interface to the VM. The NIC is connected to your virtual network. You can, of course, add more than one NIC:

```
$networkInterface = New-AzureRmNetworkInterface -Name VmNic -
ResourceGroupName $resourceGroupName -Location $location -Subnet
$subnet
$vm = Add-AzureRmVMNetworkInterface -VM $vm -Id
$networkInterface.Id
```

13. In the second-to-last step, assign the mandatory operating system disk so that the VM is able to start:

```
$DiskName = "$($vmName)_os"
$OSDiskUri = "$($StorageContext.BlobEndpoint)disks/$DiskName.vhd"
$vm = Set-AzureRmVMOSDisk -VM $vm -Name $DiskName -VhdUri
$OSDiskUri -CreateOption fromImage
```

14. Finally! You are all set to run the actual virtual machine creation:

```
$vmParameters = @{
    ResourceGroupName = $ResourceGroupName
    Location = $Location
    VM = $vm
}
New-AzureRmVM @vmParameters
```

How it works...

Virtual machine deployments combine many different resources. In this recipe, you created everything from scratch, starting with a storage account and resource groups. You created a virtual network to accommodate your virtual machines and applied a network security group for a simple level of security.

 To reuse hashtables as you have done in *Step 8*, remember to clone them. Hashtables are reference types, which would have meant that you had modified the parameters for the first rule as well.

In larger or more automated environments, you would use ARM templates instead of using a bunch of different cmdlets. Regardless of which technique you use, you should include your scripts in a source code management system such as Git.

See also

- Read more on populating the *Azure Stack Marketplace* here: `https://docs.microsoft.com/en-us/azure/azure-stack/azure-stack-marketplace`.

Creating a compute cluster with DSC

To automatically create a Hyper-V compute cluster you could use DSC. This recipe shows you how to create a two-node and domain-joined cluster. Please note that DSC is a feature of Windows PowerShell. This recipe cannot be completed using only PowerShell Core.

Getting ready

We will be using the lab VMs, `PACKT-HV1` and `PACKT-HV2`.

How to do it...

Let's perform the following steps:

1. We start the configuration data, so create a hashtable for DSC:

```
$confData = @{
    # Reserved Key first
    AllNodes = @( )
}
```

2. Inside the `AllNodes` key, add both nodes as well as the wildcard node for non-node-specific settings such as plaintext credential support:

```
@{
    NodeName = '*'
    PSDSCAllowPlaintextPassword = $true
    PSDSCAllowDomainUser = $true
}
@{
```

```
        NodeName = 'PACKT-HV1'
        Cluster = 'CLU001'
    }
    @{
        NodeName = 'PACKT-HV2'
        Cluster = 'CLU001'
    }
```

3. To the main hashtable, add one key for domain settings. These do not have to be stored with the nodes:

```
Domain = @{
    DomainName = 'contoso.com'
    DomainJoinCredential = [pscredential]::new('contoso\Install',
('Somepass1' | ConvertTo-SecureString -AsPlaintext -force))
}
```

4. Next, you can get started on the configuration itself. Start with the configuration keyword:

```
configuration TheCluster
{
    Import-DscResource -ModuleName PSDesiredStateConfiguration
    Import-DscResource -ModuleName xFailOverCluster -ModuleVersion
1.12.0.0
    Import-DscResource -ModuleName ComputerManagementDsc -
ModuleVersion 6.2.0.0
    Import-DscResource -ModuleName xHyper-V -ModuleVersion 3.16.0.0
    Import-DscResource -ModuleName StorageDsc -ModuleVersion
4.5.0.0

}
```

5. Now, add all nodes where the cluster name is CLU001:

```
node $ConfigurationData.AllNodes.Where( { $_.Cluster -eq 'CLU001'
}).NodeName
{  }
```

6. Each node needs to be joined to the domain. To do this, add the Computer resource:

```
Computer computer
{
    Name = $Node.NodeName
    DomainName = $ConfigurationData.Domain.DomainName
    Credential = $ConfigurationData.Domain.DomainJoinCredential
}
```

7. Next, we need to install a couple of features. Use a loop to add a list of features:

```
$itDepends = @()
foreach ($feature in @(...))
{
    $itDepends += "[WindowsFeature]$feature"
    WindowsFeature $feature
    {
        Name = $feature
        IncludeAllSubFeature = $true
    }
}
```

8. Configure the second hard drive to use a **GUID Partition Table (GPT)** and **Resilient File System (ReFS)** as the file system:

```
Disk DDrive
{
    DiskId = 1
    DriveLetter = 'D'
    DiskIdType = 'Number'
    PartitionStyle = 'GPT'
    FSFormat = 'ReFS'
    AllowDestructive = $true
}
```

9. Create the default directories for the VMs and disks with the `File` resource:

```
File Disks
{
    DependsOn = '[Disk]DDrive'
    DestinationPath = 'D:\Disks'
    Type = 'Directory'
    Ensure = 'Present'
}
```

10. Depending on the features and both file resources, configure the `xVMHost` resource with the modified directories:

```
xVMHost hv
{
    DependsOn = $itDepends, '[File]Disks', '[File]VMs'
    IsSingleInstance = 'Yes'
    EnableEnhancedSessionMode = $true
    VirtualHardDiskPath = 'D:\Disks'
    VirtualMachinePath = 'D:\VMs'
}
```

11. Finally, add the `xCluster` resource, depending on both domain join and feature installation:

```
xCluster $Node.Cluster
{
    Name = $Node.Cluster
    DomainAdministratorCredential =
$ConfigurationData.Domain.DomainJoinCredential
    DependsOn = $itDepends, '[Computer]computer'
    StaticIPAddress = '192.168.56.199'
}
```

12. Compile the MOF:

```
TheCluster -ConfigurationData $confData
```

13. Create and compile the LCM meta MOF:

```
[DscLocalConfigurationManager()]
configuration LcmSettings
{
    node @('PACKT-HV1', 'PACKT-HV2')
    {
        Settings
        {
            RebootNodeIfNeeded = $true
            ConfigurationMode = 'ApplyAndAutoCorrect'
        }
    }
}

LcmSettings
```

14. Create CIM sessions to both VMs:

```
$sessions = New-CimSession -ComputerName PACKT-HV1, PACKT-HV2 -
Credential $confData.Domain.DomainJoinCredential
```

15. Configure the LCM first:

```
Set-DscLocalConfigurationManager -CimSession $sessions -Path
.\LcmSettings -Verbose
```

16. Now push out the cluster config and wait:

```
Start-DscConfiguration -Force -Verbose -CimSession $sessions -Wait
-Path .\TheCluster
```

How it works...

This recipe showed you how you could create a baseline configuration for your Hyper-V environment and apply it using DSC. You started with the configuration element and added all nodes matching a filter. This is a very popular technique. Your configuration code can be kept separate from your configuration data and simply adapts to the input.

Due to the usage of the `DependsOn` resource property, you learned how to control the order of operations the LCM executes. Since many resources depend on the features or the domain membership, these were added to the list of dependencies.

If you really only want to use PowerShell Core, you could also user PowerShell Direct and copy the resulting MOF files to `C:\Windows\System32\Configuration\pending.mof` to be applied as well.

Configuring guests with DSC on Hyper-V

Often, Hyper-V guests are not configured out of the box and need network configuration, domain join, and other configurations applied.

This recipe will show you how you can use PowerShell Direct and DSC to configure VM workloads on Hyper-V.

Getting ready

Install and start PowerShell Core.

How to do it...

Let's perform the following steps:

1. Start with a little baseline configuration. Refer to the code in this book's code repository for more details:

```
configuration BaseLine
{
 Import-DscResource -ModuleName ComputerManagementDsc -
ModuleVersion 6.2.0.0
 Import-DscResource -moduleName PSDesiredStateConfiguration
 ...
}
```

2. Add the configuration data. This time, we set note-specific properties as well:

```
$confData = @{
    AllNodes = @(
        @{
            NodeName = 'NEWVM01'
            TimeZone = 'Samoa Standard Time'
        }
        ...
    }
}
```

3. Build the MOF files:

```
BaseLine -ConfigurationData $confData
```

4. In order to use PowerShell Direct, you need to use the New-PSSession cmdlet. Connect to the VMs NEWVM01 and NEWVM02 now as the local user called install using the password Somepass1:

```
$sessions = New-PSSession -VMName NEWVM01,NEWVM02 -Credential
Install
```

5. Now we can copy all necessary files to the open sessions. Start with the ComputerManagementDsc resource, which we can retrieve dynamically:

```
$mod = [System.IO.DirectoryInfo]$(Get-Module ComputerManagementDsc
-ListAvailable)[0].ModuleBase
Copy-Item -ToSession $session -Path $mod.Parent.FullName -
Destination "C:\Program Files\WindowsPowerShell\Modules" -Recurse
```

6. Copy the VM configuration to the configuration folder on each VM:

```
Copy-Item -ToSession $session -Path
".\BaseLine\$($session.ComputerName).mof" -Destination
"C:\Windows\System32\configuration\pending.mof"
```

7. Now you will just need to wait. The LCM will automatically pick up the `pending.mof` file and apply it:

```
Invoke-Command -Session $session -ScriptBlock {
    Test-DscConfiguration -Verbose -Detailed -ErrorAction
SilentlyContinue
}
```

How it works...

This recipe was similar to the previous one in that both use DSC. In this recipe, however, you saw how to bootstrap a DSC configuration when the network was not yet configured or other factors were missing. By using PowerShell Direct with PowerShell Core, you can still remotely connect to the VM and apply any configuration you like.

In *Step 5*, we made good use of the PowerShell engine and the built-in cmdlets. You can discover the installation location of any module with `Get-Module`. Notice that the path of course points to the versioned folder on PowerShell 5 and newer.

Configuring guests with DSC on Azure Stack

Azure Stack virtual machines can, of course, be configured with DSC as well. Like their brothers and sisters on the public cloud, you can use the DSC extension with any new template deployment.

This recipe shows you how to prepare a config so that it can be retrieved during a deployment.

Getting ready

Install Azure Stack, and install and start PowerShell Core.

How to do it...

Let's perform the following steps:

1. Connect to the Azure Stack portal and add the DSC marketplace item:

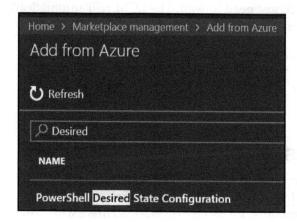

2. Create the DSC configuration baseline:

```
$cScript = {
    configuration config
    {
        . . .
    }
}
```

3. Create the configuration data:

```
$cData = {
    @{
        Files = @(
            @{
                DestinationPath = 'C:\File1'
                Type = 'File'
                Contents = 'On Azure as well'
            }
            . . .
        )
    }
}
```

4. Store both configuration data as well as the configuration script in separate files and compress the configuration into an archive:

```
$cData.ToString() | Set-Content configdata.psd1
mkdir config
$cScript.ToString() | Set-Content .\config\configscript.ps1
Compress-Archive .\config\* -DestinationPath .\config.zip
```

5. Now, you need to create a storage account to upload the configuration to:

```
New-AzureRmResourceGroup -Name alltheconfigs -Location local
$account = New-AzureRmStorageAccount -Name dscthings -
ResourceGroupName alltheconfigs -Location local -SkuName
Standard_LRS
$container = New-AzureStorageContainer -Name mofs -Context
$account.Context
```

6. Next, upload the configuration archive as well as the configuration data:

```
$content = Set-AzureStorageBlobContent -File .\config.zip -
CloudBlobContainer $container.CloudBlobContainer -Blob config.zip -
Context $account.Context -Force
$token = New-AzureStorageBlobSASToken -CloudBlob
$content.ICloudBlob -StartTime (Get-Date) -ExpiryTime (Get-
date).AddMonths(2) -Protocol HttpsOnly -Context $account.Context -
Permission r

$contentData = Set-AzureStorageBlobContent -File .\configdata.psd1
-CloudBlobContainer $container.CloudBlobContainer -Blob
configdata.psd1 -Context $account.Context -Force
$tokenData = New-AzureStorageBlobSASToken -CloudBlob
$contentData.ICloudBlob -StartTime (Get-Date) -ExpiryTime (Get-
date).AddMonths(2) -Protocol HttpsOnly -Context $account.Context -
Permission r
```

7. Create a new ARM template and refer to the code for details. Make sure that the DSC extension is configured properly:

```
"settings": {
    "configuration": {
        "url":
"$($content.ICloudBlob.StorageUri.PrimaryUri.AbsoluteUri)",
        "script": "configscript.ps1",
        "function": "config"
    },
    "configurationData": {
        "url":
"$($contentData.ICloudBlob.StorageUri.PrimaryUri.AbsoluteUri)"
```

```
        }
    },
    "protectedSettings": {
        "configurationUrlSasToken": "$token",
        "configurationDataUrlSasToken": "$tokenData"
    }
}
```

8. Deploy the ARM template, which is now using your blob SAS tokens and URIs to download the configuration and configuration data:

```
New-AzureRmResourceGroup -Name fromTemplate -Location local

$parma = @{
    Name = 'dep01'
    ResourceGroupName = 'fromTemplate'
    TemplateFile = '.\template.json'
    adminUsername = 'ScroogeMcDuck'
    adminPassword = ('MOneyM4ker!' | ConvertTo-SecureString -
AsPlainText -Force)
}
New-AzureRmResourceGroupDeployment @parma
```

How it works...

In this recipe, you used the ARM template deployment. ARM templates have a distinct benefit in that they can be checked into source code management systems such as Git or SVN. Changes to a template can trigger a new template deployment.

While this recipe used the default deployment, you can also deploy your resource group template incremental and add new resources without destroying existing ones.

In this recipe's template, you added the DSC extension to be able to configure the VM during deployment.

10
Using PowerShell with Azure and Google Cloud

Working with cloud services is an increasingly important topic. The focus has shifted steadily toward the cloud over the past couple of years. In this chapter, you will see and compare Azure and Google Cloud automation with PowerShell. AWS was intentionally left out because the AWS PowerShell experience is already very good and on par with Azure, whereas a lot more effort needs to be put into Google Cloud PowerShell.

In this chapter, we will cover the following recipes:

- Connecting to Azure
- Connecting to Google
- Exploring Azure resource groups
- Exploring Google Cloud projects
- Deploying resource group templates
- Deploying Google Cloud templates
- Using the Azure Container Registry
- Using the Google Cloud Container Registry
- Containers on Azure
- Containers on Google Cloud
- SQL on Azure
- SQL on Google Cloud

Technical requirements

This chapter's code resides in `https://github.com/PacktPublishing/Powershell-Core-6.2-Cookbook/tree/master/Chapter10`.

Connecting to Azure

This short recipe shows you how to connect to Azure and securely store your credentials.

Getting ready

Register for a free Azure account at `https://azure.microsoft.com/en-us/free/` if you have not yet done so.

How to do it...

Let's perform the following steps:

1. To work with Azure, install the Azure PowerShell module first, as follows:

   ```
   Install-Module -Name Az -Scope CurrentUser
   ```

2. Right now, starting any cmdlet will result in an error. Try it now, as follows:

   ```
   Get-AzVm
   ```

3. To begin working with Azure, you need to connect your account. Use `Connect-AzAccount` now—a login prompt will be displayed, as follows:

   ```
   Connect-AzAccount
   ```

   Simply follow the on-screen instructions, as shown in the following screenshot:

```
C:\> connect-azaccount
RNING: To sign in, use a web browser to open the page https://microsoft.com/devicelogin and enter the code DKYNYRN
```

4. If you have access to more than one subscription, select the right one, as per the following example:

```
Get-AzSubscription
```

5. And use it with `Set-AzContext`, as follows:

```
Set-AzContext -Subscription 'JHPaaS'
```

6. Start a new PowerShell session and use `Get-AzComputeResourceSku` to see the persistent context in action, as follows:

```
Get-AzComputeResourceSku | Select-Object -First 1
```

How it works...

This short recipe gave you the necessary steps to log in to your Azure account and connect it to Azure PowerShell. Your context is stored in a JSON file in your user's `AppData\Roaming\AzurePowerShell` directory and is reused automatically. This is a big improvement to earlier cmdlet versions where you manually needed to export and import the context.

Connecting to Google

In a similar way to Azure, Google Cloud requires authentication before you can do anything. While the Google Cloud PowerShell is not as advanced as Azure, it is good enough.

This recipe shows you how to connect your Google Cloud account to be used with the gcloud CLI and the `GoogleCloud` PowerShell module.

Getting ready

Register for a free account at `https://cloud.google.com/` if you haven't already done so.

How to do it...

Let's perform the following steps:

1. Start by creating a new project in your dashboard at `https://console.cloud.google.com`. This will be the first step that you need to do in a browser, as shown in the following screenshot:

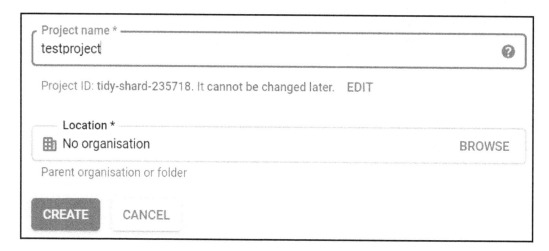

2. Next, install the necessary bits with `Install-Module`, as shown in the following example:

```
Install-Module Chocolatey
Install-ChocolateySoftware
Install-ChocolateyPackage -Name gcloudsdk
Install-Module -Name GoogleCloud -Scope CurrentUser
```

3. As with Azure, you need to authenticate before doing anything. Try retrieving your Cloud projects, as follows:

```
Get-GcpProject
```

4. Use the `gcloud` CLI now to log in and persist your token, as follows:

```
gcloud init
```

5. Now it is possible to interact with Google Cloud. Try retrieving some data, as per the following example:

```
Get-GcsBucket
```

6. To store your access token permanently, use the following `gcloud` snippet and authenticate in your browser, as per the following example:

```
gcloud auth application-default login
```

7. This way you can always retrieve a bearer token for RESTful API calls, as shown in the following example:

```
gcloud auth application-default print-access-token
```

How it works...

This recipe works in a similar way to the *Connecting to Azure* recipe. In order for the Google Cloud module to be usable, you need to authenticate first. Because multi-factor authentication is usually used, you will be redirected to a browser to insert your FIDO2 key, or to authenticate via an app.

The PowerShell module `Chocolatey` you used in *Step 2* is used to install the binary package **Google Cloud SDK** on a Windows system. If you cannot access `Chocolatey`, or if you are using Linux, please install the Google Cloud SDK manually. Access to the `gcloud` command is necessary.

As you can see in *Steps 4*, *6*, and *7*, the management experience is a bit rough around the edges. While the PowerShell module, `GoogleCloud`, exists it does not allow you to authenticate in the same easy way as the Azure PowerShell module does.

Exploring Azure resource groups

Azure resource groups are containers for all your different resources. There cannot be any resources without them. This recipe shows you how to create, update, and delete resource groups.

Getting ready

Install and start PowerShell Core.

How to do it...

Let's perform the following steps:

1. Try listing your existing resource groups first, as follows:

   ```
   Get-AzResourceGroup
   ```

2. You can create resource groups at any time to organize your resources such as virtual machines, networks, and so on, as shown in the following example:

   ```
   New-AzResourceGroup -Name JHP_Networking -Location 'West Europe'
   ```

3. By assigning tags to your resource groups, you can enable a more streamlined billing process in your organization. Try using the Tag parameter now, as shown in the following example:

   ```
   New-AzResourceGroup -Name JHP_VMDisks -Location 'West Europe' -Tag
   @{CostCenter = 48652; PrimaryOwner = 'JHP'}
   ```

4. You can, of course, modify resource groups at any time. Try tagging another resource group, as shown in the following example:

   ```
   Set-AzResourceGroup -Name JHP_Networking -Tag @{CostCenter = 4711;
   PrimaryOwner = 'SomeoneElse'}
   ```

5. If you want to append the tags, you need to retrieve the hash table first and then add new keys. Try it now and add a primary owner, as shown in the following example:

   ```
   $tags = (Get-AzResourceGroup -Name JHP_VMDisks).Tags
   $tags.PrimaryOwner = 'Mr. Big Boss'
   $tags.Purpose = 'Storage accounts'
   Set-AzResourceGroup -Name JHP_VMDisks -Tag $tags
   ```

6. You can also export entire resource groups, as shown in the following example. This is used to prepare resource group deployments:

   ```
   Export-AzResourceGroup -ResourceGroupName JHP_VMDisks -Path .
   ```

7. Removing a resource group is very simple as well. Try removing one of yours now, as per the following example:

   ```
   Remove-AzResourceGroup -ResourceGroupName JHP_VMDisks -Force
   ```

How it works...

Resource groups collect all of your resources. This recipe showed you the main operations done with them. It is always a good idea to organize your resources properly.

The great benefit of well-organized resource groups is that applying **role-based access control (RBAC)** will be a lot easier. If your networking team needs to manage virtual networks, but all virtual networks are spread over hundreds of resource groups, you will have a much harder time.

See also

- Check out the Azure resource group best practices here: `https://docs.microsoft.com/en-us/azure/portal-docs/playbooks/azure-readiness/organize-resources?tabs=AzureManagmentGroupsAndHierarchy`.

Exploring Google Cloud projects

Unfortunately, Google Cloud projects only have one cmdlet associated with them. Cloud projects are somewhat equivalent to Azure resource groups as they collect resources of different types. To do anything in the Google Cloud, you are required to use a project.

This recipe shows you how to use the one cmdlet and add the rest of the methods via REST API calls.

Getting ready

Complete the *Connecting to Google* recipe and install and start PowerShell Core.

How to do it...

Let's perform the following steps:

1. Use the single available cmdlet now to retrieve your first project, as follows:

```
Get-GcpProject
```

2. For all other resource interactions, we need to access the REST API resource, `projects`. Get started with your bearer token, as shown in the following example:

```
$baseUri =
'https://cloudresourcemanager.googleapis.com/v1/projects'
$header = @{
    Authorization = "Bearer $(gcloud.cmd auth application-default
print-access-token)"
}
```

3. To list all projects, you can now also use a RESTful GET. Try it now, as shown in the following code:

```
$projects = (Invoke-RestMethod -Method Get -Uri $baseUri -Headers
$header).Projects
```

4. To grab the details of just one specific project, you can supply it in the request URI, as shown in the following example:

```
Invoke-RestMethod -Method Get -Uri
"$baseuri/$($projects[0].projectId)" -Headers $header
```

5. To prepare a new Google Cloud project, prepare the request body. Your project needs a project name and ID and can optionally use labels as long as they are lowercase, as per the following example:

```
$body = @{
    projectId = 'uid-of-project'
    name = 'friendly-name'
    labels = @{
        owner = $env:USERNAME.ToLower()
        costcenter = '100100101'
    }
} | ConvertTo-Json
```

6. Create the project now using the POST method on the same API endpoint, as follows:

```
Invoke-RestMethod -Method Post -Uri $baseUri -Body $body -
ContentType application/json -Headers $header
```

7. As soon as the project is created, you can use it to deploy Kubernetes clusters, deploy databases, and more. To clean this one up, use the DELETE method and supply the project name in the URI, as shown in the following example:

```
Invoke-RestMethod -Method Delete -Uri "$baseUri/uid-of-project" -
Headers $header
```

How it works...

The Google Cloud cmdlets wrap around API calls and return .NET objects representing the cloud resources. What I cannot tell you is why cmdlets such as `New-GcpProject` and `Remove-GcpProject` are missing. Fortunately, PowerShell Core can always use REST.

You have seen in this recipe how you can access missing functions, as well as being able to create and delete projects. The biggest challenge with this is always the API documentation. While the API references of Google Cloud, Microsoft Azure, and Amazon AWS are particularly good, this is still not an easy task.

See also

- To learn more about the Google Cloud API, check out: `https://cloud.google.com/resource-manager/docs/apis`.

Deploying resource group templates

When working with Azure, you can deploy many resource types from so-called Azure Resource Manager templates. This approach is ideally suited for continuous integration and continuous delivery pipelines, where your entire infrastructure is defined as code. The code is then deployed on Azure whenever there are changes to the template.

This short recipe shows you how to deploy a simple resource group template to deploy a storage account.

Getting ready

Install and start PowerShell Core.

How to do it...

Let's perform the following steps:

1. Execute the following command:

```
$template = @{
    # Schema and content are mandatory
    '$schema' =
"https://schema.management.azure.com/schemas/2015-01-01/deploymentT
emplate.json#"
    contentVersion = "1.0.0.0"
}
```

2. To this hash table, add a key called `resources`, as shown in the following code. This is mandatory, otherwise there would be nothing to deploy:

```
resources = @(

)
```

3. The resources key is an array of hash tables. So, add your storage account hash table now by starting with the mandatory resource type, as shown in the following example:

```
@{
    # The type of each resource is fixed. Here, we deploy a storage
account
    type = "Microsoft.Storage/storageAccounts"
}
```

4. Next, add the name and API version keys to the table. The resource name and API version are mandatory as well. Notice that the storage account name needs to be unique in the region, as shown in the following example:

```
name = -join [char[]](1..10 | foreach {Get-Random -Minimum 97 -
Maximum 123})
apiVersion = "2018-07-01"
```

5. You can use functions inside ARM templates as well. Try retrieving the location of the resource group dynamically with the `resourceGroup()` function, as follows:

```
location = "[resourceGroup().location]"
```

6. If there are parameters or variables in your deployment, you can, of course, access them as well. Read the value of the `storageaccounttype` parameter next, as follows:

```
sku = @{
    name = "[parameters('storageaccounttype')]"
}
```

7. Because you used a parameter in the last step, you need to add a `parameters` key to your template, as follows:

```
parameters = @{
}
```

8. The `parameters` key contains key value pairs where the key is the parameter name and the value is another hash table. Add the `storageaccounttype` parameter now, and add a list of possible values to implement some validation, as shown in the following example:

```
storageaccounttype = @{
    type = "string"
    defaultValue = "Standard_LRS"
    allowedValues = @(
        "Premium_LRS",
        "Standard_LRS",
        "Standard_GRS"
    )
}
```

9. You can either store the template or use the hash table. Export it now after converting it into a JSON document, as shown in the following example:

```
$template | ConvertTo-Json | Set-Content template.json
```

10. To deploy it from a file, reference it in the next cmdlet, as shown in the following example:

```
New-AzResourceGroup WithDeployment -Location 'West europe'
New-AzResourceGroupDeployment -Name MyDeployment -ResourceGroupName
WithDeployment -Mode Complete -TemplateFile .\template.json -
storageaccounttype Standard_LRS
```

11. You can also use the hash table you created without exporting it first, as per the following example:

```
New-AzResourceGroupDeployment -Name MyDeployment -ResourceGroupName
WithDeployment -Mode Complete -TemplateObject $template -
storageaccounttype Standard_LRS
```

12. When your template is fully deployed, you can access your resource, as follows:

```
Get-AzStorageAccount -ResourceGroupName WithDeployment
```

How it works...

All resources are referenced by their type. The type consists of the resource provider, for example, `Microsoft.Storage`, and the type, which, in this recipe, was `storageAccounts`. The API version of each resource provider is very important. This defines the capabilities of the API endpoint so that you can interact both with Azure Stack as well as the Azure Cloud.

The parameters you have defined in your template are all automatically picked up and can be used as dynamic parameters in your `New-AzResourceGroupDeployment` cmdlet.

ARM templates are essentially just huge hash tables that are converted into the JSON format. In *Step 1*, you began your template by creating a hash table containing the mandatory `$schema` key. In *Steps 2 to 6*, you gradually added a very simple resource to your template, a storage account.

Using the parameters key you added in *Step 8*, you subsequently stored the settings as a JSON template and used both the template as well as the hash table with the `New-AzResourceGroupDeployment` cmdlet to deploy resources to a resource group.

See also

- Check out the treasure trove of templates at: `https://github.com/Azure/azure-quickstart-templates`.

Deploying Google Cloud templates

Where Azure uses JSON, Google Cloud uses YAML. That doesn't matter though, as PowerShell Core allows us to use cmdlets to store templates. This recipe shows you how to create instance templates and spin up new instance groups with similar VM configurations.

Getting ready

Install and start PowerShell Core.

How to do it...

Let's perform the following steps:

1. Execute the following commands:

```
$image = Get-GceImage -Family "windows-2016"
$disks = @(
    New-GceAttachedDiskConfig -SourceImage $image -Name os -
AutoDelete -Boot
    New-GceAttachedDiskConfig -SourceImage $image -Name d1 -
AutoDelete
    New-GceAttachedDiskConfig -SourceImage $image -Name d2 -
AutoDelete
)
```

2. Once executed, run the following command:

```
$templateParameter = @{
    Name = 'vm-conf1'
    Project = 'jhptestproject'
    MachineType = 'n1-standard-1'
    Description = 'Single VM template'
    Region = 'europe-west3'
    Disk = $disks
    Network = 'default'
}
Add-GceInstanceTemplate @templateParameter
```

3. To retrieve and check your template, you can use `Get-GceInstanceTemplate`, as follows:

```
Get-GceInstanceTemplate -Name vm-conf1
```

4. Execute the following command:

```
$tmpl = Get-GceInstanceTemplate -Name vm-conf1
Add-GceManagedInstanceGroup -InstanceTemplate $tmpl -Name manni -
TargetSize 4 -Zone europe-west3-a
```

5. To clean up again, you can use the `Remove-GceManagedInstanceGroup` cmdlet. Try it now, as follows:

```
Remove-GceManagedInstanceGroup -Name manni -Zone europe-west3-a
```

6. This is, of course, even more flexible with the REST API, where you can actually pass your template, as shown in the following example:

```
$template = @{
    "name" = "vm-conf1"
    "description" = ""
    "properties" = @{ ... }
        "disks" = @( ... )
        "canIpForward" = $false
        "networkInterfaces" = @( ... )
        "labels" = @{ }
        "scheduling" = @{ ... }
        "serviceAccounts" = @( ... )
    }
} | ConvertTo-Json -Depth 42
$head = @{Authorization = "Bearer $(gcloud.cmd auth application-
default print-access-token)" }

$tmp = Invoke-RestMethod -Method post -uri
https://www.googleapis.com/compute/v1/projects/jhptestproject/globa
l/instanceTemplates -Headers $head -body $template -contenttype
application/json
```

How it works...

Google Cloud instance templates work differently compared to ARM templates. These instance templates are used to deploy managed instance groups that consist of machines with the same configuration. On Azure, a template can essentially deploy anything (that is supported).

This recipe showed you how to quickly create instance templates and managed instances with PowerShell cmdlets and showed you one example of using the REST API instead. *Step 1* started by defining a list of disks that the template used. The definition was used in *Step 2* with the `Add-GceInstanceTemplate` cmdlet. You added a template that deploys VMs with the size `n1-standard-1` and your disk configuration.

Instances are deployed in an instance group. In *Step 4*, you created an instance group from your template with four similar machines. You cleaned it up again in *Step 5*.

As an alternative, *Step 6* showed you the REST equivalent of the `Add-GceInstanceTemplate` cmdlet for more flexibility.

Using the Azure Container Registry

You can deploy your own repository for Docker container images, called a registry. These private repositories are used to host your own, customized container images to deploy on Kubernetes or as Azure Container Instances.

This recipe shows you how to create the registry and prepare and push a simple container.

Getting ready

Install and start PowerShell Core.

How to do it...

Let's perform the following steps:

1. Create the container that is defined in the source code inside the `#region` tag.
2. Create a new resource group, as follows:

   ```
   New-AzResourceGroup -Name MyContainers -Location westeurope
   ```

3. Now, add the container registry resource to it, as follows:

   ```
   New-AzContainerRegistry -ResourceGroupName MyContainers -Name
   ContainersGalore -Location Westeurope -Sku Basic -EnableAdminUser
   ```

4. To retrieve the login credentials for your registry, for example, to use them with the Docker CLI, try the following cmdlet:

```
Get-AzContainerRegistryCredential -ResourceGroupName MyContainers -
Name ContainersGalore
```

5. To be able to use your registry, you need to tell the Docker CLI how to log in, as shown in the following example:

```
$containerRegistry = Get-AzContainerRegistry -ResourceGroupName
MyContainers -Name ContainersGalore
$containerCredential = $containerRegistry | Get-
AzContainerRegistryCredential
$containerCredential.Password | docker login
$containerRegistry.LoginServer -u $containerCredential.Username --
password-stdin
```

6. Tag the container you created in *Step 1* with your own repository, thereby linking to it, as shown in the following example:

```
docker tag mypolariscore
"$($containerRegistry.LoginServer)/luckynumber:v1"
```

7. Now you can push your local image to the repository with the Docker CLI, as follows:

```
docker push "$($containerRegistry.LoginServer)/luckynumber:v1"
```

8. You can now safely remove the local files with the Docker CLI, as per the following code:

```
docker rmi "$($containerRegistry.LoginServer)/luckynumber:v1"
```

How it works...

The container registry simply provides an interface for Docker and container orchestration engines such as Docker Swarm and Kubernetes to spin up new containers from a specific image. The image contains code from upstream providers such as Microsoft and your own customizations.

In this recipe, you created a container registry and pushed a container that exposes a small REST API endpoint. We will use it in the *Containers on Azure* recipe.

Using the Google Cloud Container Registry

The Google Cloud Container Registry offers the same functionality as the registry on Azure, without the flexibility. There is a predefined set of available registries on Google Cloud, depending on the region, which are created per project and not on demand.

This recipe shows you how to create a registry for the Europe region and pushes the same container that you have already pushed to Azure.

Getting ready

Install and start PowerShell Core.

How to do it...

1. Execute the following commands:

```
$project = Get-GcpProject -Name testproject
$imageName = 'eu.gcr.io/{0}/luckynumber:v1' -f $project.ProjectId
```

2. We still need to tell the Docker CLI how to authenticate. You can do it on Google Cloud with your access token, as follows:

```
gcloud auth print-access-token | docker login -u oauth2accesstoken
--password-stdin https://eu.gcr.io
```

3. You need to manually enable the registry for your project by browsing to the following URL:

```
start
"https://console.cloud.google.com/apis/api/containerregistry.google
apis.com/overview?project=$($project.ProjectId)"
```

4. Recreate your image from the previous recipe and use a different tag, linking to your Google Cloud registry, as shown in the following example:

```
docker tag mypolariscore $imageName
```

5. Push the image now, as follows:

```
docker push $imageName
```

6. And remove the local files, as follows:

```
docker rmi $imageName
```

How it works...

The Google Cloud Container Registry works exactly like the container registry on Azure, at least on the surface. While the container registry cannot be created dynamically and is tied to a project, all resources in your project can authenticate automatically against your registry. This makes deploying a Kubernetes cluster easier.

The management of images hosted on the Google Cloud registry works just like on any other registry: by using the Docker CLI.

Since the registry is automatically available, you just need to know how to access it. You started in *Step 1* by creating the correct tag for your container image, containing the registry to be used. *Step 2* then showed you how to get an access token for Google Cloud automation in order to authenticate your Docker push and pull commands.

After you enabled your registry in *Step 3*, you created and pushed your image to your very own registry in *Steps 4* to *6*.

Containers on Azure

To deploy containers on Azure, we will be using Azure Container Instances for an easier start. Using Kubernetes adds a little more complexity.

This recipe will show you how to create a new container group that uses the container image from your private Docker gallery. It is actually not much harder than starting a container on-premises.

Getting ready

Complete the *Using the Azure Container Registry* recipe, install and start PowerShell Core.

How to do it...

Let's perform the following steps:

1. Start by getting a reference to your registry as well as the credentials, as shown in the following example:

```
$containerRegistry = Get-AzContainerRegistry -ResourceGroupName
MyContainers -Name ContainersGalore
$containerCredential = $containerRegistry | Get-
AzContainerRegistryCredential
```

2. The relevant cmdlets can be explored with Get-Command, as per the following code:

```
Get-Command -Module Az.ContainerInstance
```

3. Deploy your new container group by linking to your image and supplying your registry credentials. Since port 8080 needs to be exposed, you should add it as well, as shown in the following example:

```
$param = @{
 ResourceGroupName = 'MyContainers'
 Name = 'luckynumber7'
 Image = "$($containerRegistry.LoginServer)/luckynumber:v1"
 OsType = 'Windows'
 IpAddressType = 'Public'
 Port = 8080
 RegistryCredential =
[pscredential]::new($containerCredential.UserName,
($containerCredential.Password | ConvertTo-SecureString -
AsPlainText -Force))
}

New-AzContainerGroup @param
```

4. To list your (now running) containers in a group, try the next cmdlet, as follows:

```
Get-AzContainerGroup
```

5. The API will now work. Retrieve the container group dynamically and use the public IP of your container, as per the following example:

```
$ip = (Get-AzContainerGroup).IpAddress
Invoke-RestMethod -Method Get -Uri
"http://$($ip):8080/containerizedapi"
```

6. If you are concerned that your containers had trouble starting, or you simply want to see the output, you can get logs as well. Try it, in the following way:

```
Get-AzContainerInstanceLog -ResourceGroupName MyContainers -
ContainerGroupName luckynumber7
```

7. All things have to end. Remove your container group, as follows:

```
Remove-AzContainerGroup -Name luckynumber7 -ResourceGroupName
MyContainers
```

How it works...

Azure Container Instances provides a simple starting point for your containerized applications. While it is not as flexible as Kubernetes, you often don't need all of the overhead.

This recipe showed you how to spin up and remove container groups using private or public container images. You saw how simple it was to request a public IP address by adding the IPAddressType as public and how to expose ports.

Containers on Google Cloud

Google Cloud uses Kubernetes to host your containers. This adds a bit more complexity and requires you to learn not only about Docker, but about Kubernetes as well.

This short recipe will show you how to create your first Kubernetes cluster and add nodes to the cluster.

Getting ready

Install and start PowerShell Core.

How to do it...

Let's perform the following steps:

1. This time, there are enough cmdlets available. Explore them with Get-Command, as follows:

   ```
   Get-Command -Noun Gke*
   ```

2. Start with the configuration of the individual cluster nodes that will be deployed, as shown in the following example:

   ```
   $nodeParameter = @{
       DiskSizeGb = 10
       MachineType = 'g1-small'
       ImageType = 'COS'
   }
   $nodeConfig = New-GkeNodeConfig @nodeParameter
   ```

3. Your Kubernetes pods are deployed in a node pool. Try it now, using the node configuration created earlier, as shown in the following example:

   ```
   $poolParameter = @{
       NodePoolName = 'kube001pool'
       NodeConfig = $nodeConfig
       MaximumNodesToScaleTo = 2
       MininumNodesToScaleTo = 1
       InitialNodeCount = 1
       EnableAutoUpgrade = $true
   }
   $nodePool = New-GkeNodePool @poolParameter
   ```

4. With a node pool configured, you can deploy your Kubernetes cluster, as follows:

   ```
   $clusterParameter = @{
       ClusterName = 'kube001'
       Description = 'Kubernetes cluster DEV'
       NodePool = $nodePool
       Region = 'europe-west3'
       Zone = 'europe-west3-a'
   }
   $cluster = Add-GkeCluster @clusterParameter
   ```

5. To make use of your cluster, you still need to instruct Kubernetes to run a container image. First of all, get the authentication information for Kubernetes, as follows:

```
gcloud.cmd container clusters get-credentials kube001
```

6. Now, you can run the container! Try it now, in the following way:

```
$project = Get-GcpProject -Name testproject
$imageName = 'eu.gcr.io/{0}/luckynumber:v1' -f $project.ProjectId
$clusterName = 'gke_{0}_{1}_{2}' -f $project.ProjectId,
$cluster.Locations[0], $cluster.Name

kubectl.exe run numbergenerator --image $imageName --cluster
$clusterName --port 8080
```

 If you don't have access to the kubectl command, please run: gcloud.cmd components install kubectl.

7. Your cluster was configured with a public endpoint. Since kubectl received the port parameter, your port 8080 should again be accessible, as shown in the following example:

```
Invoke-RestMethod -Uri
http://$($cluster.Endpoint):8080/containerizedapi -Method Get
```

How it works...

The node pool you deployed in this recipe is used to control the number of instances, or pods, that are deployed in your Kubernetes cluster. Each node uses a node configuration that you created in *Step 2*.

This recipe is, again, twofold. You do not only use PowerShell Core to create the resources, but also another command-line tool, kubectl, to manage the Kubernetes cluster itself.

There's more...

If you want to get started with Kubernetes, either on Azure or the Google Cloud, you need to get familiar with Kubernetes first. The documentation at https://kubernetes.io/ is great to do just that.

SQL on Azure

The Azure Cloud offers many different database management systems and database types, such as MariaDB, PostgreSQL, Cosmos DB, and Azure Tables. This recipe will show you how to create a simple managed MS SQL database on an SQL server instance.

Getting ready

Install and start PowerShell Core.

How to do it...

1. To get started with a database deployment, we still need a server. This server is a managed SQL server that is provided as a PaaS offering, as shown in the following example:

```
New-AzResourceGroup -Name SqlDatabases -Location westeurope

$adminCredential = Get-Credential -UserName sqlgrandmaster
$name = -join (1..12 | ForEach-Object { Get-Random -Min 0 -Max 9 })
New-AzSqlServer -ResourceGroupName SqlDatabases -ServerName $name -
SqlAdministratorCredentials $adminCredential -Location westeurope
```

2. If you want to be able to actually connect remotely to your SQL PaaS instance, you need to create the appropriate firewall rules to allow your Azure Virtual Networks or your own public IP, as shown in the following example:

```
$param = @{
    ResourceGroupName = 'SqlDatabases'
    ServerName = $name
    FirewallRuleName = "AllowedIPs"
    StartIpAddress = Get-PublicIpAddress
    EndIpAddress = Get-PublicIpAddress
}
$serverFirewallRule = New-AzSqlServerFirewallRule @param
```

3. Create a new, empty database now, as follows:

```
New-AzSqlDatabase -DatabaseName db01 -ServerName $name -
ResourceGroupName SqlDatabases
```

4. Often, you would rather migrate an existing database. To do this, you can import existing databases from Azure Blob storage as well. Prepare a storage blob now, as per the following example:

```
Invoke-WebRequest -Uri
"https://github.com/Microsoft/sql-server-samples/releases/download/
wide-world-importers-v1.0/WideWorldImporters-Standard.bacpac" -Out
wwi.bacpac

$storageAccountName = -join (1..10 | ForEach-Object { Get-Random -
min 0 -max 9 })
$account = New-AzStorageAccount -Name $storageAccountName -
ResourceGroupName SqlDatabases -SkuName Standard_LRS -Location
westeurope
$container = New-AzStorageContainer -Name bacpacs -Context
$account.Context
$content = Set-AzStorageBlobContent -File .\wwi.bacpac -
CloudBlobContainer $container.CloudBlobContainer -Blob 'wwi.bacpac'
-Context $account.Context -Force
```

5. Now you can use the `Import-AzSqlDatabase` cmdlet with your BACPAC file to create a new database, as shown in the following example:

```
$importParam = @{
    ResourceGroupName = "SqlDatabases"
    ServerName = $name
    DatabaseName = "db02"
    DatabaseMaxSizeBytes = 1GB
    StorageKeyType = "StorageAccessKey"
    StorageKey = ($account | Get-AzStorageAccountKey)[0].Value
    StorageUri = $content.ICloudBlob.StorageUri.PrimaryUri
    Edition = "Standard"
    ServiceObjectiveName = "S3"
    AdministratorLogin = $adminCredential.UserName
    AdministratorLoginPassword = $adminCredential.Password
}

$import = New-AzSqlDatabaseImport @importParam
```

6. The import of this particular database takes three to five minutes. You can wait for an import to finish by executing the `Get-AzSqlDatabaseImportExportStatus` cmdlet:

```
while ((Get-AzSqlDatabaseImportExportStatus -OperationStatusLink
$import.OperationStatusLink).Status -eq 'InProgress')
{
    Start-Sleep -Seconds 5
```

```
Write-Host . -NoNewLine
}
```

7. To test whether it worked, you can execute the little Pester test by executing lines 63 – 81. It should look like the following screenshot:

```
Describing Did it work?
  [+] Should not throw 1.16s
  [+] Should have 73595 orders 221ms
```

8. Explore the other features of a PaaS SQL instance now as well! There is, for example, a built-in security assessment that makes use of Advanced Threat Protection, as shown in the following example:

```
Enable-AzSqlServerAdvancedThreatProtection -ServerName $name -
ResourceGroupName SqlDatabases
$container = New-AzStorageContainer -Name vulscan -Context
$account.Context
Update-AzSqlDatabaseVulnerabilityAssessmentSettings -ServerName
$name -DatabaseName db02 -StorageAccountName
$account.StorageAccountName -ScanResultsContainerName vulscan -
ResourceGroupName SqlDatabases
Start-AzSqlDatabaseVulnerabilityAssessmentScan -ServerName $name -
DatabaseName db02 -ResourceGroupName SqlDatabases
```

How it works...

Azure usually provides databases and DBMS as **Platform as a Service (PaaS)** offerings, which means that the entire management is done by Microsoft and the fully configured SQL instance is provided to you, the user.

If you don't need the overhead of managing your own instance, this is a great service. While you, of course, will not be able to manage every little configuration item, these PaaS offerings are often sufficient.

This recipe enabled you to create your very own PaaS SQL instance and deploy an empty database. You also deployed a database from a BACPAC file containing the backup of an entire database.

SQL on Google Cloud

Like Azure, Google offers different database services such as Spanner or MariaDB as PaaS services. In this recipe, we will use the classic SQL instances which, on Google Cloud, are running MariaDB. You will see how to create a new instance and import a database dump.

Getting ready

Install and start PowerShell Core.

How to do it...

Let's perform the following steps:

1. Discover the relevant cmdlets first, as shown in the following code:

```
Get-Command -Noun GcSql*
```

2. To get started, configure the desired settings for your PaaS instance, as shown in the following example:

```
$project = Get-GcpProject -Name testproject
$param = @{
    MaintenanceWindowDay = 7
    MaintenanceWindowHour = 22
    DataDiskSizeGb = 10
    TierConfig = 'db-n1-highmem-32'
    IpConfigIpv4Enabled = $true
}
$settings = New-GcSqlSettingConfig @param
```

3. From this, you can create the instance configuration, as follows:

```
$sql = New-GcSqlInstanceConfig -Project $project -Name mysql01 -
DatabaseVer 'MYSQL_5_7' -SettingConfig $settings
```

4. With both settings configured, it is time to deploy the instance itself, as follows:

```
$sqlInstance = Add-GcSqlInstance -InstanceConfig $sql
```

5. To import an existing database, you can simply use the `Import-GcSqlInstance` cmdlet with either an SQL script or a CSV file. Create a database first from the portal, as shown by the following screenshot:

6. Then, import the database, as shown in the following code:

```
Invoke-WebRequest -Method Get -Uri
"https://raw.githubusercontent.com/datacharmer/test_db/master/emplo
yees.sql" -OutFile employees.sql
$c = Get-Content .\employees.sql | Select -First 111
$c | Set-Content .\employees.sql
Import-GcSqlInstance -Instance mysql01 -ImportFilePath
.\employees.sql -Database employees
```

7. To fill the database, you can also import individual dumps. Try it now with the `departments` table, as follows:

```
Invoke-WebRequest -Method Get -Uri
"https://raw.githubusercontent.com/datacharmer/test_db/master/load_
departments.dump" -OutFile departments.dump
Import-GcSqlInstance -Instance mysql01 -ImportFilePath
.\departments.dump -Database employees
```

8. While you can retrieve the public IP of your instance with PowerShell, you need to visit the portal for the rest. Try generating the connection string now, as follows:

```
$sqlInstance = Get-GcSqlInstance -Name mysql01
$connectionString = 'Server=myServerAddress;Database=tidy-
shard-235718:us-central1:mysql01;Uid=root;Pwd=<USE YOUR OWN>;' -f
$sqlInstance.IpAddresses[0].IpAddress
```

And visit `https://console.cloud.google.com` to manage your authentication methods, as shown by the following screenshot:

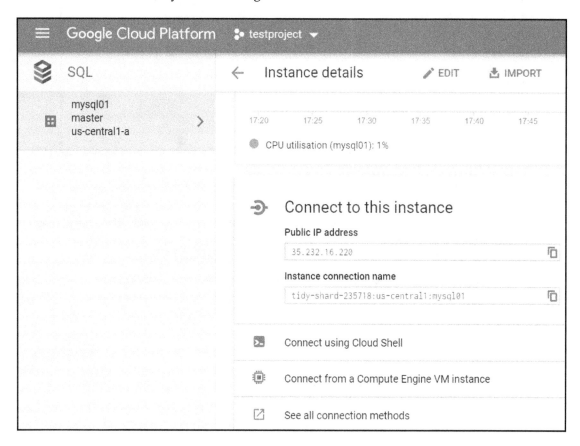

How it works...

In this recipe, you have used the GcSql cmdlets to provision a MariaDB PaaS instance. As you might have noticed in *Step 2*, you can configure important settings such as the maintenance window for the instance and the tier. Other settings, such as credentials to connect with, can only be configured within the Google Cloud Console.

MariaDB on Google Cloud can, of course, also deal with imports in the format specific to MariaDB: SQL scripts, dumps, and CSV files!

Accessing Web Services

11

This chapter will introduce you to RESTful services in a couple of different ways. From automating Azure DevOps to executing Azure automation runbooks, you will explore RESTful **Application Programming Interfaces** (**APIs**) and even provide your own.

This chapter will cover the following recipes:

- Exploring RESTful services
- Accessing Azure DevOps via REST
- Creating new Azure resource groups via REST
- Calling Azure runbooks via webhooks
- Providing a RESTful web service through PowerShell
- Creating a new team project in Azure DevOps
- Creating a new build definition in Azure DevOps

Technical requirements

This chapter's code can be found in this book's GitHub repository at `https://github.com/PacktPublishing/Powershell-Core-6.2-Cookbook/tree/master/Chapter11`.

Exploring REST services

RESTful services are everywhere and have been for some years now. PowerShell puts you in a unique position with its capabilities. Not only can you read data from services, you can also publish and delete data easily and with confidence. This first recipe shows you the most important REST methods that you can use with `Invoke-RestMethod`.

Getting ready

Install and start PowerShell Core.

How to do it...

Perform the following steps:

1. `Invoke-RestMethod` is used to access different endpoints of an API with different methods. Try the GET method first:

```
# The Invoke-RestMethod cmdlet should be your standard cmdlet to
interact with web services
$baseuri = 'https://jsonplaceholder.typicode.com'
# To read data from an API endpoint, use the GET method
Invoke-RestMethod -Method Get -Uri "$baseuri/posts"
```

2. Through routes, you can access different elements from your RESTful endpoint:

```
# There might be additional routes, like requesting a specific item
Invoke-RestMethod -Method Get -Uri "$baseuri/posts/42"

# Here, a resource has other resources linked to it. A post has
comments, for example
Invoke-RestMethod -Method Get -Uri "$baseuri/posts/42/comments"
```

3. Often, you can pass query parameters directly into the URL of your request instead of or in addition to the body:

```
Invoke-RestMethod -Method Get -Uri "$baseuri/posts?userId=3"
```

4. To create new items, the POST method should be used. Try to create a new object in the API tester:

```
$jsonBody = @{
    title = 'PowerShell rocks'
    body = 'It really does.'
    userId = 7
} | ConvertTo-Json

Invoke-RestMethod -Method Post -Uri "$baseuri/posts" -Body
$jsonBody -ContentType application/json
```

5. The PUT and PATCH methods can be used to update existing elements:

```
$jsonBody = @{
    id = 1
    title = 'PowerShell rocks'
    body = 'It really does.'
    userId = 7
} | ConvertTo-Json

Invoke-RestMethod -Method Put -Uri "$baseuri/posts/1" -Body
$jsonBody -ContentType application/json

Invoke-RestMethod -Method Patch -Uri "$baseuri/posts/1" -Body
$jsonBody -ContentType application/json
```

6. And of course, the DELETE method will get rid of an object:

```
Invoke-RestMethod -Method Delete -Uri "$baseuri/posts/42"
```

How it works...

Many, if not all, web services implement the same methods: **Create, Read, Update, and Delete** (**CRUD**). The GET method is often used to not only retrieve single elements but also all elements of a specific type, for example, all of the Azure DevOps projects of a single organization.

This recipe had you use GET (Read), POST (Create), PUT/PATCH (Update), and DELETE (Delete). Regardless of the RESTful API, these methods should stay the same. In the following recipes, you will explore different services and their implementations.

Accessing Azure DevOps via REST

Azure DevOps and Azure DevOps Server are Microsoft's cloud and on-premises solutions for hosting code projects and source code repositories and for providing build and release pipelines, as well as package feeds.

Automating the configuration of Azure DevOps is usually not that complicated, mainly due to a well-documented API. However, certain tasks are unnecessarily complicated. In this recipe, you will do some very simple tasks to explore Azure DevOps from PowerShell.

Getting ready

Install and start PowerShell Core. Register for a new account at `https://dev.azure.com` (it's free) if you don't have one already.

How to do it...

Perform the following steps:

1. To prepare for PowerShell, browse to `https://dev.azure.com`, log in, and navigate to your **Security** settings:

2. From there, create a new personal access token so that you can access the API without going through the OAuth2 authorization process:

3. Copy your personal access token! You will never see it again.

4. In this recipe, we are using basic authentication with the access token instead of a Bearer token, which is a bit harder to come by. Fill in your API key and generate the token:

```
$accessTokenString = 'YOUR TOKEN!'

# We are crafting an authorization header that bears your token
$tokenString =
[Convert]::ToBase64String([Text.Encoding]::ASCII.GetBytes(("{0}:{1}
" -f '', $accessTokenString)))
$authHeader = ("Basic {0}" -f $tokenString)
```

5. To get a list of your organization projects, you can use the "Projects" API:

```
$baseuri = 'https://dev.azure.com/<YOURUSERNAME!>'
$headers = @{ Authorization = $authHeader }

$projects = Invoke-RestMethod -Method Get -Uri
"$baseuri/_apis/projects" -UseBasicParsing -Headers $headers
$projects.value
```

6. `Invoke-RestMethod` automatically attempts to give you objects. This means that you can immediately work with them like you would with any other PowerShell object:

```
$projects.value | Format-Table Name, Visibility, State
```

7. If you already have a specific project, you can retrieve it through another route that is part of the Projects API:

```
Invoke-RestMethod -Method Get -Uri
"$baseuri/_apis/projects/PowerShellCookBook?api-version=5.0" -
UseBasicParsing -Headers $headers
```

8. Try retrieving the Git repository of a project next so that you can clone it:

```
$repo = (Invoke-RestMethod -Method Get -Uri
"$baseuri/PowerShellCookBook/_apis/git/repositories?api-
version=5.0" -UseBasicParsing -Headers $headers).value

# Test it ;)
New-Item -ItemType File -Path .\newrepo\README.md -Value 'Here be
dragons.' -Force
Set-Location -Path .\newrepo
git init
git remote add origin $repo.remoteurl
git add .
git commit -m 'initial commit'
git push -u origin --all
```

How it works...

Azure DevOps (previously Team Foundation Server and Visual Studio Team Services) provides multiple API endpoints and services. The Projects API you used in this recipe belongs to the Core service. Also part of the Core service are Teams and Processes. These three components are at the core of your Azure DevOps experience.

In this recipe, you started by creating an access token. This token is required if you cannot use multi-factor authentication for your account, for example, because getting a Bearer token isn't easy. You used this personal access token with HTTP headers, more specifically with the Authorization header.

Next, you supplied the headers to `Invoke-RestMethod` to list your Azure DevOps resources, such as projects and repositories.

See also

- The entire API reference can be found at `https://docs.microsoft.com/en-us/rest/api/azure/devops/?view=azure-devops-rest-5.0`.

Creating new Azure resource groups via REST

While you would usually interact with Azure through the **Azure Resource Manager** (**ARM**) module, C#, Ruby, Python, or other languages, you can also do some platform-agnostic scripting against the RESTful API.

Getting ready

Install and start PowerShell Core.

How to do it...

Perform the following steps:

1. To get an authentication token, there are some great functions that we don't have to recreate. Using the code from `https://gallery.technet.microsoft.com/scriptcenter/Easily-obtain-AccessToken-3ba6e593`, in its code repository, you can get authenticated:

```
$subscriptionId = (Get-AzContext).Subscription.Id
$baseUrl = "https://management.azure.com/subscriptions"
$headers = @{
    Authorization = Get-AzBearerToken
}
```

2. With the request header prepared, you can begin by listing all existing resource groups in your subscription:

```
(Invoke-RestMethod -Method Get -Uri
"$baseurl/$subscriptionId/resourcegroups?api-version=2018-05-01" -
Headers $headers).value
```

3. To add a new resource group, we will use both the request body as well as query parameters in the URI. Begin by crafting the JSON body:

```
$rgJson = @{
    location = 'westeurope'
    tags = @{
        PowerShell = 'IsAwesome'
    }
} | ConvertTo-Json

$resourceGroupName = 'PowerShellCookBook'
```

4. The JSON body can be passed to `Invoke-RestMethod` by specifying the correct content type, which is `application/json`, in this case:

```
Invoke-RestMethod -Method Put -Uri
"$baseurl/$subscriptionId/resourcegroups/$($resourceGroupName)?api-
version=2018-05-01" -Headers $headers -Body $rgJson -ContentType
application/json
```

5. By modifying the query parameters in the URI, you can directly retrieve your new resource, which in this case is a resource group:

```
Invoke-RestMethod -Method Get -Uri
"$baseurl/$subscriptionId/resourcegroups/$($resourceGroupName)?api-
version=2018-05-01" -Headers $headers
```

6. To clean up, you can use the DELETE method with the same URI. We do not need a request body:

```
Invoke-RestMethod -Method Delete -Uri
"$baseurl/$subscriptionId/resourcegroups/$($resourceGroupName)?api-
version=2018-05-01" -Headers $headers
```

How it works...

RESTful APIs provide uniform access to data, regardless of the underlying infrastructure. In PowerShell Core, `Invoke-RestMethod` is the single cmdlet you need to access them all. With Azure in particular, all resources inside your subscription can easily be accessed by providing the subscription ID and the resource API endpoint in the URL.

This recipe showed you how you can interact with Azure through the RESTful API. Explore other endpoints so that you can do things such as list all storage accounts in your subscription. You used the JSON body, as well as query parameters that are denoted by appending `?<ParameterName>=<ParameterValue>&<ParameterName2>=<Parameter2Value>` to an existing URI. The ampersand character separates individual parameters.

Calling Azure runbooks via webhooks

Azure runbooks are a great asset for your automation account. They can be scheduled like jobs and are used to automate all kinds of operations that are related to your Azure infrastructure or even your on-premises workloads.

Not only can runbooks be executed from within the portal or using PowerShell. You can also create so-called webhooks for runbooks. These are essentially little API endpoints that are used to run your runbook with parameters from anywhere and by anyone with the correct URI.

Getting ready

Install and start PowerShell Core.

How to do it...

Perform the following steps:

1. Let's create an automation account using the following commands:

```
New-AzResourceGroup -Name PowerShellCookBook -Location westeurope
New-AzAutomationAccount -ResourceGroupName PowerShellCookBook -Name
psautomate -Location westeurope -Plan Basic
```

2. Execute the following code:

```
param
(
    [object]
    $WebHookData # This parameter will later be used...
)
```

3. Next, type in the following code:

```
Write-Verbose $($WebhookData.RequestBody | ConvertFrom-Json | Out-
String)
```

4. Now, execute the following command:

```
Get-Process -Id $pid
```

5. Execute the following command:

```
$code.ToSTring() | Set-Content .\runbook.ps1

# Lastly, import the runbook
Import-AzAutomationRunbook -Path .\runbook.ps1 -Description
'Outputs request body' -Name RunLolaRun -AutomationAccountName
psautomate -ResourceGroupName PowerShellCookBook -Type PowerShell
```

6. Execute the following command:

```
Publish-AzAutomationRunbook -Name RunLolaRun -AutomationAccountName
psautomate -ResourceGroupName PowerShellCookBook
```

7. Now, type and execute the following command:

```
$parameters = @{
    Name = 'thehook'
    RunbookName = 'RunLolaRun'
    IsEnabled = $true
    ExpiryTime = [System.DateTimeOffset]::new((Get-
Date).AddMonths(1))
    AutomationAccountName = 'psautomate'
    ResourceGroupName = 'PowerShellCookBook'
}

$captainHook = New-AzAutomationWebhook @parameters
```

8. Have a look at the following command:

```
$captainHook.WebhookURI
```

9. Execute the following command:

```
$body = @{
    RunbookParam1 = 'Hello!'
    RunbookParam2 = 'All parameters will be there...'
} | ConvertTo-Json

# This will give you a job id back
```

```
$result = Invoke-RestMethod -Uri $captainHook.WebhookURI -Method
Post -Body $body -ContentType application/json
```

10. Execute the following command:

```
Get-AzAutomationJob -id $result.JobIds[0] -AutomationAccountName
psautomate -ResourceGroupName PowerShellCookBook
```

11. By executing the following command, you will retrieve the output of the runbook:

```
$jobOutput = Get-AzAutomationJobOutput -Id $result.JobIds[0] -
AutomationAccountName psautomate -ResourceGroupName
PowerShellCookBook -Stream Output |
    Get-AzAutomationJobOutputRecord

$jobVerbose = Get-AzAutomationJobOutput -Id $result.JobIds[0] -
AutomationAccountName psautomate -ResourceGroupName
PowerShellCookBook -Stream Verbose |
Get-AzAutomationJobOutputRecord
```

How it works...

Runbooks are simple scripts that you can use in your automation account to trigger scripts on a schedule easily. Runbooks can use certificates, credentials, modules, and other common resources that are stored in your automation account to authenticate against Azure or other providers.

In this recipe, you saw how to create webhooks so that you can trigger your runbooks remotely. You started by creating an automation account. This account contains all of the different automation resources. Runbooks are a part of them. In *Steps 2 to 5*, you created the runbook using simple PowerShell code, saved it, and then uploaded it to your automation account. In *Step 6*, you published the runbook so that you could use it.

Step 7 had you create a webhook for the runbook and *Step 8* showed you the result—your private webhook URI that you need to keep safe. Webhooks are used to trigger runbooks via browsing to a URL. In *Step 9*, you used `Invoke-RestMethod` to execute the runbook via its webhook.

While *Step 10* showed you how to wait for a runbook to finish, *Step 11* is more relevant in production environments. In *Step 11*, you retrieved the output of the runbook and saw how to retrieve other streams as well, such as verbose.

Providing a RESTful web service through PowerShell

PowerShell Core can also be used to host your own RESTful API. This might be a popular choice if you want to convey a status or have an interface to retrieve data that you would otherwise either need permissions for or for which you would configure **Just Enough Administration** (JEA).

This recipe shows you how to create your own endpoint to retrieve event log entries.

Getting ready

Install and start PowerShell Core.

How to do it...

Perform the following steps:

1. Execute the following commands:

```
# Begin by installing the module
Install-Module -Name Polaris -Scope CurrentUser

# Examine the module
Get-Command -Module Polaris
```

2. Execute from the source code:

```
New-PolarisGetRoute -Path "/events" -Scriptblock {
...
} -Force
```

3. Examine the source code:

```
$logName = $request.Query["LogName"]
    if ($request.Body -and $request.Body["LogName"]) { $logName =
$request.Body["LogName"]}

    $parameters = @{
        LogName = $logName
    }
```

4. Continue examining the code:

```
if ($request.Body -and $request.Body['FilterXPath'])
{
    $parameters['FilterXPath'] = $request.Body['FilterXPath']
}
```

5. Continue the examination:

```
$eventEntries = Get-WinEvent @parameters | Select-Object -Property
LogName, ProviderName, Id, Message, @{Name = 'XmlMessage';
Expression = {$_.ToXml()}}
    $Response.Send(($eventEntries | ConvertTo-Json));
```

6. Execute the following command:

```
Start-Polaris
```

7. Execute the following command:

```
$restParameters = @{
    Method = 'Get'
    Uri = 'http://localhost:8080/events?LogName=System&MaxEvents=1'
}

$eventEntry = Invoke-Restmethod @restParameters
```

8. Execute the following command:

```
([xml]$eventEntry.XmlMessage).Event.EventData.Data
```

9. Execute the following command:

```
$restParameters.Body = @{
    FilterXPath = '*[System[EventID=6005 or EventID=6006]]'
    MaxEvents = 10
} | ConvertTo-Json

$restParameters.ContentType = 'Application/Json'
$eventEntry = Invoke-Restmethod @restParameters
```

How it works...

You began by installing the great Polaris module from the PowerShell gallery and examining its contents.

In *Step 2*, you experienced that RESTful APIs usually define different routes to get to information. You can do this with Polaris for different verbs like GET, POST, PUT, PATCH, or DELETE. You started with a new get route that will later point to `http://localhost/events`.

In *Step 3*, you looked at the route's script block, examining the request. The event log name can be sent in the query or in the request body, as you can see in the code. In *Step 4*, you saw the automatic variable, `$request`, which contains the entirety of your request data. This allowed you to parse other values that we would like to see, such as the `FilterXPath` parameter, which should only be part of the body.

In *Step 5*, you saw that to get data back, the response needs to be converted into JSON. *Step 6* had you start the service. In *Step 7*, you executed `Invoke-RestMethod` to retrieve one single event. *Step 8* showed you how to retrieve the original Event XML that was sent in the JSON response to reconstruct your event as closely as possible. In *Step 9*, you used a different filter parameter, `FilterXPath`, and the maximum number of events.

There's more...

If you require more control, for example, authentication and authorization, take a look at the `New-PolarisMiddleware` cmdlet. This cmdlet effectively runs a script block for every incoming request and can be used to examine the user's token and other things.

See also

- Check out the source code of Polaris at `https://github.com/powershell/polaris`.

Creating a new team project in Azure DevOps

Azure DevOps has an excellent RESTful API that is very well-documented. One of the tasks that you would probably rather automate is the creation of new team projects with source control.

In this recipe, you will use the Projects API endpoint and your personal access token to create, update, and delete team projects.

Getting ready

Install and start PowerShell Core. Refer to the second recipe in this chapter, *Accessing Azure DevOps via REST*, in regards to the creation of a personal access token.

How to do it...

Perform the following steps:

1. Execute the following command to list all process templates:

```
$templates = (Invoke-RestMethod -Method Get -Uri
"$baseuri/_apis/process/processes?api-version=5.0" -UseBasicParsing
-Headers $headers).value
$templates | Format-Table Name, ID
```

2. Next, execute the following command in order to create the request body:

```
$jsonBody = @{
    name = "PowerShellCookBook"
    description = "The cook book repository!"
    capabilities = @{
        versioncontrol = @{
            sourceControlType = "Git"
        }
        processTemplate = @{
            templateTypeId = $templates | Where Name -eq Agile |
Select -Expand id
        }
    }
} | ConvertTo-Json
```

3. Now, execute the next command to create the new team project:

```
$response = Invoke-RestMethod -Method Post -Uri
"$baseuri/_apis/projects?api-version=5.0" -UseBasicParsing -Headers
$headers -Body $jsonBody -ContentType application/json
```

4. Try the following command next to wait for the project to get successfully created:

```
$projectIsCreating = (Invoke-RestMethod -Uri $response.Url -Headers
$headers -UseBasicParsing -Method Get).Status -ne 'succeeded'

# Wait a little for the project to get created
while ($projectIsCreating)
{
    Start-Sleep -Milliseconds 250
    $projectIsCreating = (Invoke-RestMethod -Uri $response.Url -
Headers $headers -UseBasicParsing -Method Get).Status -ne
'succeeded'
}
```

5. Execute the following command to retrieve the created project:

```
Invoke-RestMethod -Method Get -Uri
"$baseuri/_apis/projects/PowerShellCookBook?api-version=5.0" -
UseBasicParsing -Headers $headers
```

6. To get the repository URL, use the next command:

```
$repo = (Invoke-RestMethod -Method Get -Uri
"$baseuri/PowerShellCookBook/_apis/git/repositories?api-
version=5.0" -UseBasicParsing -Headers $headers).value
```

7. Lastly, use the dynamically retrieved repository URL to push code to the repository:

```
New-Item -ItemType File -Path .\newrepo\README.md -Value 'Here be
dragons.' -Force
Set-Location -Path .\newrepo
git init
git remote add origin $repo.remoteurl
git add .
git commit -m 'initial commit'
git push -u origin --all
```

How it works...

Azure DevOps has published many different API endpoints. The projects and repositories APIs are just two of them. You used both in this recipe to automate interactions with Azure DevOps. In an environment with multiple developers and the need to spin up new projects, this is an invaluable skill.

You could imagine using this in a generator context, where an entire demo project is created for you automatically. This is incidentally what Microsoft has already done with the project available at: `https://azuredevopsdemogenerator.azurewebsites.net`.

Using REST is something that you as an administrator should look into, even if development is not your strong point. RESTful APIs can be consumed on virtually any system in many different languages. Whether you are using PowerShell or Python is just a matter of choice and available tools, as long as you have mastered the basics.

In *Step 1*, you used the access token and header that you prepared in the second recipe of this chapter, *Accessing Azure DevOps via REST*. Before you deployed a team project, you retrieved a list of process templates (Agile and Scrum).

The process template reference is then used with your new project. Like many other APIs, this one also expects a well-formed request body that contains mandatory and optional parameters. You crafted the hashtable template in *Step 2*. This API requires that you add a query parameter—the API version. Since we are working with Azure DevOps and not VSTS, you used API version 5 in *Step 3*.

The project will not be created instantaneously. To wait for the project's status, in *Step 4*, you used the response URL from the previous step in the `while` loop. Then, you retrieved it directly with the GET method. You cloned your new repository in *Steps 6* and *7* and committed source code to it using Git.

Creating a new build definition in Azure DevOps

A new project will only get you so far. For many projects, whether it is a repository for **Desired State Configuration (DSC)** composite resources such as `https://github.com/automatedlab/dscworkshop` or a repository for module development such as `https://github.com/automatedlab.common`, you will require a build and release process.

This is commonly referred to as a CI/CD pipeline. **CI** is short for **Continuous Integration** and **CD** is short for either **Continuous Delivery** or **Continuous Deployment**. This recipe will enable you to automate the CI part: a build definition will kick off a new build (continuous integration) whenever a developer commits changes to code.

Getting ready

Install and start PowerShell Core. You will need to have completed the previous recipe to be able to complete this one.

How to do it...

Perform the following steps:

1. Start with the project you created in the previous recipe and store a reference to it in a variable:

```
$project = Invoke-RestMethod -Method Get -Uri
"$baseuri/_apis/projects/PowerShellCookBook?api-version=5.0" -
UseBasicParsing -Headers $headers
```

2. For a build to make sense, you should normally create some build artifacts that are going to flow down to your release pipeline. You should also include test cases if possible. We will start by cloning the repository:

```
$repo = (Invoke-RestMethod -Method Get -Uri
"$baseuri/PowerShellCookBook/_apis/git/repositories?api-
version=5.0" -UseBasicParsing -Headers $headers).value
git clone $repo.remoteurl BookRepo
cd ./BookRepo
```

3. Next, we will create the test file with `Pester`. See that last line? Execute the `Invoke` method of your script block to execute the tests as they are. Two will pass and one will fail:

```
$tests = {
    Describe 'A test suite' {
        It 'Should have meaningful tests' {
            42 | Should -Be 42
        }

        It 'should cover all code paths but not add unnecessary
tests' {
```

```
                {throw "whyyy"} | Should -Throw -Because 'Some tests
actually test the worst case as well'
            }

            It 'Might have failing tests' {
                0 | Should -Be 1
            }
        }
    }
$tests.Invoke()
```

4. Store the script block's contents in a `*.tests.ps1` file. Pester will automatically pick up these files later and execute all of the tests in them:

```
New-Item -ItemType Directory -Path ./Tests/Unit -Force
$tests.ToString() | Set-Content .\Tests\Unit\simpletest.tests.ps1
```

5. Try it out with the following command:

```
Invoke-Pester -Script .\Tests
```

6. Next, we will create a script that is used to generate your build artifacts. In this case, it is a DSC document, which as an artifact produces a **Managed Object Format** (**MOF**) file:

```
$artifactGenerator = {
    configuration PipelineConfig
    {
        File foo
        {
            DestinationPath = 'C:\foo'
            Type = 'File'
            Contents = 'Greetings from the Pipeline!'
        }
    }
}
$artifactGenerator.ToString() | Set-Content Config.ps1
```

7. To bring both tests and artifact generation together, most developers use a build script. There are plenty of great examples out there. Just look out for a file called `Build.ps1` in any Git repository. Execute the following command:

```
$buildscript = {
    ...
    $results = Invoke-Pester .\Tests -PassThru -OutputFile
TestResults.xml -OutputFormat NUnitXml
    ...
    . .\Config.ps1
```

```
        PipelineConfig -OutputPath .\BuildOutput
}
$buildscript.ToString() | Set-Content Build.ps1
```

8. Now, you need to commit and push your changes so that they are part of your repository:

```
git add .
git commit -m "added test and build script"
git push
```

9. The next steps will be a bit complicated. To create a build, we need to assemble a number of build steps. This could go as follows: run a script, publish the test results, and compile a solution. First, get all of the build steps by using the API call:

```
$buildStepResult = Invoke-RestMethod -Method Get -Uri
"$baseuri/_apis/distributedtask/tasks" -Headers $headers -
UseBasicParsing
$buildSteps = ($buildStepResult | ConvertFrom-Json -
AsHashtable).value
```

10. We just need three out of many build steps. You can filter the result with Where-Object and use Group-Object to drill down:

```
$groupedSteps = $buildSteps | Where-Object {
    $_.friendlyName -in 'PowerShell', 'Publish Test Results',
'Publish Build Artifacts' -and `
        $_.visibility -contains 'build' -and $_.runsOn -contains
'Agent'
} | Group-Object friendlyName -AsHashTable
```

11. In our build definition, we need the ID as a reference, as well as the inputs values. A PowerShell script, for instance, has different input fields compared to a publishing step:

```
# Using ID and Inputs of your steps, generate the build definition
$groupedSteps.PowerShell[0].id
$groupedSteps.PowerShell[0].inputs.name

$groupedSteps.'Publish Test Results'[0].id
$groupedSteps.'Publish Test Results'[0].inputs.name

$groupedSteps.'Publish Build Artifacts'[0].id
$groupedSteps.'Publish Build Artifacts'[0].inputs.name
```

12. Refer to the lengthy code in the book's code repository to see the entire build definition. This is a huge hashtable that we need as the JSON input for our next `Invoke-RestMethod` call:

```
$buildDefinition = @{
    name = 'CI Build'
    type = "build"
    quality = "definition"
    queue = @{}
    process = @{}
    repository = @{}
    triggers = @{}
    options = @()
    variables = @{}
} | ConvertTo-Json -Depth 42

Invoke-RestMethod -Method Post -Uri
"$baseuri/PowerShellCookBook/_apis/build/definitions?api-
version=5.0" -Body $buildDefinition -ContentType application/json -
Headers $headers
```

13. Once that call is done, you can initiate an automatic build by committing changes to the code. You could, for example, correct the failing test so that it is green:

```
(Get-Content .\Tests\Unit\simpletest.tests.ps1) -replace '0 \|
Should -Be 1', '0 | Should -Be 0' | Set-Content
.\Tests\Unit\simpletest.tests.ps1
git add .
git commit -m "Tests are OK now!"
git push
```

How it works...

This recipe had you create your build pipeline step by step. While this can also be done in the UI, and nowadays even with YAML templates, a solid automation solution is never a bad idea. Again, this is well-suited for an automated deployment.

All functionality is very well-documented in the publicly available API documentation. But as you can see in *Steps 10* to *12*, actually using the API can become highly complicated. We just added three very basic build steps. In practice, your build and release pipeline will look a lot more complicated.

If you have done everything in this recipe, you should be left with the following build result:

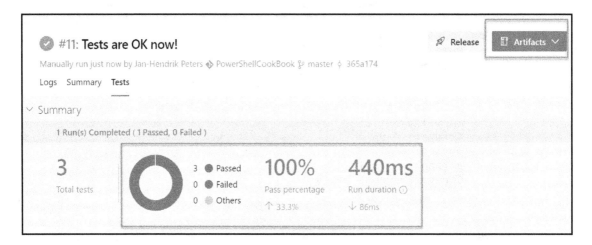

All of the test should now 100% pass and the artifacts will have been generated. Clicking on the **Artifacts** button will let you browse the artifact's drop location and download the artifacts. This enables you to do things such as look for an archive containing MOF files.

12
High-Performance Scripting

In this chapter, we will explore runspaces and parallel processing in order to be able to eke every last bit of performance out of their scripts. We will also explore the performance penalty when calling cmdlets versus .NET methods.

In this chapter, we will cover the following recipes:

- Parallelization with background jobs
- Efficiently querying the event log
- Comparing Where-Object and Where methods
- Using Active Directory cmdlets with performance in mind
- Parallelization through RunspacePools
- Exchanging variables with runspaces
- Large-scale I/O operations
- Hashtables, dictionaries, and performance

Technical requirements

This chapter requires you to deploy the lab environment that is part of this book. As an alternative, you can adapt the recipes to your own environment to improve the learning experience!

All code is available at `https://github.com/PacktPublishing/Powershell-Core-6.2-Cookbook/tree/master/Chapter12`.

Parallelization with background jobs

The term parallelization does not strictly apply to background jobs. However, jobs are a great way in PowerShell Core to run multiple operations more or less in parallel in the background.

This recipe teaches you how to use jobs and how the & operator works.

Getting ready

Install and start PowerShell Core.

How to do it...

Let's perform the following steps:

1. Discover the existing job cmdlets first:

   ```
   Get-Command -Noun Job
   ```

2. Then start a new job that lists running processes:

   ```
   Start-Job -Name MyJob -ScriptBlock { Get-Process }
   ```

3. Execute the following command to retrieve the job:

   ```
   Get-Job -Name MyJob
   ```

4. Try the following command next to receive the job's result:

   ```
   Get-Job -Name myJob | Receive-Job -Keep
   ```

5. Next, try to receive the results while removing the job at the same time:

   ```
   Get-Job -Name MyJob | Receive-Job -AutoRemoveJob -Wait
   Get-Job -Name myJob # Error
   ```

6. Add to your script in the following way:

   ```
   $throttleLimit = 10
   $collection = 1..100
   ```

7. Add a loop to your script like this:

```
foreach ($item in $collection)
{

}
```

8. Inside the loop, execute the following command:

```
$doneCount = (Get-Job -Name Queue* | Where-Object State -in
@("Completed", "Failed")).Count
$progress = ($doneCount / $collection.Count) * 100
Write-Progress -Activity 'Doing things' -Status "Working" -
CurrentOperation "($($DoneCount)/$($collection.Count))" -Id 1 -
PercentComplete $progress
```

9. Execute the following command to list all running jobs that match the name Queue*:

```
$running = @(Get-Job -Name Queue* | Where-Object { $_.State -eq
'Running' })
```

10. Try the following command now to wait for any job in order to create a queue:

```
if ($running.Count -ge $throttleLimit)
{
    $running | Wait-Job -Any | Out-Null
}
$null = Start-Job -Name "Queue$item" -ScriptBlock {Start-Sleep -
Seconds 1}
```

11. Execute the following command to wait for all remaining jobs:

```
Get-Job -Name Queue* | Wait-Job
```

12. As a new PowerShell Core feature, try the next command:

```
$job = Start-Sleep -Seconds 30 &
$job | Wait-Job
```

How it works...

In this recipe, you worked with background jobs. The job queuing mechanism, in particular, is a bit that I like to use from time to time. By creating a loop around your collection to be processed, and adding the `if` statement, you have effectively built the queue. Using the `Any` parameter of the `Wait-Job` cmdlet is very efficient here, as it simply waits for any job to finish so that the next can be queued.

Step 1 enabled you to start by listing all job-related cmdlets with `Get-Command`. In *Step 2*, you started a new job to retrieve a list of processes in the background. To retrieve only your own job, you used `Get-Job` and the `Name` parameter in *Step 3*. In *Step 4*, you used `Receive-Job` to retrieve the generated data.

If you do not want to keep the results stored, you can also retrieve them directly. *Step 5* showed you how to get all results and immediately remove the job. In *Steps 6 to 11*, you used the `Job` cmdlets to build a queuing mechanism for your background jobs.

In *Step 12*, you saw the Unix-like fork operator, the ampersand, which is used for single cmdlets.

Efficiently querying the event log

Querying the event log is an activity that Windows administrators have to do from time to time. Whether it is a misbehaving application that logs its errors to the application log, or a critical kernel event, the event log has you covered.

As we use `Get-WinEvent` on PowerShell Core, this recipe will show you how to get the most performance out of it and still have manageable and readable code. We will use the security log as an example because this log tends to grow very large, very fast. You will use filters to find out whether and where, a specific user has logged on.

Getting ready

To get ready for this recipe, log on to the lab machine, `PACKT-FS-A`, with the user **contoso\elbarto** and the password **c0waBung4!** (0 means zero), which will generate the specific event we are looking for.

How to do it...

Let's perform the following steps:

1. Have a look at the `Get-WinEvent` cmdlet by just listing the newest 10 events:

   ```
   Get-WinEvent -LogName System -MaxEvents 10
   ```

2. We want to find a malicious user logon. Start by crafting your filter hashtable, as shown in the following example:

   ```
   $logOnEvents = Get-WinEvent -FilterHashtable @{

   }
   ```

3. Inside the hashtable curly braces, add the filter for the log name, as follows:

   ```
   LogName = 'Security'
   ```

4. Now we need to filter for ID `4624`. Add this filter now, as follows:

   ```
   ID = 4624
   ```

5. To lessen the load and speed up the cmdlet's processing time, add a start time filter, as follows:

   ```
   StartTime = (Get-Date).AddDays(-1)
   ```

6. Lastly, you can filter for individual event data fields by specifying them. Add filters for the username and domain name now, as per the following example:

   ```
   TargetUserName = 'elbarto'
   TargetDomainName = 'contoso.com'
   ```

7. To make use of the list of events, you can examine their XML structure and retrieve the other data fields, as shown in the following example:

   ```
   [xml]$xmlEvent = $logOnEvents[0].ToXml()
   $ip = ($xmlEvent.Event.EventData.Data | Where-Object Name -eq
   IpAddress).InnerText
   $hostName = [Net.Dns]::GetHostByAddress($ip).HostName

   Write-Host "The infamous El Barto tagged $hostname!"
   ```

8. Events can additionally be filtered with an XML expression. Refer to the event viewer's custom view for more details. Try running the next cmdlet, as follows:

```
$xmlFilter = @"
<QueryList>
  <Query Id="0" Path="Security">
    <Select Path="Security">*[System[EventID=4624] and
EventData[Data[@Name = "TargetUserName"] = "elbarto"]]</Select>
  </Query>
  <Query Id="1" Path="System">
    <Select Path="System">*[System[(EventID=6005 or EventID=6006)
and TimeCreated[timediff(@SystemTime) <= 86400000]]]</Select>
  </Query>
</QueryList>
"@

Get-WinEvent -FilterXml $xmlFilter
```

9. The XPath filter is a bit more friendly to type and can be extracted from a larger XML filter. Try just filtering for the 4624 event and the elbarto username with the FilterXPath parameter next, as per the following example:

```
$xpathFilter = '*[System[EventID=4624] and EventData[Data[@Name =
"TargetUserName"] = "elbarto"]]'
Get-WinEvent -FilterXPath $xpathFilter -LogName Security
```

10. You could even extract all XPath queries out of an XML filter and run each query individually. Try the following code sample to see it in action:

```
foreach ($query in ([xml]$xmlFilter).QueryList.ChildNodes)
{
    Write-Host -ForegroundColor Yellow "Querying $($query.Path)" -
NoNewline
    Get-WinEvent -FilterXPath $query.Select.InnerText -LogName
$query.Path
}
```

How it works...

This recipe showed you how to hunt for specific user logins using one of the FilterHashtable, FilterXPath, or FilterXml parameters of the Get-WinEvent cmdlet. You can choose your favorite parameter yourself, as all of them have very similar run times. I like the syntax and simplicity of FilterHashtable most, though.

You also saw, in this recipe, how to work with the events that have been retrieved. The object method, ToXml, is often invaluable because this method allows you to get the original event XML back and parse it however you like.

See also

- For more technical information on *XPATH Syntax*, see: https://msdn.microsoft.com/en-us/library/ms256471(v=vs.110).aspx

Comparing Where-Object and the Where method

This recipe shows you how to apply the Where method instead of Where-Object to get results more flexibly. You will see the benefits of Where as an extension method to lists of any kind. You have already seen Where-Object in Chapters 3 and 4, so we will not go into detail on how Where-Object works. Kindly review the *Running PowerShell Core* (Chapter 3, *Working with Objects*) and *Filtering data* (Chapter 4, *Mastering the Pipeline*) recipes if you are unsure about how Where-Object works.

Getting ready

Install and start PowerShell Core.

How to do it...

Let's perform the following steps:

1. Start by reading more on the Where method. Would you have found the following help topic yourself? Take a look:

   ```
   Get-Help about_arrays
   ```

2. Try using the Where method to filter for processes consuming more than 150 MB RAM, as shown in the following example:

   ```
   $filterScript = {$_.WorkingSet -gt 150MB}
   (Get-Process).Where($filterScript)
   ```

3. The `Where` method allows you to specify a selection mode. Use the following line of code to find out just how many different selection modes there are:

```
[enum]::GetNames([System.Management.Automation.WhereOperatorSelecti
onMode])
```

4. Use the selection mode, `First`, to select the first two elements, as per the following example:

```
(Get-Process).Where($filterScript, 'First', 2)
```

5. Now try to select the last two elements, as follows:

```
(Get-Process).Where($filterScript, 'Last', 2)
```

6. Now use `SkipUntil` and `Until`. Do you notice, in the following example, how these selection modes differ? Check it out:

```
(Get-Process).Where($filterScript, 'SkipUntil')
(Get-Process).Where($filterScript, 'Until')
```

7. My personal favorite is the `Split` mode. Try splitting your collection into two separate collections, using the same filter script, as shown in the following example:

```
$online, $offline = (Get-ADComputer -Filter *).Where({Test-
Connection $_.DnsHostName -Count 1 -Quiet}, 'Split')

Invoke-Command -ComputerName $online.DnsHostName -Credential
contoso\Install -ScriptBlock { 'We love the Where() method!'}
```

How it works...

This recipe showed you each selection mode of the Where method in action. While all of them are very useful, I personally like to use the `First` and `Last` parameters to quickly grab a couple of items. The `Split` parameter, though, is the icing on the proverbial cake. In this recipe, you assigned two different variables in one go. Each variable contained part of the results.

The syntax of `Where` is not hard to learn; it is still easy to read even for those unfamiliar with it and it performs better than `Where-Object`. Give it a try!

Using Active Directory cmdlets with performance in mind

Often, administrators in a Windows environment will query the Active Directory for information. Whether it is the members of a group, all computers in a specific organizational unit, or all disabled user accounts, the Active Directory cmdlets have you covered.

This recipe shows you how to filter efficiently using the Active Directory cmdlets by searching for users in an **Organizational Unit** (**OU**) and for all disabled accounts using Lightweight Directory Access Protocol filters and PowerShell native filters.

Getting ready

Install and start PowerShell Core. This recipe assumes you are working on PACKT-DC1.

How to do it...

Let's perform the following steps:

1. First of all, try to retrieve just one single user. This operation is very quick, as shown in the following example:

   ```
   Get-ADUser -Identity install
   ```

2. But now watch what happens when, instead, you filter with Where-Object, as shown in the following example:

   ```
   Get-ADUser -Filter * | Where-Object -Property SamAccountName -eq
   install
   ```

3. Often, you already know which OU you want to look in. To speed up processing, you can specify the OU as the search base for your cmdlet, as follows:

   ```
   Get-ADUser -Filter * -SearchBase $orgUnit -SearchScope Subtree
   ```

4. In countless examples on the internet, you will find LDAP filters being used. While this recipe will not cover those, you can try a comparatively simple filter, as follows:

```
Get-ADUser -LDAPFilter
'(&(objectclass=user)(useraccountcontrol:1.2.840.113556.1.4.803:=2)
)'
```

5. As opposed to the `LDAPFilter` parameter, there is a parameter that is simply called `Filter`. Try using it now to see which of those you like better, as shown in the following example:

```
Get-ADUser -Filter 'Enabled -eq $false'
```

6. With the Active Directory it is, essentially, like other modules: there is always the right tool for the job. So, instead of taking a hammer to drive in screws, use the next line of code to reliably get disabled accounts, as follows:

```
Search-ADAccount -AccountDisabled -UsersOnly
```

How it works...

This recipe showed you once again that filtering as early as possible is necessary with PowerShell, unless you have too much time on your hands. The search base in *Step 3* is often a good way to narrow things down. By specifying the proper search scope, you can speed things up even further, if you don't require recursion, for example.

The `LDAPFilter` in *Step 4* is another thing entirely. This seemingly simple filter used the ampersand to combine the next two expressions with a logical AND. The object class needs to be user, and a flag needs to be set. This is another reason why I detest the LDAP filter. The OID in the second pair of parentheses, `1.2.840.113556.1.4.803`, is the LDAP matching rule (bitwise `AND`). This is then used to check whether the decimal value 2 is set as the value of the `useraccountcontrol` flag. This value simply means *disabled*.

See also

- You can learn more about ADSI filters here: https://docs.microsoft.com/en-us/windows/desktop/adsi/search-filter-syntax

Parallelization through runspace pools

Real, proper parallelization in PowerShell Core (and Windows PowerShell, for that matter) can be achieved in many different ways. You could, for example, use the threading namespace of .NET and try multi-threading yourself. Or you could use the more PowerShell-y way of using runspaces and their built-in throttling capabilities.

This recipe shows you how to convert long-running scripts into parallel executed runspace jobs so that you can benefit from powerful multi-threaded processors.

Getting ready

Install and start PowerShell Core.

How to do it...

Let's perform the following steps:

1. Execute the following command to install the module AutomatedLab.Common:

    ```
    Install-Module AutomatedLab.Common -Scope CurrentUser
    ```

2. Next, create a new runspace pool:

    ```
    $pool = New-RunspacePool -ThrottleLimit 10
    ```

3. Now, create a loop around some files and start a job for each file:

    ```
    $jobs = Get-ChildItem -Recurse -File -Path $PSHOME | Foreach-Object
    {
     Start-RunspaceJob -ScriptBlock {
     param ( $Path )
     Get-FileHash @PSBoundParameters
     } -Argument $_.FullName -RunspacePool $pool
    }
    ```

4. Wait for all jobs to finish:

    ```
    $jobs | Wait-RunspaceJob
    ```

5. Or try to receive the job objects again:

    ```
    $jobs | Wait-RunspaceJob -PassThru
    ```

6. Next, receive the results from all runspace jobs:

```
$pool | Receive-RunspaceJob
```

7. Clear up the runspace pool when you are done:

```
$pool | Remove-RunspacePool
```

8. The following code ties all previous steps together:

```
$start = Get-Date
$pool = New-RunspacePool -ThrottleLimit 10
Get-ChildItem -Recurse -File -Path $PSHOME | Foreach-Object {
    Start-RunspaceJob -ScriptBlock {
        param ( $Path )
        Get-FileHash @PSBoundParameters
    } -Argument $_.FullName -RunspacePool $pool
} | Wait-RunspaceJob
$pool | Remove-RunspacePool
(Get-Date) - $start
```

9. Lastly, compare the following output to the output of step 8:

```
$start = Get-Date
Get-ChildItem -Recurse -File -Path $PSHOME | Get-FileHash
(Get-Date) - $start
```

How it works...

A runspace is an instance of the PowerShell engine within a process, for example, `pwsh.exe`. This process could also be a .NET core tool using the PowerShell class. The runspace contains the execution context of your PowerShell command or script, such as variables, functions, and imported modules.

A runspace pool is, quite literally, a pool of runspaces. With the throttle limit, or the maximum number of concurrent pools, you can control how many pools exist at any given time. New jobs are automatically queued as soon as a runspace has finished processing its job, which is what you did in *Step 3* of the recipe.

In *Step 1*, you installed the auxiliary module, `AutomatedLab.Common`, first, which contains cmdlets to interact with runspaces. To be able to start queuing jobs to be executed on different threads, you will need a runspace pool. You did this in *Step 2* and created one with a maximum number of 10 runspaces.

In *Step 3*, you calculated some file hashes, combining a traditional `ForEach-Object` loop and runspaces to see the performance increase. You waited for all jobs to finish by executing `Wait-RunspaceJob` in *Steps 4* and *5*. In *Step 6*, to receive all job results, you used the `Receive-RunspaceJob` cmdlet.

Step 8 tied the previous steps together and had you gather file hashes for the directory stored in the variable, `$PSHOME`. In comparison, you executed the traditional combination of `Get-ChildItem` and `Get-FileHash` in *Step 9*.

Exchanging variables with runspaces

While the previous recipe, *Parallelization through runspace pools,* showed you the benefits of runspace pools, this recipe will show you something else. Maybe you asked yourself: So, how can I access variables from within my runspace pool without worrying about resource conflicts when the variable is modified from within 10 different runspaces?

This recipe teaches you how to implement thread-safe access to local variables from within runspaces using the singleton pattern from software development.

Getting ready

Install and start PowerShell Core.

How to do it...

Let's perform the following steps:

1. Find the following code in the recipe's script and highlight and execute it:

   ```
   function Lock-Object
   {
   ...
   }
   ```

2. Execute the following command:

   ```
   $Definition = Get-Content Function:\Lock-Object -ErrorAction Stop
   $SessionStateFunction = New-Object
   System.Management.Automation.Runspaces.SessionStateFunctionEntry -
   ArgumentList 'Lock-Object', $Definition
   ```

3. Execute the following command:

```
$arrayList = New-Object System.Collections.ArrayList
```

4. Execute the following command:

```
$sessionstate =
[System.Management.Automation.Runspaces.InitialSessionState]::Creat
eDefault()
$sessionstate.Commands.Add($SessionStateFunction)
$sessionstate.Variables.Add(
    (New-Object
System.Management.Automation.Runspaces.SessionStateVariableEntry('a
rrayList', $arrayList, $null))
)
```

5. Execute the following command:

```
$hashPaths = $PSHome, "$home/Downloads"
$runspacepool = [runspacefactory]::CreateRunspacePool(1,
$hashPaths.Count, $sessionstate, $Host)
$runspacepool.Open()
$Handles = @()
$Shells = @()
```

6. Add to your code, as follows:

```
foreach ($path in $hashPaths)
{
...
}
```

7. Add to your code, as follows:

```
$posh = [powershell]::Create()
$posh.RunspacePool = $runspacepool
```

8. Add to your code and execute the loop, as follows:

```
Lock-Object $arrayList.SyncRoot {
    $null = $arraylist.Add($hash)
}
```

9. Execute the following command:

```
1..5 | % {$arrayList.Count}
```

10. Execute the following command:

```
$arrayList | Select -First 10
```

How it works...

The `Lock-Object` cmdlet essentially works like the lock keyword in the thread-safe singleton implementation in C#. A singleton is a class of which only one instance can be spawned, ever. This design pattern is used, for example, for container classes that are instantiated once, and which are afterward only referred to by their instance.

The session state, as also explained in the previous recipe, contains all available functions, variables, cmdlets, and other resources that a runspace might use. By importing `Lock-Object` into the runspace, we make it usable.

First of all, you loaded the `Lock-Object` function courtesy of Boe Prox into memory, by selecting it fully and pressing the *F8* key or *Run Selection*. Afterward, to make this function work in a runspace, you added it to the session state by creating a new session state function entry. In *Step 3*, you just created an object that is accessed from multiple runspaces at the same time.

Next, you created the initial session state and added the shared variable reference to it. In *Step 5*, you created the runspace pool manually using the `RunspaceFactory` .NET class and added the previously created session state. In *Step 7*, you then created new PowerShell runspaces and associated them with the runspace pool for throttling.

To your PowerShell instance, you then added your runspace script. This script can be anything you like, of course, but any time you are accessing the shared variable, you must wrap it in `Lock-Object`. In *Step 8*, you did this with the `ArrayList` created earlier.

Now, in the background, the file hashes were happily created. This, of course, does not take very long. If you were quick enough, you could see the count rising in *Step 9* by getting the list's `Count` property value. In *Step 10*, you saw the result, which was unsorted, because the file hash calculations for both paths were processed truly parallel.

See also

- To read more about the singleton pattern, have a look at: `https://csharpindepth.com/articles/Singleton`.
- Also, kindly give Boe Prox's site, *Learn PowerShell*, a visit, in particular to read up on his *Lock-Object* implementation: `http://learn-powershell.net/2013/04/19/sharing-variables-and-live-objects-between-powershell-runspaces/`.

Large-scale IO operations

Storing output in some shape or form is a very common task in PowerShell. However, many administrators either don't know how to do it efficiently or are forgetful and don't remember that PowerShell actually has a pretty efficient operator for file output.

This recipe shows you how to read large files first, before demonstrating how you can also write large amounts of text very efficiently using different methods.

Getting ready

Install and start PowerShell Core.

How to do it...

Let's perform the following steps:

1. On a Windows system, the component-based servicing logs tend to get pretty big. If you are on a Windows system, try accessing such a log now (on a busy Linux system, use, for example, `/var/log/messages`), as shown in the following example:

```
$biggestLog = Get-ChildItem -Path /Windows/Logs/CBS/*.log -File |
Sort-Object Length -Bottom 1
```

2. First of all, try using the `Get-Content` cmdlet without any parameters at all, as follows:

```
$content = $biggestLog | Get-Content
```

3. Now, add the `ReadCount` parameter, as follows, and observe the difference in execution time:

```
$contentReadCount = $biggestLog | Get-Content -ReadCount 1000
```

4. Lastly, use the `Raw` parameter, as follows:

```
$content2 = $biggestLog | Get-Content -Raw
```

5. So why do we not always use `ReadCount` or `Raw` if they are so much faster? Compare the results of the following three lines of code with each other:

```
$content.Count # 166000 individual objects
$contentReadCount.Count # 166 objects each containing 1000 lines
$content2.Count # 1 Object
```

6. The `Raw` parameter is very useful when you are looking for strings spanning multiple lines of text. Try finding a string, for example, `ServerStandardEvalCorEdition`, in the following output:

```
$result = $content | Select-String -Pattern
"ServerStandardEvalCorEdition" # Slow
$result = $content -match "ServerStandardEvalCorEdition" # Medium
$result = $content2 -match "ServerStandardEvalCorEdition" # Fast
```

7. For the other way round, kindly execute the following steps on the domain controller, `PACKT-DC1`, if you do not have access to an Active Directory environment. First, grab all users and prepare a format for the output, as follows:

```
$users = Get-ADUser -Filter * -Properties PasswordLastSet
$userString = "{0}: {1:yyyy-MM-dd}"
```

8. The first, and most commonly used technique to generate output is the `+=` operator. This, however, is extremely inefficient in terms of processing, as shown in the following example:

```
foreach ($user in $users)
{
  $text += [string]::Format($userString,
$user.SamAccountName, $user.PasswordLastSet)
}
```

9. Next up, there is the ultra-fast unary join operator, `-join`. Try it now, as follows, and notice the incredible speed:

```
$text = -join $users.SamAccountName
```

10. Lastly, a good middle ground can be a .NET `StringBuilder` object. Try creating an instance of this class now using the new method and add to your text with the `Append` method, as shown in the following example:

```
$sb = [System.Text.StringBuilder]::new()

foreach ($user in $users)
{
   [Void]$sb.Append([string]::Format($userString,
$user.SamAccountName,$user.PasswordLastSet))
}
$text = $sb.ToString()
```

How it works...

In .NET (and .NET Core), a string is immutable and effectively read-only once it is created. This was done for improved performance. If you extend these immutable strings with + and +=, however, the opposite happens. Because the string has to be created from scratch with the new value, this operation will get very costly.

The `StringBuilder` class is specialized precisely for its name: building strings. It can do this very well and, of course, can be used in PowerShell Core without problems. In this recipe, you also saw the join operator. You might not have seen the unary join operation before, which simply concatenates strings. It is even faster than `StringBuilder`, but not nearly as flexible. This recipe is, again, a matter of the right tool for the job.

See also

- A little more background on strings in the .NET Framework can be found at: https://support.microsoft.com/en-us/help/306822/how-to-improve-string-concatenation-performance-in-visual-c.

Hashtables, dictionaries, and performance

Hashtables and dictionaries are very popular in PowerShell Core. There are many cmdlets that you have already seen, such as `Group-Object` or `Get-WinEvent`, which work with hashtables. Hashtables are found when using splatting, and a special dictionary is used for the automatic variable, `PSDefaultParameterValues`, which defines key-value pairs for cmdlets and their defaults.

This recipe will show you another reason for preferring hashtables over other constructions: *speed*.

Getting ready

Install and start PowerShell Core. This recipe assumes you are using the `ActiveDirectory` module, either directly on `PACKT-DC1` or imported from it.

How to do it...

Let's perform the following steps:

1. Start with an empty hashtable declaration and assign our 5998 users to the hashtable. The key should be the unique `SamAccountName` and the value should be the entire object, as shown in the following example:

    ```
    $hashtable = @{ }
    Get-ADUser -Filter * | ForEach-Object
    {$hashtable.Add($_.SamAccountName, $_)}
    ```

2. Try locating our user, El Barto, in the table using the key and notice the time it takes, as follows:

    ```
    $foundYou = $hashtable.elbarto # Total milliseconds: 0.4 !
    ```

3. Now try to find the value, the entire ActiveDirectory user, in the table and notice how long that takes in comparison, as shown in the following example:

    ```
    $hashtable.ContainsValue($foundYou) # Total milliseconds: 21.6 !
    ```

4. Hashtables are not only fast; they are also conveniently accessed using the dot-notation. Next, create a hashtable using `Group-Object`, as per the following example:

    ```
    $allTheEvents = Get-WinEvent -LogName System |
        Group-Object -Property LevelDisplayName -AsHashTable -AsString
    ```

5. Now try to access all `Warnings` in the event log at once, as follows:

    ```
    $allTheEvents.Warning
    ```

6. As always, you can get creative with your cmdlets. Use the `EventID`, as follows, for another, convenient way to access events:

```
$allTheEvents = Get-WinEvent -LogName Security | Group-Object -
Property EventID
$allTheEvents.4624
```

7. If not only speed, but type safety also matters to you, you can even create a dictionary that has type definitions applied for both keys and values. Try creating a dictionary where all keys must be strings and all values must be processes, as shown in the following example:

```
$dictionary = New-Object -TypeName
'System.Collections.Generic.Dictionary[string,System.Diagnostics.Pr
ocess]'
```

8. What happens now when you store wrong data? Try using a wrong key and a wrong value next, as per the following example:

```
$dictionary[(Get-Date)] = Get-Process -Id $pid # (Get-Date) is
converted to a string
$dictionary.SomeProcess = Get-Item .            # Terminates.
```

How it works...

Hashtables implement the .NET interface IDictionary that is generically available for all dictionary types, such as the ordered dictionary, the dictionary, or, for that matter, the hashtable.

In this recipe you used the hashtable to quickly access data by a unique and well-known key: you created a table of users indexed by their `SamAccountName`, which should be unique enough. Accessing your data now is very quick, and nothing compared to lookups in lists with filter methods such as `Where-Object`.

Other Books You May Enjoy

If you enjoyed this book, you may be interested in these other books by Packt:

Learn PowerShell Core 6.0
David das Neves, Jan-Hendrik Peters

ISBN: 978-1-78883-898-6

- Get to grips with Powershell Core 6.0
- Explore basic and advanced PowerShell scripting techniques
- Get to grips with Windows PowerShell Security
- Work with centralization and DevOps with PowerShell
- Implement PowerShell in your organization through real-life examples
- Learn to create GUIs and use DSC in production

PowerShell 6.0 Linux Administration Cookbook

Prashanth Jayaram, Ram Iyer

ISBN: 978-1-78913-723-1

- Leverage the object model of the shell, which is based on .NET Core
- Administer computers locally as well as remotely using PowerShell over OpenSSH
- Get to grips with advanced concepts of PowerShell functions
- Use PowerShell for administration on the cloud
- Know the best practices pertaining to PowerShell scripts and functions
- Exploit the cross-platform capabilities of PowerShell to manage scheduled jobs, Docker containers and SQL Databases

Leave a review - let other readers know what you think

Please share your thoughts on this book with others by leaving a review on the site that you bought it from. If you purchased the book from Amazon, please leave us an honest review on this book's Amazon page. This is vital so that other potential readers can see and use your unbiased opinion to make purchasing decisions, we can understand what our customers think about our products, and our authors can see your feedback on the title that they have worked with Packt to create. It will only take a few minutes of your time, but is valuable to other potential customers, our authors, and Packt. Thank you!

Index